Hitler:
The Survival Myth

Also by Donald M. McKale:
The Nazi Party Courts
The Swastika Outside Germany

Hitler:
The Survival Myth

Donald M. McKale

STEIN AND DAY/*Publishers*/New York

For Susan Ruth

First published in 1981
Copyright © 1981 by Donald M. McKale
All rights reserved
Designed by Louis A. Ditizio
Printed in the United States of America
STEIN AND DAY/ *Publishers*/ Scarborough House
Briarcliff Manor, N.Y. 10510

Library of Congress Cataloging in Publication Data

McKale, Donald M   1943–
    Hitler, the survival myth.

    Bibliography: p.
    Includes index.
    1.   Hitler, Adolf, 1889–1945—Death and burial.
2.   Heads of state—Germany—Biography. I.   Title.
DD247.H5M18   943.086′092′4 [B]   80-5405
ISBN 0-8128-2724-4

Contents

Illustrations between pages 102 and 103

Preface

Even the keenest observer of history has wondered at one time or another whether Adolf Hitler really died, cowering in his bunker beneath Berlin at the end of World War II. And possibly he has imagined Hitler having escaped with other Nazis to the jungles and remote corners of Latin America. The alleged survival of the Nazi warlord, who had brought such mass grief and death, became one of the postwar world's most popular and treasured myths. First for political reasons, his enemies and followers refused to admit that he had died. More recently for entertainment, perhaps revealing the darker side of the human soul, a multitude of stories have hit book-shops, the cinema, and television. These envision the Nazi dictator slipping away from the Russians in Berlin, or the diabolical production of his exact genetic duplicate, thus bringing him back to life.

Students in my European history classes and other persons generally fascinated with World War II still want to know what happened to Hitler. I find this amazing, especially because it has been thirty-five years since the world last saw him alive. Inasmuch as a host of investigators and historians far more able than I have tried to solve the mystery of how he died, and a definitive answer is still wanting, I decided to explore why the puzzle arose and persists, apparently, even to the present day. Equally important, I wanted to find out what this riddle tells us about ourselves and about the postwar era.

To my knowledge, this is the only book of its kind. It is not a piece of fiction alleging Hitler's survival, nor is it an effort to prove his death (though the reader will surely spot my viewpoint on the subject). In a sense, it combines both approaches, telling the "story of a story." I have traced not only what fate historians and the Allied governments (including the Soviets) thought had befallen Hitler in 1945, but especially what the popular press believed happened to him and the resulting legends and myths. What did the public know about his demise and when? I do not pretend to discuss every story about his destiny that has been dreamed up since the war. That would be impossible. But if, by contrasting the principal figments of man's imagination (and setting forth their dubious origins) with near eye-witness and factual accounts of his death, I contribute to a rational decision by the reader as to what end Hitler met, that will be reward aplenty.

I have also discovered that the issue of who was to blame for the world's bewilderment over Hitler's fate was not as clear-cut as the West has generally believed. Since the end of the war, Western historians have passionately insisted that the mystery surrounding his death in the bunker on April 30, 1945, resulted from the suppression of the facts of his suicide by the Soviet Union. Most writers have pointed to June 5-6 and 9, 1945, barely a month after Hitler's death, when the Russians issued to the world two contradictory versions of what had happened to him. Since the Red Army had captured Berlin, it has been claimed by Anglo-American and German writers, the Russians had controlled and manipulated the evidence about the dictator's fate for their own political purposes.

Hugh Trevor-Roper, in the introduction to the third edition of his superb study, *The Last Days of Hitler,* wrote: "For years after 9th June the official Russian doctrine remained unchanged, apparently unchangeable, by the evidence. It was never allowed that Hitler might be dead. It was assumed and sometimes openly stated, that he was alive."[1] In his book, *Ten Days to Die,* the Nuremberg judge, Michael Musmanno, argued, "Russia must accept much of the blame (to the extent that it still exists) that Hitler did not die in May 1945."

More recently, Werner Maser, the German historian and Hitler biographer, declared that till the publication in 1968 of the Russian autopsy report on Hitler's charred remains, saying the dictator had died from poison, Soviet writers had "continued to assert that Hitler had committed suicide by shooting himself." Moscow had practiced willful deception, concluded Maser. The body which the Red Army had discovered and examined in May 1945, he said, had not been Hitler's. The autopsy report had therefore been a fraud.[2]

"To the disgrace of Soviet historians," added the journalists James O'Donnell and Uwe Bahnsen in 1975, "a thoroughly unnecessary cloud of distorted histories has for the past thirty years surrounded the entire official report of the events in the Fuehrerbunker on that final day." O'Donnell and Bahnsen complained, moreover, about the "scanty Soviet memoir literature over Berlin in 1945." Textbooks on German history and Western accounts of Hitler's death still repudiate or ignore the Russian evidence.[3]

Trevor-Roper was right in asserting that Soviet policy on Hitler's death had been one of confusion and duplicity. The Kremlin consciously tried during 1945 to maintain the fiction of his survival. But it could be added to this accusation against the Russians that the role of the West in the controversy had not been entirely without fault. As the following pages show, the idea among the public that the Nazi Fuehrer might escape the Allies became popular in the United States during the war, American leaders contributed to this view with their published remarks in 1945, and the Western press indiscriminantly printed in 1945 and after every postwar rumor of Hitler's supposed whereabouts. Nor did the West, except for Trevor-Roper, seem willing to acknowledge the steady flow of signs from the Soviet Union after 1945 hinting at Hitler's death.[4] These culminated in 1968 with the publication (albeit unofficially through a Soviet journalist) of the autopsy report on the Fuehrer's remains. The scholarly world, which is still debating precisely how Hitler ended his frightful career, is plagued by such traditional differences. Consequently, it is my view that the myth of Hitler's fate is no longer whether or not he survived. Rather, it is the belief, which is also a product of the "Cold War," that the Western and Russian interpretations of his death cannot be reconciled.

For those millions who died or suffered because of Hitler, it is sad that the legend which said he had survived the war rose and, for a time, even flourished. Since both Nazi and Russian statements at the beginning of May 1945 had indicated that he had made his final stand in Berlin, the burden of proof for producing him—dead or alive— should have fallen to the Soviet Union. Considering the magnitude of his crimes and the world's justifiable passion for revenge against him, the Russians had at the least a moral obligation to inform the world of what they had discovered about his fate. The factors, both in and outside the Soviet Union, which prevented that from happening are in part the subject of this study.

Donald M. McKale
Clemson, South Carolina
August 1980

Acknowledgments

I gathered material for this study, either directly or by correspondence, from a host of libraries, archives, and individuals in this country, England, Germany, and Israel: the National Archives and Records Service, Washington, D.C. (John Mendelsohn); the Library of Congress (Arnold Price); the National Library of Medicine, Bethesda, Maryland; the Georgia College Library, Milledgeville, Georgia (Nancy Dyer); the Clemson University Library, Clemson, South Carolina; the University of Georgia Library, Athens, Georgia; the Emory University Library, Atlanta, Georgia; the Hoover Institution, Stanford, California (Agnes Peterson); the Leo Baeck Institute, New York (Sybil Milton); the Yivo Institute for Jewish Research, New York (Dina Abramowicz); the British Library, London; the Institute for Contemporary History and Wiener Library, London (Gita Johnson and Janet Langmaid); the British Imperial War Museum, London (T.C. Charman); the School of Slavonic and East European Studies, University of London; the Archive of the Heim und Welt Verlag, Hannover, West Germany (Gert Kramer and Sigrun Meyer); the Zeitungsarchiv of the Bundespresse- und Informationsamt, Bonn, West Germany; the Institut fuer Zeitgeschichte, Munich (Erna Danzl); the Bundesarchiv, Koblenz (F.P. Kahlenberg); and the Jerusalem Archives (Martin Sieff).

I owe a special debt of thanks to Professor Hugh Trevor-Roper, author of *The Last Days of Hitler,* for his suggestions and correspondence regarding this project. My good colleague and friend at Georgia College, Professor William I. Hair, encouraged me to finish the study, and was kind enough to read the entire manuscript. Professors Paul S. George and Larry Elowitz of Georgia College, and Philip Bolton of Milledgeville, Georgia, also read the work. Translations of several sources were made by Mr. Gordon Harris, the School of Slavonic and East European Studies, University of London; Professor Dennis J. Dunn, Southwest Texas State University; and Professor Jean Guitton, Georgia College.

From the Georgia College Foundation and the College's Faculty Research Committee, I received research grants for travel to libraries and archives in this country and abroad. I am very grateful for their support. Thanks to a helpful teaching schedule at Clemson University, I completed the writing of the book earlier than I expected.

Finally, for enduring my lengthy periods of isolation and my lack of sociability as I worked on the study, I owe the most to my wife, Janna, and children, Emily, David, and Susan.

D.M.M.

Hitler:
The Survival Myth

1

Introduction: A Myth in the Making

It was the afternoon of May 1, 1945. Everyone waited in suspense. Around the world, people lingered near a radio or looked for the latest newspaper. They expected any moment the biggest news in six years. As the Battle of Berlin reached its flaming finale, and the Red Army fought its way toward the Brandenburg Gate and nearby Chancellery building that had been the office of Adolf Hitler, speculation mounted on the whereabouts of the Nazi tyrant. Was he in Berlin? Had he fled Germany? Was he still alive? Most important, would the Allies, after the worst war and anguish in history, be cheated out of capturing and taking revenge on the archfiend who had planned such destruction? The world wanted to know.

Suddenly, early that evening, Allied monitoring stations picked up a signal from Hamburg radio, one of the last vocal remnants of Hitler's battered empire. It had a vital announcement for the German people, it said, that would be broadcast later that night. There was no hint of what might come. It repeated a stand-by alert at 9:40, followed by dramatic strains from the last part of Hitler's favorite Wagnerian opera that ended in an orgy of destruction, *Goetterdaemmerung*. Again the announcer urged listeners to stay tuned. Seconds later, the startling news. "It is reported from the Fuehrer's headquarters that our Fuehrer, Adolf Hitler," the announcer began, "fighting to the last breath against Bolshevism, fell for Germany this afternoon in his operational headquarters in the Reich Chancellery." The previous day (April 30), continued the bulletin, Hitler had appointed Grand Admiral Karl Doenitz, head of the German Navy and a dedicated Nazi, as his successor.

3

Doenitz then spoke. Vowing to persist in the war, he praised Hitler's courage and bravery. "Our Fuehrer Adolf Hitler is dead," he mourned. "The German people bow in deepest sorrow and respect. Early he had recognized the terrible danger of Bolshevism and had dedicated his life to the fight against it. His fighting having ended, he died a hero's death in the capital of the German Reich, after having led an unmistakably straight and steady life."

Perhaps as an omen of the mystery and controversy that would follow his announcement, a ghostly voice interrupted Doenitz. When he declared that Hitler had died a "hero's death," the voice shouted across the airwaves, "This is a lie!" As he lauded Hitler for being one of the key figures in German history, the voice broke in, "The greatest of all fascists. His death calls on us to act, so strike now!" Seconds later, as Doenitz urged his people to fight on, the voice cried, "Rise against Doenitz. The struggle is not worthwhile if crime wins."

Where the phantom voice originated, one could only guess. Since a bulky radio transmitter was necessary for such interference, it was unlikely that it came from a private German citizen who would have found it difficult, even in the last days of the war, to conceal the apparatus from the Nazi authorities. It may have been the work of a Nazi resistance group, or possibly an Allied official monitoring the broadcast and wishing either to urge the Hamburg listeners to surrender or to disrupt Doenitz's message. Or it may have been an engineer in the Hamburg station who saw no reason to prolong Germany's agony.

The Nazis were determined to impress on the world that Hitler's death, as his life, had been an act of supreme valor. Although Doenitz had been vague on the subject, one easily assumed from his words that Hitler had died fighting on the Berlin barricades against the hated Russians. In his "Order of the Day," broadcast shortly thereafter to German troops, he again eulogized the fallen dictator. "Faithful to his [Hitler's] great ideal to save the nations of Europe from Bolshevism," said the Admiral, "he has given his life and has met a hero's death."[1] As many had feared, the seed of a Hitler legend had been firmly planted. And the nearly triumphant Allies had no evidence to combat it.

Such stunning news spread quickly. "The day is ours, the bloody dog is dead," the BBC quoted from Shakespeare's *Richard III*. "The paperhanger is dead," shouted a newsboy in New York City, "Hitler, the big bum, is finished!" Thousands in the world's largest city rushed for newsstands. Many of the crowds, however, moved on when they learned that the source of the death account had been the Nazis.

"If Hitler is Dead, Good Riddance," exulted a headline in *The Atlanta Constitution*. Never had the world known such pleasure over the reported death of one man. "As for Hitler himself," said the editorial that followed, "the world will demand positive proof of his death. We shall want most certainly to examine his alleged body, and until his identity is established beyond the shadow of a doubt by experts we shall precede on the premise that he is alive." Calling Hitler "history's greatest criminal," the paper asserted that if he had not gone to his grave, as Americans hoped, "let us search him out into the ends of the earth and see that he gets just punishment for his unprecedented crimes against humanity."

This mixture of joy and doubt seemed typical of the immediate reaction to the Nazi announcement. While the tendency was to accept that Hitler had met his end, a feeling of uneasiness could be sensed and opinions differed on the meaning of his demise. Part of the disquietude rested on the suspicion that he had not departed the world courageously, as the Nazis had described. "The story that Hitler died the heroic death of a soldier in battle," London's *Evening Standard* sneered, "is completely discounted."

Although the world principally concerned itself with ending the war and suffering, a monomania on Hitler's fate swept it in the next several weeks. Fascination with what had happened to him spanned national boundaries and social classes. It would prompt thoughts from Europeans, Russians, Americans, diplomats, government leaders, and people in the streets. Human nature probably dictated that this would be the case. For six years, Hitler had been the arch villain in history, and it seemed somehow unnatural for him to have died so suddenly. Euphoria over his reported end would soon turn into mass skepticism, especially as the Russian and Allied governments failed to produce his body or agree on its whereabouts.

Yet such doubt had been growing for nearly a year. The uncertainty with which the world greeted the Nazi death report of May 1, 1945, had deep historical roots. Hitler's trail during the last months of the war had been a cold and confusing one for his enemies. "Hitler's death," a British astrologer had prophesied with frightening accuracy at the beginning of the war, "will not be disclosed to the public or to the world at large. A veil of secrecy will surround it. Moreover, he will not be spared a violent and painful end."[2]

As the war had turned against Germany, Hitler's enemies had naturally wondered: what would happen to him? Would he be captured and punished, as the Allied governments hoped? "Suicide," American intelligence had secretly concluded, "is the most likely possibility." "Hitler ought to be shot or hanged," said 40 percent of Americans polled during the war. His future had aroused a great deal of curiosity and disagreement.[3] And out of this fascination with his sheer evil and his destiny had sprouted that mythomania which would accompany the Nazi announcement on May 1, 1945, that he had ended his life a "hero" in Berlin. That he might live beyond the war was an idea planted firmly in the West, even while he had lived. The famous postwar theories of a Hitler "double" dying in the Fuehrer's place, of Nazis escaping to Argentina or Spain, and of a future Nazi rebirth—all had been advanced in the last year of the war.

The world had slowly been caught in those final months, as had the Germans previously, between the view of Hitler's apparent talent for survival amidst danger and of Nazi propaganda, renowned for its falsehoods and exaggeration. After nearly falling victim to an assassin's bomb that had exploded at his headquarters on July 20, 1944, Hitler had virtually disappeared. Except for the claims of Joseph Goebbels, diminutive Propaganda Minister and master of the art of untruth, that Hitler had outlived the blast because of Divine Providence, the Nazis said nothing about his physical condition or whereabouts. Occasionally they published a photo of him, "evidently an effort to give reassurance to the German people," explained the London *Daily Telegraph.*[4]

Outside Europe, speculation had grown. "Was Hitler in the latter stages of paranoia?" "Had he been seriously injured in the bomb plot?" "Had he been partially paralyzed by a stroke?" "Or," asked some observers, "had he disappeared with his notorious hangman and police chief, Heinrich Himmler, to complete plans for a postwar Nazi comeback and for unleashing World War III?" A book titled *The Nazis Go Underground,* stressed that Hitler would "never be saved, no matter what." Anti-Nazi, it unwittingly contributed to the slow mythologizing in the West of his fate. Those who knew him, it said, believed he would "fight to the last," holding out in his retreat in the Bavarian mountains near Berchtesgaden, even after his armies had surrendered.

But if he decided differently, the book theorized, he would either kill himself or be destroyed by his followers, who needed a "dead Fuehrer" as a future martyr. Other leading Nazis would flee by submarine to Argentina, to banks "full of stocks and bonds as well as gold and jewels belonging to Nazis or to the party." Why Latin America? Because large German minorities lived there, and the Nazis had received wide publicity in the 1930s from trying to organize party groups among them. In 1938 and 1939, the Nazi party had been outlawed in Brazil and Argentina.

A novel, *Phantom Victory,* published at the end of 1944, also discussed such future Nazi activity. It forecast that the Nazis, although defeated, would outsmart the naive British and Americans after the war and by 1960 build a powerful "Fourth Reich." Aiding this German revival would be disagreements among the Western Allies and the Soviet Union, especially over the occupation of Germany.

And what happened to Hitler in the book? By allowing an understudy or double, Hermann Kulicke, to be captured by the Allies, he escaped. When Kulicke was identified as a hoax, a rash of reports surfaced that the "real" Hitler had been seized near Magdeburg, then in Upper Bavaria, and finally in numerous cities and villages that sported "phony" Hitlers. As to other Nazis, Hermann Goering, Hitler's portly *Luftwaffe* (Air Force) commander and Reich Marshal, had flown to Sweden, which refused to hand him over to the Allies. Similarly, Goebbels had fled to Spain and lived in luxury under General Franco's protection. And Himmler was recognized as a bank clerk in Buenos Aires and executed by a mob.

Hitler, *The New York Times* had warned in October 1944, could escape the Allies with a variety of facial disguises. How would he look, asked the paper, "without his mustache and his dark lock, his hair cut short and dyed fair or ginger or white, and wearing horn-rimmed glasses and perhaps a bowler hat?" To prevent such deception, it suggested the Allies publish a list of Nazi leaders whose reported death "they will accept only tentatively." But, it added cynically, "Two men might be left out of the wanted list—Hermann Goering, whose fatness is a certain guarantee against any change by successful make-up, and Joseph Goebbels, who, even if he altered his features, would still be betrayed by his clubfoot."

The arrival of 1945 had brought further calamities for Hitler. A last desperate Nazi counteroffensive, the "Battle of the Bulge," failed in Belgium and France. Germany found itself entrapped. The Anglo-American armies pushed across France toward the Rhine River. The Russians drove relentlessly from the east. Even with the war hopelessly lost, Hitler would not admit defeat. In two radio broadcasts monitored in the West, one on New Year's and the other on January 30, he gave no hint from which of his headquarters he had spoken. The speeches lasted barely twenty minutes. It was unquestionably Hitler who spoke, but he could only muster a mere shadow of the emotion he once did.

The first conjecture could now be heard in the West on when Germany would surrender and on Hitler, his whereabouts and punishment after the war. Three Jesuit priests, having just arrived in Rome from Austria, told newsmen, "Hitler is hiding in a small monastery outside Salzburg. He had a large gash on the left side of his scalp, which he had received in the bomb plot." The International Red Cross in Switzerland, which had been in contact with Hitler's Elite Guard (the SS) about the treatment of prisoners in German concentration camps, had heard that "the Fuehrer is in poor health." Two German Army officers captured by the Americans testified, "We saw the Fuehrer several months ago. He was weak and rarely traveled anywhere except from his bunker headquarters to a war briefing room." A Nazi diplomat, also an American captive, declared, "Hitler is still very much alive. I saw him only hours after the bomb exploded in his presence. His escape was simply miraculous."

Observed *The New York Times,* "There are a thousand and one guesses as to how the Fuehrer is going to meet the end of his proud Nazi Reich." In London, bold headlines on April 11, 1945, had said that Hitler would die soon and be replaced by Himmler. British Foreign Secretary, Anthony Eden, appeared before the House of Commons, and laughed off rumors that Hitler had been assassinated and that the British were responsible. Endless talk could also be heard that he had killed himself, especially as reports appeared in the

German press, including an article by Goebbels, condemning the suicides of despairing German officials. The *Los Angeles Times* scoffed, "The world can expect more mass suicides as the Allied war machine grinds on—perhaps of Hitler, Himmler, Goebbels and the rest of the mangy Nazi crew who lack the nerve to face their fate as prisoners."

The only information even remotely reliable in those desperate April days had dealt with the military situation. The Russians, beginning their final march on Berlin from the east in the early hours of April 16, emphasized that they would soon link up with American forces moving across central and southern Germany from the west. Berlin's sole escape corridor southward between the Russians and Americans narrowed rapidly.

The bitter conquest of the Reich yielded no greater shock than the Allied liberation of the Nazi death camps. Already the Soviet Union had uncovered several of the worst camps in Poland, where it estimated several million Jews and others had been gassed by the Nazis. American troops freed the camp at Buchenwald in central Germany, and further north the British liberated 40,000 prisoners at Belsen. "Yanks Discover Prisoners Burned Alive," "Full Horror of German Atrocities," headlines across the United States told the grisly story. Edward R. Murrow delivered a CBS radio broadcast from amid the stench of death and the starvation at Buchenwald. "The manner of death seems unimportant," he had said. "Murder has been done. God knows how many men and boys have died here during the last twelve years."

Such reports could not help but feed the passion to capture Hitler and his fellow "rat pack" of criminals, and punish them. Once the war ended, the Allies and the newly organized United Nations had already decided, the Nazi leaders would be brought to trial for "war crimes." Across the United States, sentiment swelled for the most rigorous punishment of the Nazi Fuehrer. "Hitler and his fellow war criminals must be brought to justice," demanded the *Philadelphia Inquirer*. "It should be made a world-wide, inflexible rule," the *Washington Times-Herald* asserted, "that leaders of nations which lose wars are just to be hanged, without ifs, ands or buts. The precedent established by the hanging of Hitler would be of value to the world now and later on." "Hitler will be made prisoner of war like other Nazi officials, if he doesn't resist," the American Secretary of War, Henry Stimson, had assured a news conference on April 19. "Our troops will do their duty."

The British agreed. "I recommend that leading Nazis, including Hitler, be shot without trial," said the Archbishop of York. A poll of Londoners showed they thought "shooting is too good" for Hitler. "We want him exhibited in zoos and in devastated countries," said more than a third of those sampled, "and receipts should be given to charity." In the House of Commons, Foreign Secretary Eden was questioned about whether His Majesty's government considered Hitler a major war criminal. "Will it be the duty of a British soldier who sees Hitler to shoot him or bring him back alive?" he was asked. To laughter and cheers, he replied, "I am quite content to leave that to the judgment of the British soldier."

But where had the Nazi tyrant gone? Why had he vanished so completely? The mystery had built in the last week and a half of April to a crescendo, as the Russians ripped into Berlin with two gigantic armies and the Americans pushed south of the capital toward Bavaria and to within thirty miles of the Soviet forces. Allied strategy had seemed to indicate a belief that Hitler and the remnants of his government were either in Berlin or in the Bavarian mountains. As this riddle grew, it had helped to ensure that when the first official announcement of Hitler's fate came, as it did from the Nazis on May 1, 1945, the news would be received with widespread skepticism.

While Goebbels and the few remaining Nazi radio stations worshipped their Fuehrer on his fifty-sixth birthday, April 20, reports surfaced in the West that the German leadership had been reduced to bitter quarreling over where and how the last battles of the war were to be fought. Hitler, these contended, now argued for at least part of the government staying in Berlin. Himmler, on the other hand, insisted that everything valuable be rushed to Bavaria and southern Germany. Allied headquarters in Paris illustrated the growing American concern for this so-called "redoubt," and described it as "that general area where Hitler and his more fanatical followers are thought to be preparing to make their last stand." By April 25, American forces heading toward the area had swept southeast (away from Berlin) to within seventy-five miles of Munich.

The focus on Berlin or Bavaria as Hitler's hideout did not quiet the other stories of his whereabouts. "Today's best rumor," an Associated Press report began, "is of the phantom train said to have been seen to enter the Harz forest" with "perhaps" Goebbels and Hitler aboard. The Free Dutch radio, operated by Nazi resisters in Holland, declared that Hitler had escaped to a "northern redoubt" in Mecklenburg. Still other reports, based on "French sources," said he had asked his ally, Japan, for permission to hide in Tokyo so he could continue the war from there. Unconfirmed stories that Goering and Goebbels had left Berlin also encouraged the thought that he might not be in the capital.

"A double posing as Hitler will die in Berlin," theorized anti-Nazis calling themselves the Free German Press Service. "A carefully coached grocer resembling Hitler has been sent to the city in the Fuehrer's place to die on the barricades," they cautioned. They identified the substitute as August Bartholdy of Saxony, trained even to speak like Hitler after spending long hours with the dictator at Berchtesgaden. "The double will act as Hitler's trump card," warned the anti-Nazis, "creating a hero legend around the Fuehrer's death while Hitler himself goes underground." Wherever the Nazi leader chose to spend his last days, Anglo-American commanders were officially directed to "search out, arrest, and hold him."

Meanwhile, as Soviet and German communiques indicated Berlin had reached its death throes and that the Red Army had virtually encircled the city by April 25, the Nazis insisted that Hitler now personally led its defense. "The Fuehrer is in Berlin and has decided to stay there in this grave hour," said the Nazi newspaper, the *Voelkischer Beobachter,* and the crippled German radio system. "Merely by his presence in the capital," they argued, "he will stem the Russian advance and protect Europe from the despised Asiatic Bolshevism." Hamburg radio gave the world its first details of the Fuehrer's whereabouts on April 26. "He is directing the defense of Berlin from an underground headquarters," the radio said, "and is receiving hourly reports on the trend of the battle."[5] Boasted Werner Naumann, an official in the German Propaganda Ministry, "Hitler and Goebbels are endeavoring to outdo each other in feats of personal bravery."

Partly in response to this fulsome worship, *The New York Times* called Hitler "the fading Fuehrer" and suggested he had been persuaded to stay in Berlin by Goebbels. Hitler's last stand in Berlin, the *Times* guessed, would be "in the service of the legend which the Nazis have been diligently building up about him and themselves." This was the myth "that they are shining knights in armor leading Europe in a crusade against Bolshevism." The paper cautioned the Allies that the tale of Hitler at the barricades against the Red Armies might be a German venture to create differences between the Western Powers and the Russians. But, it concluded, the Nazi legend would fail, because Hitler's battle against Bolshevism had only been a scheme for his plan of conquest. "His armor has long since been smeared with the blood of millions of victims slain. He has already surpassed Attila and Genghis Khan as a symbol of monstrous savagery."

The Fuehrer was also on the minds of the Russians, who described Berlin as a "living hell." Marshals G. K. Zhukov and Ivan Konev, commanders of the massive Red Armies swarming over the city, had received orders to take Hitler alive, "if possible." Moscow radio stressed the belief, however, already publicized in the West, that Hitler had escaped to Bavaria to gather the surviving Nazi faithful and organize a "children's army." The broadcast said that a few days earlier, Hitler had received the Nazi Youth leader, Artur Axmann, at his secret headquarters. Axmann had been ordered to recruit thousands of "children," according to the Russians, "who are to be brought to the Bavarian redoubt and there trained and organized into death battalions." A less detailed Russian story had Hitler fleeing Berlin and "probably" leaving a double to die in his place.[6]

Some observers were pleased with the apparent Russian and Western unity in agreeing that Hitler might be somewhere in the Bavarian Alps. But the statements by the Kremlin had both propaganda and military-strategic implications. Since differences had already risen between the Soviets and Anglo-Americans, especially over what the Russians had called Western "benevolence" toward the Nazis,[7] Moscow may have been aiming at discrediting both its allies and the Germans. On the one hand, it could not admit publicly to believing the enemy's claim that Hitler was in Berlin. To have done so would have been to legitimize Nazi propaganda portraying Hitler as an anti-Bolshevik Hercules.

On the other hand, by subscribing to the southern redoubt theory, the Soviets placed a greater responsibility on the Western Allies, and particularly on the Americans heading into Bavaria, for finding Hitler. Correspondingly, they lessened their own accountability for uncovering him by implying that he was not in the Reich capital. Through a careful stroke of propaganda, Moscow had shifted the onus of finding Hitler onto its allies, something it would repeat after the war had ended. But the British and Americans, because they had first publicized the notion that Hitler could be in the south, had presented the Soviets with this tool to use against them. Already Hitler's destiny had become entwined in "Cold War" propaganda.

That Hitler was in Bavaria was suggested anew by an announcement over Hamburg radio on the evening of April 26 that Goering had resigned his offices. The Reich Marshal, having previously been mentioned to succeed Hitler, had "been suffering from heart trouble for some time" and had "asked the Fuehrer to be relieved of his command." Hitler had acquiesced, the Nazis explained, replacing Goering as Luftwaffe chief with General Ritter von Greim. The latter had visited the Fuehrer's headquarters personally and been promoted to Field Marshal.[8]

In the West, the resignation had been interpreted that Goering had committed suicide to avoid execution by his rival, Himmler. It was now presumed that Himmler had grown more powerful daily and persuaded Hitler to flee to Bavaria. The Allies took no chances; their massive air strikes reportedly demolished Hitler's mountain chalet at Berchtesgaden. "Whether Hitler was there is, of course, not known," the *Los Angeles Times* had commented, "but if he was there he got at the least a good shaking up."

Other stories had appeared in these final days to tie Himmler to Hitler. These included a series of surprising reports of April 28 and 29, linking Himmler to a German peace initiative and to suggestions that Hitler may already have died. According to Swedish, British, and Russian sources, Himmler had met secretly in Denmark and northern Germany with Count Folke Bernadotte, a Swedish Red Cross official, and offered to surrender to the Anglo-Americans. Included in the rumors was information from Himmler that "Hitler is dying and may not live another twenty-four hours."

While this version of what had happened to Hitler was not new to the Allied governments,[9] it surprised the Western press. Added to the question of whether Hitler was in Berlin or Bavaria was now the view that he lay on his deathbed—or, as some guessed, he had already died, and probably at the hand of his vicious police henchman. Lending credence to this interpretation of supreme villainy were tales, popular for years, about Nazi treachery and infighting for power among Hitler's lieutenants.

The spectacular news of Himmler's diplomacy had combined with other events to signal to an anxious world that a Nazi surrender might be imminent. Along the Elbe River, seventy-five miles south of Berlin, the American and Soviet Armies had met, fastening the eastern and western battlefronts together and slicing what remained of Hitler's Reich in half. Anti-Hitler revolts had been reported in several German cities still held by the Nazis. And a broadcast from Italy said that Hitler's ally, Benito Mussolini, and other Fascist leaders had been executed by Italian patriots. The Duce had been shot and his body publicly displayed and defiled. Such news had been more than the Americans, also embroiled in the war in the Pacific, could take. They were overcome with ecstasy by a news story that said the Germans had capitulated, only to learn they had rejoiced over a bogus peace. The Nazis were continuing their senseless struggle.

Nevertheless, exciting news was not lacking. Daily communiques from Moscow indicated that the Soviets had nearly conquered Berlin. In rapid succession, they had captured since April 26 Spandau, Potsdam, Tempelhof Airport, parts of the Charlottenburg and Moabit districts, and the heart of the city except for a pocket of twenty-five square miles. This area held the Reich's administrative district, including its ministry buildings, Reichstag ("Parliament"), and Hitler's Chancellery. The huge Chancellery building sat surrounded by some of the most famous and, formerly, beautiful avenues in Europe. Once used by Hitler to lavishly entertain foreign heads of state and diplomats, it faced the Wilhelmstrasse and was encircled by Under den Linden, the East-West Axis (the main avenue leading into Berlin), the Brandenburg Gate, and the large park, the Tiergarten.

But the Russians now shelled these landmarks with artillery, mortars, and tanks, and pounded them from the air with low-flying fighter planes, whose pilots had trouble finding their way through the smoking ruins. Bulletins from Moscow described Red infantry units scrambling over wreckage and mopping up block after block of buildings. Other troops fought underground through fanatically contested and utterly black subway tunnels. The tubes linked concrete cellars into which thousands of frightened Berliners had poured for refuge. "So many tanks are in Berlin that they choked the streets," reported Soviet newsmen on the scene.

By the evening of April 29, the troops of Marshal Zhukov's First White Russian Army had struck to within a half mile of the ruined Chancellery and Reichstag. As they approached the Tiergarten from the north and west, they discovered that the Nazis had converted the park into a huge fortress. The next day, April 30, the Soviets delighted in reporting their storming and capturing the gutted remains of the Reichstag building. Moscow made a trophy out of the Parliament; when it had burned in 1933, Hitler had used the fire to dramatize his hatred for Communism, by arresting German Communists and eventually outlawing their party.

The Russians were now reportedly at the Brandenburg Gate, built by the Hohenzollerns at the end of the eighteenth century and symbol of the authoritarianism and power of the old Prussian monarchy. Both ends of the mile-long Unter den Linden, which ran eastward from the Gate, had fallen to the Russians. Red shock troops started battling their way into the eastern end of the Nazi-infested Tiergarten.[10] According to both the Germans and Soviets, it was there that Hitler and Goebbels now directed the city's defense from a heavily fortified underground headquarters.

The world had waited, holding its breath. Would the Russians find Hitler? When would Berlin fall? If the final Nazi radio broadcasts had told the truth, most observers thought, Hitler should be captured in his battered capital, dead or alive. "Hitler is in Berlin and will die there," a German officer arrested in Magdeburg, Kurt Dittmar, had reaffirmed to the Allies. "There is an epidemic of suicides among Nazi officers and SS troops in the capital," reported the Russians. Swiss radio, quoting "high military circles in Munich," said in startling fashion that "Hitler died in his underground shelter in the Berlin Tiergarten yesterday, April 29."

No one could say for certain. Only the Russians knew what had happened in the besieged capital. The Americans were fighting their way into southern Germany, the British into the north. And the Nazis, notorious for their propaganda and lies, could not be trusted. Then it had suddenly come: the electrifying announcement over Hamburg radio on the evening of May 1, 1945. A world nearly exhausted from the past week's blizzard of news bulletins sounding the imminent death of Hitler and his hated regime, heard what it had fought for six years to achieve. Hitler had died in Berlin. "Fighting to the last breath against Bolshevism," a Nazi announcer had proclaimed, the Fuehrer had fallen "for Germany this afternoon in his operational headquarters in the Reich Chancellery." Although few who soon learned the news realized it, a myth had been born that would fascinate the world for the next generation.

2

A Hero's Death or Suicide?

The first word from the Kremlin came early on the morning of May 2. It disappointed the West. Vague, like the Nazi bulletin a few hours earlier, it indicated Hitler had neither died nor been taken prisoner by the Red Army in Berlin. In a radio broadcast to the Russian people, and later published in the government press, the Soviet news agency Tass said the Germans "asserted that" Hitler had died at noon the previous day, after having named Doenitz his successor. The German report had left Moscow wary. "These German radio announcements," warned the Tass statement, "apparently represent a new Fascist trick." Then came the most confusing and disconcerting part of the message. "By spreading the news of Hitler's death," Tass said, "the German Fascists apparently wish to give Hitler the means of leaving the stage and going 'underground.'"[1]

Other Soviet broadcasts echoed the idea that the Nazis had deceived the world by proclaiming Hitler dead in Berlin. Stalin, in his "Order of the Day" to Russians on May 1, said the "Hitlerite adventurers" would "resort" to all kinds of "tricks" in search of "a way out of their hopeless plight." A few hours later, a Soviet broadcast to Europe (in German) discussed the May Day enthusiasm in Russia and condemned the report of Hitler's demise. "It's the Nazis' last attempt to split the Allies," it fumed. Then, referring to Himmler's peace move, the radio argued, "The offer to surrender to the U.S.A and Britain, but not to the U.S.S.R., is a similar attempt which has also failed. Trying to make capital out of Hitler's corpse will backfire on the Germans."

But would it do the same to the Russians? They too seemed anxious to tie "Hitler's corpse" to politics and propaganda. While this appeared to be an official but cautious view from the Kremlin, not every Russian agreed with it. Colonel Piluigen, a Soviet war correspondent attached to the British Army near Bremen, accepted the German statement that Hitler had perished. As he heard the Nazi bulletin on the evening of May 1, he was sitting in a tavern, trying to relax with a beer from the rigor and tension of the day. Jumping to his feet, he lifted high his glass and shouted in Russian, "To the death of Hitler!" Piluigen and fellow Allied correspondents sitting and cheering around him had no doubt about the truth of the news. Had he met a hero's death? "Absolutely not," they all agreed, "he was too much of a coward."[2]

The information, or lack thereof, from Moscow caught the West by surprise. Not only had the Soviet Union mentioned nothing of its armies in Berlin having located the Nazi Fuehrer, but it raised again the disturbing prospect that he might have escaped. Furthermore, the Kremlin had been painfully imprecise. Had the Red soldiers not found Hitler? Did they have evidence that he had gone "underground"? The world had been left even more perplexed and uneasy about the German version of Hitler's destiny. Wittingly or not, the Russians had struck a powerful blow for those convinced that he had survived.

Meanwhile, as the Russian statements became known, world headlines on May 1 and 2 carried lengthy obituaries. In Palestine, the home for thousands of European Jews who had fled Nazi persecution, papers were certain that "Hitler died this afternoon."[3] *Le Monde* described him as "cruel" and "indifferent to human life," and "one of the most astonishing as well as sinister figures of history." "His appearance was not imposing," said the Paris paper, "yet he was still impressive to his people." It feared, however, "that Hitler will appear to future generations to be a great man."

"Few men in the whole of history and none in modern times have been the cause of human suffering on so large a scale as Hitler, who died in Berlin yesterday," read *The Times* (London). While admitting that he had possessed some "most remarkable talents," the paper declared that "he became in the eyes of virtually the whole world an incarnation of absolute evil." "The ultimate source of his power for evil," it continued, had been "his uncanny subtle and acute understanding of the mind of his own people." Even in death, the personality and wickedness of the Fuehrer captivated his enemies.

Reactions from diplomats at the United Nations meeting in San Francisco were more restrained. Lord Halifax, Britain's Ambassador to the United States, pointed up the lack of frenzied excitement about Hitler at the gathering. "Isn't it remarkable," he asked reporters who had stopped him at his hotel, "how calmly people take such news?" A few blocks away, a Chinese delegate remarked at a luncheon, "Dictators die easily these days." In London, the British Foreign Office said that it believed Hitler had died, but it declined to comment on the accuracy of the Nazi report.

The European capitals, ravaged by the war and Nazi occupation, buzzed with conjecture. "Caution must be the watchword about Hitler's death," newspapers and radio commentators urged their audiences throughout May 2 and 3. The many rumors of his fate that had deluged the world in the last days of April now took their toll. "Remember such stories," said Italian radio, "all come from a suspect source—from Germany itself." Of the bulletin stating Hitler had gone to the grave while defending Berlin, it warned, "This is the last effort of German propaganda to sow dissension among the Allies, or at least to build up the myth of Hitler the hero." The Brussels paper, *Le Soir,* also reminding its readers of the previous rumors, suggested, "Hitler has probably retreated to some hideout from which he will emerge one day as another Antichrist." On the other hand, the Austrians were indifferent about whether Hitler had only just died or whether he had been dead for several days. "The main thing," said Austrian radio, "is that Hitler has been cast on the muck-heap of history."

While most other Europeans agreed, they were nagged by the fear, possibly encouraged by the Soviet statements, that the German report of Hitler's end would have serious propaganda consequences. Doenitz, they suspected, had cleverly formulated a Nazi "stab-in-the back" legend, not unlike the myth that had arisen after World War I, to explain Germany's defeat. The Americans and British, so Doenitz had seemed to say, had knifed Hitler in the back as he had battled to protect Europe and the Western world from Bolshevism. The legend, however, had uncommonly short legs. Hitler had never solely fought "Bolshevism." On the contrary, he had created the situation which, in an incredibly short time, had made the Soviet Union a world power. Germany lay in ruins and occupied by foreign powers, and eastern Europe had been overrun by Red soldiers.

The French, having suffered through German invasions in 1870, 1914, and 1940, were concerned about another legend. "The Nazis," lamented a Parisian as he thought of rebuilding his nation following four years of German rule, "have purposely fostered a Hitler myth that will become the heart of a future Nazi resurgence." In so doing, it was asserted, Hitler's followers had plagiarized the legend of the medieval German king, Frederick Barbarossa. According to the Barbarossa story, well known to the French through Victor Hugo's drama, *Les Burgraves,* the king had not died while on a Christian Crusade to the Holy Land. Instead, after a miraculous escape, he had made for Germany, there to retire to a mountain cave.

Then, awakening from a cataleptic sleep, he would emerge as Germany's savior each time it was on the verge of collapsing under its enemies' attacks. The Germans, a French broadcast warned, wished to transform Hitler into a modern Barbarossa:

> How pleased the Fuehrer would have been to pass from history to legend through the golden gates of popular poetry! How useful it would have been for the survival of Nazism and how exalting to the imperialistic dreams of future generations, to foster the idea of his mysterious disappearance! To become a mythological figure and a symbol of hope for a nation! And to disappear just when he would have had to account for the disaster into which he had precipitated his country, thus fostering the belief that had he been there, disaster could have been avoided and that his miraculous return would restore power and prosperity.[4]

This European reaction to the report of Hitler's end found sympathy in the United States. In New York, some said "It's another Nazi fake," or "They're trying to palm off a Hitler double." French sailors in Times Square were more confident, predicting "It is the end of the pig. He will roast in hell." A young bobby-socks blonde expressed the feeling of many when she noted, "Too bad he's dead. He should have been tortured." A former American soldier, crippled by machine gun

fire in the Philippines, said, "If it's true, it's the greatest thing I ever heard."

Another observed, "Hitler's headstone should be a skunk. But he shouldn't be buried. He will contaminate the good earth." Mayor Fiorello La Guardia, who had once nominated Hitler for the Chamber of Horrors, shouted into a police car radio as he rode through Manhattan, "That's the best news I've heard. Look for anything to happen now." On a more somber note, a Bronx rabbi, concerned with Hitler's legacy, said, "He leaves behind him a ruined and agonized world, the monument to his madness. God save humanity from the seeds of his tyranny and terror."

A "man-in-the-street" survey by the *Los Angeles Times* produced a headline that screamed, "Happy Grins Greet Hitler Death Report." "Hitler's dead?" asked a local nurse. "Why that's wonderful!" Then she caught herself momentarily. "I guess that's a terrible thing to say about someone," she confessed, "but I am awfully glad he's dead. He started the war. Let the war finish him." Men of the cloth were even quick to find meaning in Hitler's destruction. A Methodist preacher in San Francisco, sermonizing on "the fall of the dictators," declared, "The law of sowing and reaping is as eternal as the law of gravity."

On a more official note, the Illinois Legislature pronounced Hitler dead on May 3. By dying, the assembly stated, "he has brought joy to all men." Said a resolution adopted by the jubilant politicians, "We hereby commend Adolf Hitler on the one good act of his career, and declare him dead so we may not be deprived of the celebration to which we are so justly entitled, and condemn him for not having died fifty-six years ago."[5]

Despite the overwhelming denunciation of Hitler, the Nazi military remnant that continued fighting in pockets in Germany, Austria, and Czechoslovakia, insisted that their fallen leader had died a gallant death. "He had displayed the courage of a true soldier," they said. One of their broadcasts on May 2 added to Doenitz's statement and boldly asserted, "When the enemy advanced to the heart of the Reich capital, Hitler himself took up arms and fell while leading his soldiers." Seconds later, the Nazi commentator said something unusual. Amidst praising Hitler, he conceded that the Fuehrer had probably not been infallible, as his followers had always maintained, but that he

may have made a few mistakes. "We can calmly await the judgment which history will pass on Adolf Hitler," it was maintained. "Perhaps it will be shown that he had some faults, as everybody has, but it will also have to be admitted that he was one of the greatest European men who might have led our continent towards a great future had his contemporaries understood him."

Other German broadcasts, like that from Flensburg (where Doenitz had established his headquarters) on May 5, repeated that Hitler had been a martyr. He had died "on the afternoon of May 1st" in the Reich Chancellery, it contended, showing a final time "that the fight against Bolshevism and its destruction were tantamount to the preservation of western civilisation." Concluded the Flensburg message, "In choosing a soldier's death he set an example of inexorable willpower and singleness of purpose."[6]

As this Nazi campaign to immortalize Hitler continued, the Allies became concerned. A captured German diplomat heightened their apprehension. "The Nazis will soon announce that Hitler's body has been cremated," he forecast. "The aim," said the prisoner, "is to prevent disproof of the assertion that Hitler died a hero's death." Such talk about his bravery prompted the first official Anglo-American comment on the report of his demise. Supreme Allied headquarters in Paris contradicted on May 2 the Nazi claim of his heroic passing. As evidence, General Eisenhower cited a secret meeting of April 24 between Himmler and Count Bernadotte. Himmler, Eisenhower said, had told the Swedish emissary that Germany was "finished" and "Hitler was dying." Also present was a German general, Schellenberg, who had interjected into the talks, "The Fuehrer is suffering from a brain hemorrhage and can live no longer than two more days."

This was confirmed that afternoon by President Truman.[7] "The United States is in possession of official information that Hitler is dead," he told a packed room of reporters at the White House. But asked how he had died, Truman replied, "That is unknown." When questioned about the source for his statement, moreover, he refused to explain. Pressed to elaborate on what the President had said, White House officials were equally non-committal. Only Secretary of War Stimson seemed unequivocal, telling newsmen later, "Hitler has met his end."

Despite their honest opinions, the statements of the American

leaders added to the bewilderment and controversy. Neither Eisenhower nor Truman had been able to offer proof that Hitler was deceased. They could not even enlighten the world on how he had died. By denying the German story of Hitler's "manly" death, Eisenhower left the impression that the Nazi tyrant may not have met his end. American newspapers reported the General's remarks with vague headlines like "Heroic Death Story is a Lie" and "No Hero's Death, Says Eisenhower." Further, the President's treating of Hitler's death as a fact, his basing his view on alleged "official information," and his rejecting of pleas to reveal his evidence, hardly clarified the mystery.

Truman's source may have been the Russians. Several hours after his news conference, Moscow broadcast an official communique that said Berlin, "center of German imperialism and hotbed of German aggression," had fallen to the Red Army on the afternoon of May 2. General Helmut Weidling, commander of the Berlin defenses, had surrendered the German garrison in the center of the capital. Within hours, said the communique, the Soviets had taken prisoner "more than 70,000 German officers and men." Among the captured were Weidling; Vice Admiral Erich Voss, representative of the German Navy and Doenitz at Hitler's headquarters; and Hans Fritsche, head of the radio section in the German Propaganda Ministry. Later broadcasts announced the seizure of Hitler's personal pilot, Hans Bauer, and SS officials like the chief of Hitler's Chancellery Guard, Wilhelm Mohnke, and Johann Rattenhuber.

But a spectacular new version of Hitler's destruction lay nearly hidden in the announcement of Nazi Berlin's conquest. The Fuehrer, according to Fritsche, one of the German prisoners, had taken his own life, not dying at the head of his troops battling Bolshevism. Moscow, in its usual blunt and colorless language, reported simply, "Fritsche stated during interrogation that Hitler, Goebbels, and the newly appointed Chief of the General Staff, Infantry General [Hans] Krebs, had committed suicide."[8]

This became instant news. Now, instead of the previous days' polemics over whether Hitler had been in Bavaria or Berlin, a different explanation of his alleged death in the former Nazi capital confronted the world. Earlier, the Nazis contended he had died in battle, the Americans that he had succumbed to a serious illness. Now the

Soviets said that he had put himself to death. And how? They did not elaborate. Nor did they say anything of the whereabouts of Hitler's remains; if the Russians had the body, they kept silent. The only thing certain was that Moscow controlled the evidence. British and American soldiers still fought miles from Berlin, and it would be July before Stalin would allow them into the city.

The Russian account again left the world begging for the truth. "Suicide," said an American who had just heard about Fritsche's statement, "is more in character for Goebbels, whose brilliant mind was as twisted as his club foot." William Shirer, a former American press correspondent in Germany and fast becoming a chief spokesman of hate against the Germans as a people, thought Hitler had been an "evil genius" whose career and regime "were built on lies." "Now lies surround him in death," he said. What about the German people? They would remember only Hitler's death and the battle of Berlin, Shirer concluded, but "will be too stupid to remember the suicide."

To some observers, like Germany's allies and sympathizers, the new Soviet announcement and the other versions made it clear Hitler had somehow expired in Berlin. Japan, after claiming Hitler had been killed by Red Army artillery fire, sent condolences to the German Ambassador in Tokyo. Similar feelings were expressed by the Prime Minister of neutral Ireland, Eamon de Valera, to the German Legation in Dublin. Portugal, also neutral, ordered two days of mourning for Hitler, and a memorial service was held in a Lisbon church. Fumed an angry American columnist, "Even neutrality can be carried too far. The tears which were shed for Hitler wouldn't have watered a baby cactus."

Others took the differing stories of Hitler's death to mean that he had not perished. For those who had been deeply involved in the war or the terrible suffering it had caused, it seemed impossible that he had suddenly gone. "The peace of the grave," it was felt by many Americans, "is too good for him." "I want him alive," said one, a postman in Miami, "so that we can torture him as he has done to us." If this archfiend were indeed gone, how could the world have its justifiable revenge against him? Still others, caught up in the excitement and drama of the war, realized that if Hitler were alive, the war would probably continue. Yet it appeared somehow abnormal for the bloodiest and deadliest war in history to have wound down so quickly. Only the previous winter, the Western Allies had fought desperately to defeat the Germans in the Battle of the Bulge in Belgium. When Hitler had supposedly died, summer had not even arrived.

Most Allied authorities, tired of what they called too many "Nazi tricks," reserved comment on the issue. They would believe Hitler dead when they saw his body. Still, thoughts of a "dead Hitler" made for cheerful talk among American soldiers in Paris. A Chicago pilot shot by the Nazis and left to die, said, "I hope the sonuvabitch was as scared of dying as I was when that SS officer let me have it through the stomach." A bit later, he added, "Now they say Hitler is dead. Maybe he is. If he is, I don't believe he died heroically. Mussolini died at least something like a dictator, but somehow I can't figure Hitler dying in action." Another soldier noted, "I wish I was the guy who killed him. I'd killed him a little slower."[9]

The soldiers were not alone in their skepticism. A New York astrologist, Helene Paul, read the headlines of Hitler's reported demise and said, "It can't be so." Using the same horoscope Hitler was said to have consulted at crucial times, she concluded, "Mathematically accurate calculations show without question that he left Germany a week ago and fled with a large sum of money." Where had he gone? "That," she said, "is not in the horoscope."

Public opinion was also bombarded in the early days of May by an increasingly uncertain western press. As the war continued and no confirmation of Hitler's death came from Berlin, concern spread that no matter what had happened to him, the dangerous legend surrounding his end that some had once prophesied had been born. Shirer thought it a mystery that Hitler had not left behind a political testament for later Nazis. "Only one thing bothers me about Hitler's death," he said. "I was sure that just before he killed himself he would issue a grandiose proclamation, a final testament in which he would recapitulate all the Nazi nonsense in which most Germans believed. But Hitler died without leaving a word, which is most unlike him." Such a final revelation from the Fuehrer, he guessed, could have "become a sort of Bible to Germans if they should ever recover their present catastrophe and begin again on the job that first the Kaiser and then Hitler failed to finish."[10]

Shirer and other western journalists were convinced that World War II had been a "holy war," a mighty collision between the powers of good (democracy) and evil (Nazism). They emphasized that the Germans had purposely tried to delay their defeat through deception in Hitler's death and creating the myth of his martyrdom. Explained *Le Monde,* such a myth would "serve the regrouping of the followers and the revival of Nazism after the war." The last triumph of a great enemy of the public peace, like Hitler, it asserted, had always been the formation of a legend. "Napoleon," a British paper noted, "had done it at St. Helena—Napoleon the lover of peace, the maker of laws, the unifier of Europe, forced by perfidious Albion to make war for the freedom of Europe. Hitler had been casting himself in this role for some time."

It was the obligation of the press, the latter felt, not to permit this to happen. "It is our duty," said another crusading paper, the London *Evening Standard,* "to see that there shall be no bearers of the legend." Louis Lochner, chief of the former Associated Press office in Berlin, argued that Goebbels had carefully staged "the legend of Hitler's meeting a hero's death." Then he sketched the following possible scenario: "Doenitz's announcement by no means ends our troubles with Hitler. They may only have begun. There may be a state funeral for him, and photographers may have the opportunity to produce pictures of a dead man labeled Hitler. Then, some day later, a resurrected Hitler may again stir the world."

The crusade against untruth became a difficult one. Indeed impossible, especially as more of Hitler's generals and key officials were taken prisoner and voiced their opinions. Field Marshal Gerd von Rundstedt, former commander of German forces in the West and held by the British, told reporters, "I feel satisfied the Fuehrer is dead." But not by suicide. "Either the Fuehrer was wounded and died as a result of these wounds and possibly even fell fighting, or he died under the impact of the pressure of events upon his soul. Never, never will I believe he put an end to his own life. That was not in accordance with his nature." Was Hitler still alive and hiding? "Impossible," came the quick retort, "anyway, where would he go?" Added the Marshal, "I last saw Hitler in Berlin on March 12, and he was shaking as if he had the palsy."

Another German prisoner, Erwin Giesing, a physician who claimed to have examined Hitler after the bomb had exploded at his headquarters in July 1944, doubted that the Fuehrer had gone to the grave. "I saw him for the last time on February 15," said Giesing from a prison cell in Bavaria, "and found he was sound of heart and lungs and for a man of fifty-six he was above average in health. At the time, Hitler told me that if the war went against Germany, he would die leading his troops." The doctor totally discounted Himmler's theory that Hitler could have died from ill health, possibly a brain hemorrhage. Instead, he believed it possible the dictator was alive and hiding. Perhaps hoping to inflate his importance with his captors, he alleged, "I am the only living person who could positively identify the Fuehrer's body." Other doctors who had known Hitler equally well, he maintained, were Karl Brandt and Theodore Morell, "but they had probably been killed." Giesing also said he had X-rays of the Fuehrer, taken after the July bomb plot.[11]

Another type of prisoner, the frail and tormented souls newly liberated from Nazi concentration camps, reacted differently. At the Buchenwald camp near Weimar, where one would have expected a celebration at the word of Hitler's death, there was apathy. The former prisoners, many nearing death themselves from malnutrition and mistreatment, discredited the report, expecting anything from the Nazi oppressor. "He was such a crook," whispered one feebly. "I think he was incapable even of dying honestly," added another. A Russian prisoner cried uncontrollably, "Hitler has escaped with a quick end, but he caused such suffering for millions. I hate it."

The appearance of ever new stories about Hitler's demise proved most frustrating to those wishing to stop what they believed to be a potentially dangerous legend. One came from a Paris radio broadcast, quoting "well informed sources," which reported that Hitler had been assassinated on the night of April 21-22, after a showdown quarrel with his leaders over continuing the war. This version, too, glorified the Fuehrer. His own generals and other subordinates, it said, had stabbed Germany's heroic Siegfried in the back. Hitler had allegedly presided over a war council meeting on April 21, attended by several field marshals, Himmler, Goering, and Goebbels. The atmosphere had become so tense that when Himmler, Goering and one of the marshals were invited to return alone the next day, each feared he would be executed like those who had opposed Hitler in the July plot.

During the night, so the Paris broadcast said, only a few hours before the second meeting, an explosion ripped Hitler's private apartments. He and his guard corps had been killed.

This tale seemed tied to the western idea, popular for some days, that it had been Himmler, and to a lesser extent Doenitz, who had been in control of the remnants of the Nazi government. Upon Hitler's murder, Himmler had allegedly seized command and Goering had fled to Norway.[12] The story, moreover, prompted a further piece of speculation in the West. Hitler, Goebbels, and Goering, so the view went, had been murdered by members of the Himmler-Doenitz clique. Thus the vanquished Germans were reduced to sheer villainy and treachery—another example of their total wickedness.

Meanwhile, even though Berlin and the German armies in the Netherlands, Denmark, and northern Germany had been conquered, the Nazis persisted in portraying their battle as the last defense of western civilization from Asiatic Bolshevism. Reports from the German-controlled Czech radio said that Himmler and Martin Bormann, Hitler's private secretary and the Nazi official closest to the Fuehrer in the last years of the war, were hiding in Prague, seeking to hold together the dwindling German pocket there. But on May 6, the German Command in Bohemia and Moravia broadcast that Hitler's "most intimate assistants have also met a hero's death at the Fuehrer's side in the final battle for Berlin." These included Goebbels, his wife and children; Bormann; General Hans Krebs, the last German Chief of Staff; General Wilhelm Burgdorf, an Army adjutant at Hitler's headquarters; and Werner Naumann, Goebbels' assistant in the Propaganda Ministry. "The struggle for the Reich Chancellery building was waged with the utmost grimness down to the last moment," the broadcast noted, describing the Battle of Berlin. "The Soviets report that it was nothing but a heap of rubble when Soviet forces occupied the Government quarter."

Thus, a week after the Nazi announcement of Hitler's death, the world seemed further than ever from learning what had really happened to him. Had he died a "hero's death," fighting for the Western Christian world against Communism? Or had he killed himself, thereby swindling the world out of even the barest measure of revenge, his capture and deliberate execution? No one knew what to believe; the Nazis had made lies so much a part of their politics, and the reports of

Hitler's fate had varied so widely for weeks. Nor had the Russians, with their contradictory statements about "fascist tricks" and Hitler's suicide, helped to clear up the mystery.

As the fighting in Europe came within hours of ending, suspicion spread that the master Nazi trickster was pulling one last great hoax on the world. Although Hitler's armies had been beaten, the possibility existed that he had saved himself, and was perhaps preparing the way for his return to power at a later and more opportune time. Had he escaped, laughing at the headlines and news flashes? "The world would likely never know," answered an American paper, "if, when or how Adolf Hitler had died."

3

Missing: The Corpse

Dead or alive, he had to be found. German and Russian reports of his demise had flooded the world's airwaves and newspapers on May 1 and 2. Differences in the Nazi and Communist versions had left the West wondering. Stories already circulated in England and the United States that Hitler had stood heroically against the Communists and that he had likely escaped to freedom.

Each prospect threatened a world that had spent six agonizing, death-filled years to rid itself of the Nazi curse. Should either be discovered as, true, there would surely be political consequences. Fears had already spread of a resurrection of Nazism after the war. These gave credence to Allied spokesmen, and particularly the Russians, who demanded the division and harshest suppression of Germany. Furthermore, the killer of millions had to be punished for his unspeakable crimes. The nations, families, and friends of the masses he had tormented craved revenge; they would not rest till Hitler's fate had been determined.

To find the answer, the Allies had to force Germany's full surrender. This came on May 7, 1945, at Allied headquarters in France. At the insistence of the Soviet Union, the Germans repeated the formal submission the next day in Berlin. The Armageddon in Europe had finally ended. While finishing the greatest war in history was uppermost to the Allies, and especially to the Americans still battling the Japanese, the issue was left curiously unsettled because the war's chief perpetrator had not been found. Nor had his Nazi associates, called by Americans the "rats of Europe," been captured and punished. To be sure, the world in which Hitler had lived was dead. But what about him?

The Soviet reports coming out of Berlin were chaotic. They indicated that perhaps the Russians had not totally subdued the city or that they were having difficulty locating Hitler's last headquarters among the rubble. For a week after the release of Fritsche's statement that Hitler had died by his own hand, Soviet news accounts told the world that the dictator was nowhere in evidence. It appeared that the Soviet press and radio might even be indulging in the same speculation as that of the Western media. However, events of May and early June 1945 illustrated something much different. The Kremlin, and especially Stalin, seem to have become as concerned with tying the Hitler mystery to their demands in Germany and eastern Europe as with finding the Nazi leader. Ironically, while Hitler had portrayed himself as Europe's only hope against Communism, his strange disappearance (among many other factors) would favor postwar Soviet expansion in Europe.

Most Western observers were convinced that the Russians would soon find Hitler's body or explain conclusively what had happened to him. Moscow, it was assumed, had every reason to do so. Except for the Jews, the Russians had suffered more at the hands of the Nazis than anyone. But the Anglo-American concept of justice, having been satisfied with the discovery of Hitler's corpse or with his capture and trial, differed from that of the Soviet Union and its leaders. Although the latter wanted Hitler dead and buried, Stalin's hatred and suspicion of the Germans dictated that the Nazi leader would be kept alive, at least in spirit and propaganda. A "live" Hitler could be a warning to future Russian generations never to trust the Germans. It would also be valuable in Moscow's relations with the West.

On May 3 the Soviet commentator, Nikolai Tikhonov, boldly announced on the front page of the Communist party paper, *Pravda,* that Hitler was not in Berlin. Soviet police, he said, were combing the wreckage of the devastated capital for "war criminals." Disclosing that the Russians were not persuaded Hitler had committed suicide, as Fritsche had told them, Tikhonov referred to a tenacious hunt for his body. The riddle of his whereabouts, he vowed, would soon be solved:

The Fascists always were fond of mysteries. What of their latest—the Fuehrer's final mystery? "Hitler committed suicide." "Goebbels committed suicide." We shall find out the truth. We shall discover whether it is a case of bankrupt gamblers blowing out their brains, or a piece of cheap mystification.

Hitler himself is no more. Whether he has fled to the devil in hell, or to the embraces of some Fascist protector, he is no more. He has crossed himself out of life. And we shall find out what really happened to him. Yes, if he fled we shall unearth him, wherever he tries to hide.[1]

The next day, Russian dispatches from Berlin told of how Soviet troops had smashed into Hitler's burning Chancellery. Smoke and flame hung so thick that the soldiers were forced to leave the building without completing their search for him. According to the Soviet Army paper, *Red Star,* the bodies of Hitler, Goebbels, and Goering (if he too had joined Hitler in self-destruction), would be hard to identify in the flaming building. The story strengthened the view in Moscow that if Hitler had killed himself, he had not done so in the Chancellery.

The Russian population considered the mystery a lively issue. Since Berlin had fallen, the whereabouts of Hitler had become the burning question among the Russian people. Suspicion of the Nazis was deep-rooted; the people had expected anything in the last dramatic moments of the war. A poll of Moscow citizens, published by the Associated Press, showed that most thought Hitler and Goebbels had fled Germany. A policeman said, "Hitler's hidden. I don't think he's dead." Remarked a navy lieutenant, "I'm sure he's hiding in a submarine. He's going to do a Jules Verne." A Red Air Force captain had just returned to Moscow from Berlin: "I don't think he's dead. It's a Nazi trick. I'm sure he's safe." Revenge was also on the minds of the Muscovites. Claimed a Red Army private, "I have been wounded five times. I blame Hitler for each wound. If he is dead it is too bad because death is too good for him." The survey especially illustrated the popularity and prestige of the victorious Red Army. "Marshal Zhukov is there [in Berlin]," said many of those questioned. "He will find out everything today or tomorrow."

Still other accounts, less publicized, appeared to stress that Hitler and his top aides had died. Goebbels' radio expert, Fritsche, having earlier declared that Hitler and Goebbels had killed themselves, told Soviet interrogators that Hitler's body had been hidden at a place where it could not be found. Moscow radio added that most Berliners questioned by Red soldiers believed Hitler had shot himself and his Propaganda Minister had taken poison. Several Russian newspapers mentioned the possibility that Hitler's remains had been cremated by the fires raging through his bunker headquarters below the Chancellery.[2]

The hunt in Berlin continued. By May 7 and 8, scores of rain-soaked bodies (it had been drizzling in the city for more than a week) had been found in the Chancellery courtyard, the Reichstag, and other public buildings. High ranking Nazis, including officials of the General Staff, SS, and party, had killed themselves rather than be taken prisoner by the Red Army. None of the bodies, claimed *Pravda,* was that of Hitler or Goebbels. "The Soviet Army, and our Western friends," it said, "want to see the Fuehrer's corpse life size." "The myth of Hitler's 'heroic death,'" guaranteed the paper, "will be exposed."

Meanwhile, Moscow radio seemed to confirm that the dragnet for Hitler had experienced difficulties. Or, perhaps its contradictory statements betrayed a lack of coordination of the Soviet media. Whatever the reason, the radio called on the evening of May 5 for "rough justice" for captured Nazi leaders. "The fate of Hitler himself still remains doubtful," it added. But two days later, a commentary beamed into eastern Europe, vast areas of which had been overrun by Red soldiers, asserted without explanation that "Adolf Hitler [had] ended his career in a cowardly manner."[3]

Announcements of the next few days multiplied the confusion. According to the Tass war correspondent, Piluigen, an unidentified Russian general had said that the Soviets had found in Berlin the bullet-torn and battered body of a man recognized as Hitler. Photographs had been taken of the body from all angles for study in Moscow. Those of Hitler's domestic staff who had fallen into Russian hands had also viewed the body. All but one of the chauffeurs and maidservants had testified that the corpse was Hitler's. The lone dissenter had declared emphatically that the body was not that of Hitler, but one of his cooks. Claiming that he had known the cook intimately, the servant had asserted that the "cook double" had been murdered because of his startling likeness to Hitler, allowing the latter to escape from Berlin. The bodies of Goebbels and his family had also been uncovered, related Piluigen, but Goebbels was so badly burned that he was hardly recognizable.

Two days later, on May 10, the Soviets released an equally ambiguous report, but it appeared to confirm the discovery of the carcasses. Four badly charred corpses had been found, it said, "one of which might be that of Adolf Hitler, war criminal No. 1," and each measured and photographed by experts. But the Russians were beginning to doubt, said the report, that Hitler's corpse would ever be found. Instead, they thought that he might have been killed by the people around him as Berlin fell, and the flames that had swept his underground headquarters had probably destroyed his remains.[4]

His bunker beneath the Chancellery had also been located by Red soldiers. An elaborate hideaway, the Russians described it, a virtual "underground city." Entry to it was through a concrete tower in the Chancellery garden, where the bodies of many top Nazis who had committed suicide had lain. A narrow door in the tower led to Hitler's den, far below the ground. There the Soviets had come upon a fortress of several floors and thick concrete walls that had housed Hitler and Goebbels in their final days.[5] A suffocating smoke made working in the passages and rooms difficult. Nevertheless, the Russians admitted unearthing one of Goebbels' suitcases full of documents, and finding a plan to evacuate Hitler and his court from Berlin.

Near the Chancellery, Nazi prisoners had been seized. "Most are serfs from Hitler's immediate entourage," said the Russians, "and when speaking of their master they are careful not to drop an unnecessary word." Some captives freely cursed the Fuehrer—"the custom in Berlin today," snorted one Russian account. "When interrogated about what happened to Hitler and Goebbels, the prisoners contradict each other hopelessly. Their improbable stories have only one purpose—to cover up all traces of the criminals."

Such reports, although not saying conclusively that one of the bodies in Berlin was Hitler's, raised hopes in the West that he had died. "The bodies of Goebbels, his wife, and children," *Red Star* added to the optimism, "have been discovered in the bunker and virtually identified." Prime Minister Churchill, asked in the House of Commons his view of whether Hitler was still around, replied that he agreed with the "general opinion" that Hitler was deceased. But, he cautioned, "I shall not make guesses. When we have anything particular, I shall be quite ready to announce it."

The Prime Minister, as the other Allied leaders, had to rely on the Soviet Union for their information. With a couple of exceptions, Nazi officials captured by the British and Americans in western Germany were rarely more helpful than their Russian-held counterparts in Berlin. They too told a melange of stories about what happened to their Fuehrer. Only a few had been in a position to know his fate with fair certainty, but they ventured guesses nonetheless. And most of their opinions were printed by eager journalists.

Nazis from the highest ranks, like Goering and Himmler, to a few of Hitler's stenographers, secretaries, and doctors fell into Anglo-American hands throughout May and the beginning of June 1945. Some doubted the story of Hitler's end. "If Hitler would tell me himself, I wouldn't believe it," said Hjalmar Schacht, one of the experts responsible for financing German rearmament in the 1930s. Yet the bulk of the captives felt Hitler was no more. From a prison in Austria, former commander of German forces in Italy and North Africa, Field Marshal Albert Kesselring, told interrogators, "Hitler could have escaped to south Germany, but he chose instead to stay in Berlin, because he was a brave man." The Marshal's only regret over Hitler was that the latter, a "genius," had been overburdened by his responsibilities. "Sometimes the ideas of a genius are misunderstood," he added.

It was the surprising surrender of Goering to the Americans on May 9 that brought the world its first account of Hitler's last days from one of his closest lieutenants. A rotund figure notorious for his bluff and braggadocio, and "the one with all the medals" as an American newsman described Goering, the former Reich Marshal and Luftwaffe commander gave his version of why Hitler had relieved him of his offices two weeks before. "I was sentenced by Hitler to die on April 24," he said, "after suggesting that I take over leadership of the Reich." As the Allied armies were threatening that day to cut Germany in half, Goering had been in Berchtesgaden. "I called the Fuehrer by phone," he said, "and reminded him that if anything happened to him, he had designated me to take command of the government." But Hitler, having looked with increasing disfavor on the Air Force since its failures in Britain and elsewhere in the war, flew into a rage when Goering hinted at the succession. Three days later, on April 27, Goering had been captured by SS troops and told he would be executed. "Only my loyal Luftwaffe troops saved me," boasted the Reich Marshal.

"I am convinced Hitler died," he said. Maintaining he had last seen the Fuehrer in Berlin on April 22, as Russian forces were hammering into the city, he confirmed in part that Hitler had been in the capital directing its defense. "The Fuehrer," he told Allied newsmen, "came to a sudden realization on the twenty-second that the war was lost." What did Goering think had happened to his chief? "He had been ill with a brain disorder," came the answer without elaboration, "and he may have shot himself."[6]

Another key figure in the Hitler saga was Gerhard Herrgesell, taken into custody by the Americans. One of Hitler's private stenographers, he had attended the military conferences held twice daily between Hitler and his High Command since September 1942. Herrgesell had also been present in the bunker when President Roosevelt's death was announced, and he was a scribe for the last such conference held in the Berlin shelter on April 22, 1945. On the evening of the twenty-second, he and another stenographer had flown out of Berlin at Hitler's orders. Once captured, they led the Americans to shorthand notes of the military meetings, sent in mid-April for safety from Berlin to Berchtesgaden.

Of Hitler's last days, the stenographers contributed more details to Goering's patchwork story. Theirs would become an increasingly familiar account, as they told of desperate efforts by Hitler's court to persuade him to leave Berlin. "His stubbornness gradually changed to bitterness," they related, "prompting him to attack and accuse of treason the leaders of his own Armed Forces." Goering had been the first to catch the Fuehrer's wrath; he and the Luftwaffe were berated by Hitler in a meeting on April 20, the Fuehrer's birthday, whereupon Goering had chosen to leave Berlin for the south. "Hitler's secretary, Bormann," said the stenographers, "was especially anxious to push Goering out of Hitler's inner circle." As the Russians now penetrated the Berlin suburbs, causing grave concern among those in the Fuehrerbunker, tension had also dominated a second meeting on Hitler's birthday.

Hours later, on April 21, several of Hitler's military advisers, including Doenitz, had left the bunker. Whether Hitler would remain in Berlin, nothing had been said. At noon, Goebbels entered the underground sanctuary and reported that the Russians had pushed into the Prezlauer Allee, a mere twenty-minute walk from the Chancellery. "He told Hitler they had the city surrounded," said Herrgesell, "but the Fuehrer continued to study a map and ignored his Minister."

The decisive military conferences had been held on the afternoon of April 22. Present were Hitler; Field Marshal Wilhelm Keitel, chief of the Armed Forces High Command; General Alfred Jodl, adviser on strategy and operations; Bormann; and several stenographers. "Hitler suddenly shocked the others by proclaiming the war was 'irretrievably lost,'" related Herrgesell. Hitler had lashed out at the Army, saying, "I lost confidence in the Wehrmacht quite a while ago. I am even losing confidence in the Waffen SS, for the first time." What convinced him that his Elite Guard had lost heart had been the failure of SS troops to hold the Russians north of Berlin.

"Then," Herrgesell recounted the dramatic episode, "Hitler repeatedly expressed his determination to stay in Berlin, and said he wanted to die there. He thought it would be the greatest service he could render to the honor of the German nation. Angry and excited, he paced the floor almost constantly, walking back and forth, sometimes smacking his fist into his hand." Despite protests of opposition from Bormann and Keitel to his staying in the capital, his view prevailed. He had then suggested, in a "vague and uncertain" voice, that his subordinates go to southern Germany to form a government, possibly with Goering as his "successor."

Showing his blind faith in Hitler, Herrgesell told his American interrogators that he thought the German leader had died a hero's death. "I don't believe the Fuehrer remained in the cellar," he theorized. "I believe he went out, possibly several times, looking for death to which he was now so completely resigned, and that he may have died by artillery fire." Questioned about American intelligence reports that Hitler had been killed and his body destroyed by his personal SS adjutant, Otto Guensche, Herrgesell conceded the possibility. "Hitler was never out of Guensche's sight," he said. "Hitler wanted to make certain he died instantly. He said he did not want to be wounded. He did not want to be captured by the Russians nor did he want his corpse to fall into their hands."[7] Although few suspected it at the time, the world had its first nearly accurate account of Hitler's final days, through April 22.

Hitler's presence in Berlin was substantiated by Theodore Morell, another captured Nazi, who had once been presumed dead by the Allies. Having served as the Fuehrer's personal physician since 1937, Morell was an ailing man of fifty-nine years when seized by the Americans. Recovering in a Bavarian hospital, he explained to newsmen, "I last saw Hitler on April 21 in the Fuehrerbunker." Hitler's drive was kept at a feverish pitch throughout the war, Morell said, by giving him injections of glucose, vitamins, and caffein. "Such infusions," said Morell, "were necessary to offset the Fuehrer's high expenditure of nervous and physical energy, but I deny that he ever resorted to using narcotics, as some have said about him." His patient had suffered severely from colitis, Morell continued, and had begun in 1943 experiencing tremors in his left arm and leg. The vibrations became especially noticeable when the dictator felt overly tired or emotionally upset. "The Fuehrer is probably no longer alive," Morell said, "but I am certain he did not commit suicide. He instead probably succumbed to some natural ailment, such as coronary sclerosis or angina pectoris."

Hitler, after Morell had recommended more injections, had allegedly expelled the doctor from the bunker on April 21. His face "unhealthy red and bloated" and "hands trembling," Hitler had screamed at Morell, suspecting the doctor of trying to dope him so that Bormann and Keitel could take him out of doomed Berlin. "I left for Munich the next day," Morell recalled. Shortly after his capture, another of Hitler's physicians, Karl Brandt, was arrested. While Hitler had nothing physically wrong with him, Brandt testified, he had suffered from headaches and stomach disorders. Brandt said he had no knowledge of Morell's injections.[8]

Such news seemed to affirm that Hitler, in his final days, had been in Berlin and had possibly suffered from poor health. Arrests of other top Nazis produced little. "The Fuehrer is probably dead," Robert Ley, the drunken and slothful head of the Nazi Labor Front, told his American captors. "But we Nazis will continue," he bragged, "because you don't know who most of us are." Likewise, nothing useful had come from the capture and brief interrogation of the potentate of

Nazi terror, Himmler. Excepting Hitler, he was the biggest catch of the war.

Having shaved his mustache, placed a patch over one eye, put on civilian clothes, and given himself forged identification papers and two bodyguards, Himmler had fled to northern Germany. Forty miles west of Hamburg, British soldiers seized him on May 23. It had been his Gestapo mind that betrayed him. He made his military pass too carefully, and since practically no one in that part of the Reich had papers of any kind, he was arrested and questioned. Finally, disgusted at being treated as any menial prisoner, he had torn off his patch, put on glasses, and announced who he really was. While angrily protesting being searched, he bit into a phial of poison hidden in his mouth. The potassium cyanide, or "rat poisoning," as the American magazine *Newsweek,* called it, killed him instantly. A few days later, his body was hurried off to an unknown grave. No one cared to remember where the oppressor who had led the despised Gestapo and SS had been buried.

The capture of Himmler, Goering, and the others became an immediate sore spot with the Russians. They accused the West of pampering such prisoners and according them easy treatment. "Imprisonment for them means a hotel with comfortable service," grumbled Moscow radio. "They are treated to dinners, they are swamped by interviews. The greater the number of skull and cross-bones on the shoulders of the Hitlerite robbers, the greater the care shown them." The Americans, apparently caught unprepared by such blunt criticism, banned at the end of May 1945 news interviews with the captives. "A new kind of censorship at the source is coming into practice," *The New York Times* reacted, "so that the American people are being deprived of information to which they are entitled."

Something else had doubtlessly disturbed the Russians. This was the evidence, mounting each moment now, that Hitler had spent the last days of the war in Berlin. Whether or not he had expired there was another matter, but since the city was in Soviet hands, pressure intensified for Moscow either to find the Nazi ruler or explain what had happened to him. There were potential questions. Could, for example, the Western Allies use the mystery as a future weapon in gaining access to Berlin, the heart of central Europe that Red soldiers had sacrificed so much to conquer? The Russians may also have been uncomfortable about the widespread praise of Hitler and the view among Nazi prisoners that one day their philosophy would be revived.

For whatever reason, Moscow directed the commanders of the Red Army in Berlin in mid-May to keep quiet on the Hitler question. Nothing further could be discussed about the Fuehrerbunker or about what Soviet troops had found there. The gag order, said *Pravda,* would aid the job of Soviet experts investigating the shelter. Conjecturing again that Hitler may have fled, the paper noted, "The indescribable confusion that reigns in Hitler's headquarters proved a desperate escape" by the Fuehrer's staff.[9]

This silence was likely tied to several broader and more important issues that had surfaced by May, dividing the Russians and their Western Allies. For the British and Americans, a key fear had become the future expansion of Soviet influence in eastern Europe, especially in Poland and Germany. Of equal concern to the United States was its continued war against Japan. Stalin and Moscow, on the other hand, had suspicions of the powerful Anglo-American presence in western Europe and of a potential German resurgence. Both the Western powers and the Soviet Union wished to reorganize the continent as closely as possible in accord with their own security.

A new battle now unfolded, eventually termed the "Cold War" by some, between the one-time allies. Its weapons were propaganda and threats, backed by huge armies occupying special zones in Germany and soldiers stationed in other parts of Europe. Till the spheres of influence throughout Europe could be settled, it was in the Kremlin's best interest to remain mute on Hitler, and possibly even keep him "alive" for propaganda purposes. As accusations and demands spewed forth from both sides, the belief that Hitler had survived became a convenient tool for Moscow.

It especially served the Russians in the controversies that arose over the control of Berlin and the governing of Germany. After the Nazi surrender, the Soviet Union showed no signs of wanting to share the capital. It seemed to believe Berlin was the heart of Germany, and to rule it meant they possessed a kind of psychological hold on the rest of the country. Consequently, no Western troops or journalists were allowed into the city. Another problem involved the zones in Germany to be occupied by the Allies. Zones of occupation had been agreed on by the Allies during the war. A Russian zone was established that included Berlin and borders roughly the same as those of the present German Democratic Republic. When Germany surrendered, however, the American and British armies held land far into the area designated for the Russians. Churchill, obsessed with the presence of Communist troops in eastern and central Europe and with Britain's vanishing position on the continent, opposed the Allies withdrawing from the Soviet territory. "The Soviet menace, to my eyes," he later recalled, "had already replaced the Nazi foe. But no comradeship against it existed." His remark referred to his American ally, still tied down in the war in the Pacific and more agreeable to a movement of its troops back into the American zone.

Stalin knew of or at least suspected Churchill's hostility, despite the secrecy with which the Anglo-Americans had discussed their respective views during April and May.[10] This may have been the prime source for the sudden propaganda barrage of the Russians in mid-May, claiming the Nazis now planned a new war with the aid of sympathetic elements in the West. The latter included Spain and Argentina, accused by the Soviets of harboring "Nazi rats" and Italian Fascists. Citing statements by Nazi prisoners like Goering, Rundstedt, and Kesselring, blaming Hitler for the war and absolving themselves from any responsibility, Moscow radio complained, "There is system in what they are doing, and the stuff is deliberate poison. These criminals should not be allowed to continue their efforts to pave the way for a third world war."

From this accusation, the Russians found it a short jump to demand the harshest punishment of the "war criminals" and German people. Nor was it hard for them to justify their continued occupation of Germany and eastern Europe. Their suspicion of a Nazi revival, though erroneous inasmuch as the German Army had been smashed, had become genuine. What aggravated Soviet fears, moreover, was the product of their own refusal to join the United Nations War Crimes Commission, formed to plan and organize the punishment of the Nazis. That most leading Nazis were streaming to western Germany to escape what they feared would be a more stern Communist retribution, and falling into Anglo-American hands, angered Moscow.

Russia's principal recourse was to urge a hard line against the

Germans. "How do they [the Allies] prepare to punish the Hitlerite criminals?" questioned a hostile Tass, as it reviewed the Allies' handling of Doenitz (arrested by the British on May 23), Keitel, and other German generals. Especially galling to the Russians was a British suggestion that Doenitz and the High Command be used as temporary intermediaries in controlling and administering the remainder of the German forces. Moscow radio called repeatedly for the instant execution of Hitler (once he was found), Himmler, and Doenitz.

In the Soviet view, such slackness on the part of the Allies and the anxiety over renewed German aggression, justified the expanding Russian influence in eastern Europe. So had the enormous Russian sacrifice in the war. "In the victory over Germany," contended Ilya Ehrenburg, the Soviet journalist, "we had military friends but, all the same, the whole world sees their liberator in our people. We were alone when we saw the invader in our land. The English were then at home in their island, America was not in the war and France had been defeated." A Moscow broadcast on May 16 stressed, "The Soviet Union prefers to create a firm unshakeable peace rather than to fight an enemy invasion." It reproached those who opposed Russia's efforts "to organize a firm peace in Eastern Europe." Such people had forgotten that Britain, "with the English Channel," and America, "with two oceans," had "a much greater security even in our century than the nations on the continent of Europe or Asia."[11]

What solicited the most sympathy in the West were the Russians' virulent anti-German feelings, aroused by the continued reports of the Nazi concentration camps. With their mass graves, living skeletons, and torture chambers, the camps horrified the world. A British parliamentary delegation visited Buchenwald; news articles and photographs were published of Dachau and Belsen. One angry reader wrote *The Atlanta Constitution,* praising the sending of American congressmen and journalists "to see the Hun 'murder farms.'" Moscow broadcast a report on the death camp at Auschwitz. Four million persons had perished there, it said, in elaborate death factories that included gas chambers and crematories. The Germans, except for those who had themselves suffered in these human slaughterhouses, professed shock and surprise. "We knew of the camps," they said, "but not what was going on inside." This was not always a credible argument. Inhabitants of towns near Belsen were forced by the British to see the ghastly spectacle first-hand. At Dachau, the Americans did the same, showing a film about that camp to the German public.

In condemning the Germans as a people, emotions reached the breaking point in both the United States and Russia. "Even now, when he has surrendered, the enemy remains an enemy," a Soviet broadcast on May 14 bellowed. "He has not renounced his banditry, his bestial ideology, his thirst for domination. He will not change." Nearly half of America wanted the Nazi prisoners executed, according to public opinion polls in May and June 1945. "Kill them," "Hang them," "Wipe them off the face of the earth," were typical American feelings. Some surveyed said, "I want them to die slowly" and "They should be put on public display in cages." A letter to the *San Francisco Chronicle* raved, "The Germans are a war-loving people, the Americans a peace-loving nation." Even in Latin America, postwar passions ran high. A Colombian student, after having impersonated the corpse of Hitler in a "Victory over Europe" parade, died from stab wounds inflicted by a mob.

The possibility that Hitler had survived enhanced public nervousness over a rebirth of Nazism and heightened the calls for crushing the threat by taking the severest of measures against the Germans. At the end of May and during the early days of June, the Russians, and especially Stalin, appear to have decided on what their explanation to the world would be regarding the Nazi leader. Instead of publishing an official version of their findings, they kept afloat the impression he might have escaped Berlin by issuing a string of contradictory statements.

Such pronouncements may also have resulted from differences of opinion between Stalin and his commanders in Berlin. Frequent reports from Red Army correspondents in the German capital several weeks before, suggesting Hitler might have killed himself, hinted that the Army thought it had located his remains and therefore crowned its brilliant victory with a final, master stroke of success. But the hush order to the Berlin command in mid-May indicated Stalin and the political leadership had other ideas. Perhaps the Kremlin genuinely suspected Hitler had survived. Or, what seems equally plausible, it saw strategic diplomatic and political advantages in saying so.

The Russians broke their silence on Hitler at the end of May. Fresh stories started coming out of Berlin, none supported by evidence. A team of Soviet detectives reported concluding that if Hitler had died, he had not expired in the ruins of his Chancellery. Far underground and about five hundred meters from his bunker, the Russians had found a super-secret concrete shelter. Germans had hidden there until May 9. Under cross-examination, those who had told of Hitler's death had twisted their stories, clashed in details, and finally admitted that none of them had actually seen the Fuehrer end his life.

But the tale of one of his bodyguards, an SS officer not identified to the West by the Russians, had caught their attention. The officer claimed to the Soviets that he had seen Hitler as late as April 27, sitting in his personal apartment in the Fuehrerbunker. "Hitler fidgeted on a sofa," said the SS man, "and he asked me about casualties near the Chancellery, where fighting was heavy." Then the Nazi leader had begun one of his angry harangues, his voice even ringing above the din of battle outside. He had allegedly predicted that after he died, Russia and the Western Allies would quarrel over power in Europe. "The conflict must come," the Russians quoted him as telling the SS officer. "But when it comes I must be alive to lead the German people, to help them arise from defeat, to lead them to final victory. Germany can hope for the future only if the whole world thinks I am dead."

Meanwhile, an Allied official in Paris quoted a Russian general as saying Hitler had died from "a mercy injection of some sort." The needle had supposedly been administered by "a Dr. Morell." Hitler, the Soviet officer had told American intelligence, had been paralyzed and delirious with pain in the last days of his life. This account was based, the Russian said, on the interrogation of three persons close to the Fuehrer. Again, however, the Soviets identified none of their sources.

It was now three weeks since the German surrender, and there was still no proof of Hitler's death. Above all, no corpse. Nor would the world probably discover one, Stalin himself suddenly informed the Americans on May 26. The Russian Premier made his remarkable statement privately to Harry Hopkins, a special adviser to President Truman, who had flown to Moscow at the end of May. Hopkins' mission was to confer with Stalin on the alarming conflicts in policy having arisen between the Soviet and American delegates at the San Francisco Conference. The envoy was also to discuss an upcoming meeting of the Allied military leaders tentatively scheduled for Berlin.

They talked about Hitler briefly on two occasions during the eleven-day visit. At their first meeting on May 26, Hopkins said he hoped the Russians would find Hitler's body. However, Stalin doubted that the Fuehrer had been finished. "In my opinion," he replied, "Hitler is not dead but is hiding somewhere." These words triggered an immediate, spontaneous discussion. Stalin would demonstrate his incredibly mistrustful nature, and Hopkins an unwillingness to question the viewpoint of the Russian leader.

Soviet doctors thought they had identified the body of Goebbels and Hitler's chauffeur, said the Premier. But he, personally, even doubted if Goebbels had died. Bormann, Goebbels, Hitler, and "probably" Krebs, had escaped and were in hiding. Hopkins seemed to accept what was said, neither doubting the assertions nor disagreeing with them. He knew the Germans had several large submarines, he said, but "no trace of them had been found." His "hope," Hopkins added, was that "we would track Hitler down wherever he might be."

The exchange proceeded. Stalin answered that he knew of the submarines. They "had been running back and forth between Germany and Japan, taking gold and negotiable assets from Germany to Japan." His intelligence service, he said, had been commanded "to look into the matter of these submarines." However, he conceded, it had failed to discover anything. He had therefore concluded that it was "possible" Hitler and company had "gone in them to Japan."[12]

While Hopkins was in Moscow, the Soviet and Allied military commanders held their first postwar meeting in Berlin. Zhukov of Russia, Bernard Montgomery of Britain, Eisenhower of the United States, and de Lattre de Tassigny of France, issued a declaration from the German capital on June 5, 1945, saying that their nations now possessed supreme authority in Germany. But problems erupted at this initial meeting. When Eisenhower proposed that the Allied Control Council for administering Germany be created and headquartered in Berlin, Zhukov refused to consider the suggestion till he had discussed it with his government. Zhukov, as the Americans noted, leaned heavily for advice during the session on Andrei Vishinsky, Stalin's Deputy Foreign Minister, who was present. With Vishinsky's approval, Zhukov hinted that the Council could be established only after Anglo-American troops had been withdrawn from the Soviet zone in Germany.

Montgomery, still hoping with Churchill to persuade the Americans to delay moving the troops out of the Soviet territory, informed Zhukov that the job would take at least three weeks. That was fine, replied the Russian, because it would give each Allied commander time to gather his Control Council staffs. Berlin now appeared as inaccessible as ever to the West. The Soviet Union was still not ready to share the city or to erect four power rule in Germany. Montgomery and Eisenhower left the meeting that evening. Although the four commanders had been cordial enough to one another, their gathering had unveiled the substantive differences and tension among the Allies over Germany. American papers, concerned about what had happened, published headlines like "U.S. Deplores Lack of Agent in Berlin" and "First Meeting of Allied Rulers Ends Abruptly."

Nevertheless, the next day, June 6, the Soviet authorities in Berlin held a surprising off-the-record press conference with Western newsmen. The handful of correspondents invited to the meeting waited in a small, dingy room at Russian headquarters, wondering why they had been called together. One of Zhukov's staff officers and a translator entered. Without the prompting of a Soviet political functionary such as Vishinsky, the officer told the reporters the shocking news: Hitler's body had been found and identified with fair certainty.

This caught the newsmen unprepared. Each leaned forward in dusty and uncomfortable chairs to hear more. Quickly, the spokesman asked them not to quote him directly. Hitler's corpse, smoke-blackened and charred, he said, had been one of four uncovered on May 3 and 4 in the ruins of the Fuehrerbunker. Each carcass had been examined by Soviet Army doctors, but the bodies were badly burned, probably by Red Army flame throwers involved in the conquest of the underground sanctuary. After careful analysis of teeth and other features, the physicians had singled out one corpse they believed almost surely to be that of the Fuehrer. Asked why no official announcement of the discovery had been made by Moscow, the officer responded that as long as any element of uncertainty existed, the Russians did not wish to state definitely that Hitler's remains had been found.

There were other details of the discovery. Study of the body presumed to be Hitler's, he said, had shown the dictator probably died of poisoning. Whether the death mixture had been self-administered or given Hitler by a henchman, no one knew. This seemed to support an earlier Russian statement, saying the Nazi leader had died of injections from Morell, one of his doctors. It also tallied with an obscure Soviet report of May 10 that had said four badly incinerated bodies had been located in Berlin, "one of which might be that of Adolf Hitler."

The Russian officer also mentioned a telegram allegedly sent by Goebbels to Doenitz on the evening of May 1, informing the new German head of state that Hitler had ended his life at 3:30 that afternoon.[13] The Propaganda Minister, added the Russian, had shortly thereafter followed the Fuehrer's example and committed suicide himself. The officer substantiated earlier Soviet reports that the bodies of Goebbels and his family had been found in or near the Fuehrerbunker, all having died of poison. Nothing more could be said, announced the Russian spokesman. No further questions. The briefing had ended.

Instantly, the mystery of Adolf Hitler appeared solved. This was as close as the Russians had come to presenting a conclusive report on their investigation in Berlin. Why, in light of the earlier hush order from Moscow, had the Russians suddenly chosen to divulge their startling information? As with most of what they did in these tense days, one can only guess. That it had been the Red Army which did the talking was significant. Had the news conference been an innocent effort by Zhukov to inform the world of what the Army knew? Since the beginning of the hunt for Hitler, *Red Star* had been more confident of his death than *Pravda* and the other government publications. Maybe Zhukov thought there was nothing wrong with such an announcement, made in an unofficial manner and without his presence. Or, was it more likely that the Army sought through this bold statement to assert its independence from the politicians in Moscow, including Stalin? Could it have resulted from a problem of communication between the Army and government? Had Zhukov received word of Stalin's position on the issue, as told to the American emissary, Hopkins? And most diabolical of all, was the incident orchestrated by Moscow, and possibly even by Stalin himself, with the intention of purposely confusing the world about Hitler in the coming days?

None of the newsmen at the meeting questioned the origins of this dramatic Soviet statement. "Hitler Took Poison and Died in Fire," a British paper headlined. "Hitler's Body Thought Found," noted a less confident American counterpart. Indeed, serious questions remained. If the Soviets had found a part of Hitler's corpse, what had they done with it? Why had they not shown it to the rest of the world? An opinion poll in the United States said that two Americans in three did not believe the Fuehrer had met his end. "In death—if he is dead—as in life," observed the pithy *San Francisco Chronicle,* "Adolf Hitler is still making trouble for the free world."

4

"He could have flown away"

"I plan to leave tomorrow, stopping in Berlin and going on to Frankfurt," the aging envoy said to Stalin. In conquered Berlin, added Harry Hopkins, he looked forward to what for him would be a "pleasant spectacle." "I might even be able to find Hitler's body," he smiled and joked. The Russian dictator was not amused. "Hitler is still alive, I am sure," he answered. It was June 6, 1945, the day the Soviet command in Berlin had announced unofficially that Hitler's remains had been discovered.

With Stalin's permission, Hopkins flew the next day to the German capital. His party landed at Tempelhof Airport in a ruined city, still totally occupied by the Red Army. "We toured the ruins, smelled the odor of death everywhere, inspected the bunker where Hitler committed suicide," one of Hopkins' advisers wrote later. "The Russians there did not doubt Hitler's death."

Or did they? Marshal Zhukov, with no warning, appeared on June 9 before a hastily arranged press conference in the city. At his side were Vishinsky, Soviet Deputy Foreign Minister, and General Nikolai Bezarin, Russia's commandant of Berlin. The meeting was for Western newsmen having just arrived in the capital as the first foreign journalists to spend more than a day there. What occurred at the gathering left the world aghast, especially in view of what Zhukov's aide had said on June 6. Statements by the Marshal and those beside him would be considered in the West for the next quarter of a century as the official Russian view of Hitler's fate.

Zhukov, despite what the world had been told by one of his own staff three days before, that Hitler's body had most likely been found and identified by the Red Army, announced the opposite. A British reporter asked him, "Have you any idea or opinion about what happened to Hitler?" That was as doubtful as ever, replied the commander of the Soviet occupation forces. "The circumstances are very mysterious," he chose his words carefully. "We know from diaries we have found, belonging to aides of the German commander-in-chief, that two days before the fall of Berlin Hitler married a cinema actress, Eva Braun." Then came the totally unexpected: "We did not identify the body of Hitler. I can say nothing definite about his fate. He could have flown away from Berlin at the very last moment. The state of the runway would have allowed him to do so."

The newsmen present sat dazed. This startling remark, hinting that Hitler had escaped, was the hottest news story since the Nazi report of Hitler's end a month before. In the following days, Zhukov's electrifying words would be published and read around the world. Equally surprising was the announcement that Hitler and Eva Braun, who had scarcely been heard of even in Germany, had married. Of further interest to the Western Allies were the diaries of German officials mentioned by Zhukov, since such records were the first hard pieces of evidence made public from the Russian investigation into Hitler's whereabouts.

Zhukov had first discussed Eva Braun at a press conference on May 8, calling her "Hitler's secretary." News accounts about her love affair with the Fuehrer, based on the story of the wife of a janitor at Hitler's apartment in Munich, had been published at the same time. Eva Braun had been called by Hitler to Berlin a month earlier, the talkative Frau had told journalists. "They were obviously much in love and you can be sure that wherever Hitler is—dead or alive—Eva is at his side," she ventured.

Word of the marriage produced instant speculation. Several British papers said the couple had begun their affair in 1932 and that Eva Braun had become engaged to her lover seven years later. "I saw the Fuehrer for the last time on April 22, and Eva Braun was with him," the stenographer, Herrgesell, had told the Allies. The Russians also disclosed that they had found a partly burned letter in the Fuehrer-bunker, written by Eva to her parents. Although they might not hear from her for a long while, the note had allegedly said, they were not to worry. Vishinsky could not resist a personal comment about the newlyweds. "The interesting question is," he told the stunned newsmen on June 9, "whether Eva is a boy or girl. Anything could be expected from Hitler."

Bezarin seconded Zhukov's assertion that Hitler had not been found. "My personal opinion," he said, "is that he has disappeared somewhere in Europe. Perhaps he is in Spain with Franco. He had the possibility of taking off and getting away." Then he described, without much explanation, the Russian search for the Nazi leader. "There are all sorts of people who were close to him who say he was killed by an exploding shell. My own troops who took his Ministry found bodies." In Hitler's Chancellery, in fact, Bezarin's investigators found too many bodies they thought were the Fuehrer's.

"It got to be a joke," he laughed. "Everytime I would find a pair of pants, I would say 'these are Hitler's.'" He added that a special Soviet commission had reviewed the affair. The Russian-appointed mayor of Berlin, an elderly German Marxist, Arthur Werner, could throw no light on the subject. "Hitler—we just don't know," he said at the press conference, following the cue of the Russians. "There are many Germans who say that he has found refuge in another country."

Zhukov, strengthening what had been said, added that the Russians had not come across Bormann's body. Hitler's personal secretary and head of the Nazi party organization had been reported with the Fuehrer in the bunker. Zhukov was even indefinite on Goebbels, whom the Soviets had earlier said they had identified. Bezarin conceded, however, "Goebbels evidently killed himself with a gun and so did his wife. They poisoned their children beforehand. Of course I cannot positively confirm that we have found their bodies."[1]

How could this dramatic Soviet reversal between June 6 and 9 on what had happened to Hitler be explained? Historians and others have long debated the turnabout and its significance. But given the many contradictory statements of the Russians since May 1, the events of early June should not have been so shocking and considered so counter to previous Russian policy. While Zhukov was holding his press conference on June 9, the Soviets published more impressive evidence the same day that said Hitler had met his end. This information, however, would go virtually unnoticed in the West for nearly a decade, while the world chose to seize on Zhukov's vague and unsubstantiated statement.

Nevertheless, Zhukov had apparently changed his mind, at least publicly, after June 6. Why? Because the Soviets have published no military or political records on the subject, we can only guess at the reasons. One may have been pressure exerted on Russian headquarters in Berlin from Moscow, center of Soviet orthodoxy and Stalin. The Premier ordered Vishinsky to put Zhukov in his place, some have theorized, after the Marshal had authorized the announcement on June 6 that Hitlers' remains had been located. Except for the off-the-record news conference that day, held by one of Zhukov's aides, the Deputy Foreign Minister had always been at the important postwar meetings involving the Russian commander and his staff. For example, as early as May 8, at the Russian ceremony in Berlin for the signing of the German surrender, the Americans had noticed Vishinsky's presence. "Vishinsky might just as well have remained standing as he was constantly bobbing up to whisper instructions in Zhukov's ear," an American official attending the festivities had observed.

Other facts suggest Vishinsky was Stalin's mouthpiece. During Hopkins' mission to Moscow, Stalin had assured him, "The political arm of the Soviet government completely controls the military and therefore Vishinsky, who is in Berlin at this time, will really speak for Moscow." When Zhukov visited Eisenhower's headquarters at Frankfurt on June 10, the Marshal made a speech about the soldier's duty to obey his political leadership. Vishinsky sat next to him.

It seems plausible that Stalin had corrected his Army leader.[2] Why? Some historians have argued that Stalin's dogmatic view of his own greatness and infallibility and his intense desire for revenge led him to declare Hitler alive. The Nazi leader had survived because Stalin said so. A "live" Hitler could be punished for his murder of millions of Russians and for his near destruction of Stalin's regime.

One could also not discount the instinctive suspicious nature of the Premier. Like all tyrants, he feared for his power and always looked for rivals to suppress. This had been frightfully apparent in his pre-war purges of Soviet government and Communist party officials. Equally, he mistrusted other nations. Schooled by Marxist ideology and the conspiratorial Russian revolutionary experience, he believed in the inevitability of a clash between the Soviet Union and what he called Western "capitalist imperialism." So Stalin may have been persuaded that his arch fascist enemy, Hitler, who Moscow had maintained was a tool of German capitalism who plutocrats had placed in power to protect the Reich from Bolshevism, still lived and sought to trick him.

Just as likely, he may have seen the Hitler mystery as a "political" question. He judged it necessary, whatever the proof (or lack thereof), to contend that Hitler had not died a hero in ruined Berlin, but had instead slunk away into hiding. He may have thought that if Hitler was admitted dead, if Nazism revived in Germany, this could lead to the identifying of holy places, shrines, and relics, raising the spirit among the Germans of a new anti-Bolshevik crusade. Such a threat was much on the minds of Kremlin leaders in the summer of 1945.

Subsequent history has seemed to support this view. Probably because of the fear of the revival of a cult of Hitler in Germany, it became Soviet policy after 1945 to de-emphasize the Nazi era. Especially, little reference would be made to the German dictator personally, either in Russian propaganda or historical writing. In contrast to the Western world after the war, which insisted that it had destroyed the terrible monster, Hitler, the Soviet Union asserted that it had defeated German "capitalism" or "nationalism." The charismatic personality of the Nazi leader, possibly because it frightened the Kremlin, has never received much attention from the Soviets.

This curious shift regarding Hitler's final lot may also have been a sign of tension in Russian politics. Stalin had long exhibited a fear of his own military leaders, as proven by his crushing of the officer class in the 1930s. Despite his purge of the Army, the record of the Russian high command had been good in the war, especially after 1941. Zhukov had built a brilliant list of achievements. Guiding the capture of Berlin had been a final trophy after his successful defense of Leningrad and Moscow and his victories at Stalingrad and Kursk.

Stalin had tried to undercut Zhukov's popularity and power during the Battle of Berlin, however, by forcing him to share the glory of conquering the capital with a rival Soviet commander, Konev. After the war, the Marshal had been more celebrated than ever, except by Stalin. At a banquet in the Kremlin, Stalin had toasted the Russian people and its political leadership (which included himself), but he said nothing of the Army's role in the triumph over Germany. This was left to his subordinates, like Foreign Minister Vyacheslav Molotov. Zhukov may also have appeared suspect to Stalin because the Marshal openly admired Eisenhower, once praising him as "one of the greatest generals of all time."

About the only feat Zhukov and the Army had not achieved had been the capture of Hitler, dead or alive. Stalin, by insisting the Nazi Fuehrer might still be living, was able to tarnish the luster of his successful generals. In his thinking, they had failed to deliver what would have been the supreme symbol of the war. Stalin wished to seize from the Army control of this political issue; in his contest with the military, Hitler "alive" was more useful.[3] As a further de-emphasis of the Army, he presented himself on June 27, 1945, with the title of Generalissimo. And one by one the triumphant officers were withdrawn from their commands. Zhukov would be snatched away from Germany in November, and sent to obscure posts first in Odessa, and then the Urals. Only after Stalin's death would the Marshal return briefly to prominence.

Hinting that Hitler and his closest aides had escaped probably related directly to Russia's political ambitions in Europe. Between June 5–6 and 9, as Zhukov had performed his about-face, a new wave of Soviet claims rose to counter Allied pressure in the governing of Berlin and Germany and the much publicized danger of a Nazi rebirth. Each charge aimed at bolstering what the Russians believed to be their rights in Germany, eastern Europe, and elsewhere, while undermining Anglo-American demands. Zhukov's press conference on June 9, asserting Hitler was alive and therefore still a danger, could not help but legitimize and enhance the Soviet position. With Hitler having survived and Nazism yet a menace, so the impression was planted, was it not safer for Russia to retain its newly won power in Europe?

At issue among the Allies during this crucial week was the occupation of Germany. On June 6, only a day after the first meeting of the Allied commanders in Berlin, where Zhukov had pushed for the Anglo-American withdrawal from the Soviet zone in Germany, Moscow newspapers published maps of the zone. These showed that the Soviet Union would hold roughly half of Germany on a line running well west of Berlin and including large areas in American and British hands. A further point of contention was Berlin. Tass said that the former German capital would be divided into four areas of occupation. But this sharply contradicted the Allied declaration on the defeated Germany, signed on June 5, which had spoken of a "greater Berlin" commanded in rotation by the Allies.

The Soviets also alleged that the declaration had been "a program for the disarmament and demilitarization of the German state." Justifying Russia's seizure of German factories and industrial plants as reparations, Moscow argued for "the destruction of German militarism and Fascism." Fear of a renewed Nazism assumed phobic proportions. On June 8, the Soviets reported "a Nazi plan envisaging the restoration of the Hitlerite Empire in 1950." This was even more threatening, it said, since "ticklish problems are already arising" to divide the Allies.

Kremlin broadcasts especially singled out for criticism the British commander, Montgomery, who had opposed the evacuation of the Western Allies from the Soviet zone without receiving concessions from the Russians. What further exacerbated the Russians was Montgomery's decision to use remnants of the German High Command to aid in administering the vast numbers of German prisoners of war in the British zone. Following orders sent through German commanders, the prisoners were moved into areas along the north German coast, with their backs to the sea. There they were documented, checked, and slowly demobilized.[4]

Something else strengthened the view that Zhukov's words of June 9 carried political and propaganda overtones. This involved the way the Soviets publicized the puzzle of Hitler's whereabouts. During June 9 and 10, the Russian press and radio issued opposing statements on the riddle. Moscow broadcast on the evening of June 9 to England and North America Zhukov's comment that Hitler could "have flown away from Berlin at the very last moment." That same day, both *Red Star* and Moscow radio released stories saying the Nazi dictator had committed suicide two days before Berlin had surrendered.

Red Star, in a lengthy article titled "The Last Days of Berlin," discussed a meeting in the devastated city in the early morning of May 1, 1945, between the last chief of the German High Command, Krebs, and the Russian General, Vasily Chuikov. The account, remarkable for its detail, said Krebs had crossed the smoke-filled and rubble-strewn battleline to Chuikov's headquarters around four o'clock. His mission had been to ask the Russians for a truce and to begin arrangements for the surrender of what little remained of the Nazi garrison in the heart of the city.

This story also illustrated that already on May 1, hours before the Nazi announcement over Hamburg radio that Hitler had died, the Soviets had learned of the death. "I am authorized to inform the Soviet Command, and through them, the Soviet Government," *Red Star* quoted the tall, tired, and pale Krebs as telling Chuikov, "that yesterday on 30th April, the German Fuehrer, Adolf Hitler, voluntarily left this world." After a pause, he had told the Russians that Hitler had named a government to succeed him. "In his Will," said Krebs, "the Fuehrer appointed Grand Admiral Doenitz his successor, and Dr. Goebbels is appointed head of the new German government. I have the honor to represent this new government, and am reporting to you with a personal message from Goebbels."

"The German government," continued the Nazi commander, "considers further resistance in Berlin useless and asks that the Soviet Union agree to a one-day cease fire in order to prepare the conditions of our capitulation." Chuikov, with Red troops owning nearly all of Berlin and the Allies having overrun most of Germany, refused. He insisted instead on Germany's unconditional surrender. Krebs had then requested permission to return to his headquarters to confer with Goebbels.

At a second meeting hours later between Krebs and Chuikov, the German officer had repeated that his headquarters wished to surrender, but asked that the new Doenitz-Goebbels government be officially recognized by the Soviets and the Allies. Krebs had also pleaded that the part of Berlin still in German hands (merely a few square miles) be left to the rule of the new Nazi regime. "A government without territory," Krebs had said to the Russians, "would be as ridiculous as the London Polish government." Chuikov again rejected the appeal. Krebs went back to Goebbels. About forty-five minutes later, Russian infantry and tanks had resumed their attack on the city. Suddenly, amidst the smoke and dust raising a black curtain over the capital, the Soviets had noticed a German general creeping alongside the ruins in the center of the city with a white flag in his hand. He was taken prisoner and identified himself as Helmuth Weidling, chief of the Berlin garrison. In minutes, Weidling sat before Chuikov, informing the Russian commander that both Goebbels and Krebs had killed themselves and that he wished to capitulate. It was now May 2.

Weidling too, said *Red Star,* had confirmed to the Russians what Krebs had told them: Hitler had died. In an order to the last Nazi holdouts to lay down their arms, he noted:

> Soldiers, officers, generals, on 30th April the Fuehrer ended his life, leaving us, who had sworn allegiance to him, to ourselves. You think that, in accordance with the Fuehrer's orders, you still have to fight for Berlin, although the lack of heavy artillery and ammunition, and the general conditions, render the fight senseless, and every hour of our fight increases the terrible suffering of Berlin's civil population and of our wounded? Everyone who now perishes for Berlin is making a vain sacrifice.[5]

Thus, at the moment Zhukov had astounded the world with his press conference, offering no proof for his pronouncement that Hitler "could have flown away" from Berlin, Moscow published thorough accounts asserting the Fuehrer had gone to his grave. Why? Again, alas, we have no solid evidence, but can only conjecture. Perhaps the *Red Star* article was another effort of the Red Army (like its statement of June 6) to acquit itself in the controversy. Or possibly, by proclaiming both sides of the story, the Kremlin sought to protect itself in the future against the accusations that it had not found the leading Nazi criminal and that it had allowed him to get away. The duplicity might also have originated to confuse an already bewildered world and add credibility to Soviet postwar political demands. Even coincidence may have played a role, but that seemed far less likely in June, when Moscow clarified its propaganda campaign on Germany and Europe, than in the chaotic days of May.

Equally puzzling was why the West chose to widely publicize Zhukov's statement and virtually ignore the other, more substantial, version. About the only paper to mention the *Red Star* essay was London's *Evening Standard.*[6] Zhukov's stature and popularity notwithstanding, it is curious that his public remarks should have been considered so much more official than those of his Army's paper or Moscow radio. This was especially true in light of Stalin's coordination of the Soviet government and press and the observance in the West of Vishinsky's influence over Zhukov. Nevertheless, a war-weary, fearful, and doubting world had been overwhelmed by the uncertainty which the Russian marshal offered. Today, thirty-five years later, June 9, 1945, appears not to have been that radically different or inconsistent with previous Russian policy on Hitler's fate.[7] It was as dubious as ever.

Zhukov's announcement intensified the Hitler mystery. It injected new elements into the popular belief Hitler had survived, and in the mind of the public it shifted part of the burden for finding him away from Russia to the Western Allies. Intended or not, it became a shrewd piece of psychological manipulation and propaganda. News of Hitler's marriage to Eva Braun, for example, spawned sensational stories about their romance and her beauty, and contributed elements to the mythology that he had survived.

Assuming that a powerful dictator would court only the most voluptuous women, and recalling that Hitler had often entertained movie actresses, news magazines instantly described Eva Braun as "the blond and curvesome Munich secretary" and "a sensuous blonde" with "extremely beautiful legs." One of Hitler's butlers claimed to have played the accordion while the couple had made love by candlelight at Berchtesgaden. Other reports, from "friends of Eva," said she had held out on the Fuehrer and often met secretly with an SS officer.

The wildest rumor came from Sweden. It asserted that the Fuehrer and Eva had produced two children, a five-year-old boy and a four-year-old girl. Their eleventh-hour wedding, just as Berlin fell, said the report, had been performed to legitimize the young ones. Who had been the source of the story, no one knew.[8] Allied officials in Germany, when questioned, refused to comment on whether they were hunting for the alleged offspring. This tale would later be resurrected to lend credence to the view that Hitler had escaped. "Hitler or his children," muttered an editorial in the *San Francisco Chronicle,* "may be expected to bob up from time to time when somebody works up enough imagination." The children, so the scenario would go, had given him a further reason to flee Berlin—he would train them as his successors.

Another reaction to the Russian press conference came from Spain, accused of harboring the fugitive Hitler. The Soviet Union had implied that the former Nazi chief and Spain's dictator, Franco, were still allies from the days when the Germans had backed Franco's forces against the Soviet-supported Madrid government in the Spanish Civil War. During World War II, however, except for Spanish volunteers called the Blue Division that had fought with the Nazis on the Eastern front, the ungrateful Franco had refused to join the Nazi side, angering and frustrating Hitler. Yet Moscow used the controversy over what had happened to the Fuehrer as a propaganda stick with which to beat its old adversary, Franco.

Answering the Russian charge, Madrid issued a curt statement. "Hitler, married or single, alive or dead," it said, "is not on Spanish soil, nor would he be allowed here, and if he entered he would not receive shelter." But the denial was undermined a few days later, when a demonstration of fascist youths in Barcelona, determined to hold a memorial service for Hitler and Mussolini, ended in violence and wide publicity.

Zhukov's contention even caught the Western Allies unprepared. Eisenhower, when questioned in London about what had been said, voiced his astonishment at the Soviets doubting Hitler was finished. "I just took it as a fact that he was," he said, "and I thought it was impossible for him to be anything else." "But I know this," he added, "if Hitler is not dead, he is suffering more than if he were because he is being hunted for his life and will be fearful every minute that he is going to be caught."

The General's response gave little hint of what the Allies had done to solve the mystery. Nor did he push the Russians for even the slightest shred of proof of Zhukov's allegation. He appeared dazed by it all; his equivocation could only have encouraged the public's acceptance of what the Russians had said.[9] Eisenhower's record, in this regard, was to deteriorate. Four months later he made the unfortunate pronouncement that he thought Hitler was alive.

In the meantime, a parade of new stories hit the headlines in mid-June, purporting to explain the Nazi Feuhrer's disappearance.

An American serviceman who had flown Harry Hopkins from Moscow to Berlin on June 7 and been one of the first Americans to tour Hitler's bunker, stated that Hitler had cheated the grave. The bunker was intact, he said later, but "there was a lot of litter around." "There was no way you could tell if Hitler had died there," he continued, "no bloodstains or anything, and I personally think he got out before the Russians got there."

Versions of what had happened to the dictator now became an epidemic. One said that in spite of the Russians maintaining he had not been found, the Red Army had captured and sent him to Moscow, where he would soon become an adviser to Stalin for "western affairs." Another had him rescued during the siege of Berlin from the Chancellery by one of his master spies (later said to be Otto Skorzeny), and whisked off to Spain to live closely guarded in a remote Andalusian castle.

A few Germans, most of them deranged and sent to hospitals, thought they had seen the Fuehrer fighting in Berlin. In the last days, a doctor declared, "I looked after the Fuehrer in the Tiergarten." Others alleged to have seen him drive away from the Chancellery in an armored Mercedes. Nazi pilots claimed the honor of having spirited their hero to safety. One, a Lieutenant Arthur Mackensen, told in detail how he had flown the Fuehrer on May 5 from Berlin to Denmark. "Hitler," said the thoroughly confused pilot, "departed from Denmark for an unknown destination, but only after a speech that was received by a farewell party of Nazis with a rousing 'Heil Hitler!'" The British reported at the end of June 1945 uncovering a large German plane near Travemuende, west of Luebeck. "We were ordered in the last weeks of the war to keep the craft ready to carry Hitler non-stop to Japan," said an idle ground crew waiting nearby.

None of these stories were ever proven, but they found eager audiences, some anxious to discover the truth while others wished for drama and excitement. The latter came easily enough, as on June 26. Late that night, a mysterious voice from an unknown transmitter broke over the radio waves in Germany, crying, "Attention Germans! Hitler is alive and safe!" A bit later, the voice proclaimed, "In revenge the Fuehrer lives to gather around himself any of his most loyal collaborators for striking at the enemy." Instantly, Moscow announced that the transmitter had been discovered in the Anglo-American zone (which was untrue), thus providing what the Soviets called "fresh evidence to support the assumption that Hitler really managed to get away."[10]

Discovering the truth about Hitler became another matter altogether. One demanding to know what had really happened was an American officer, Major George Eliot. He publicly called on the Western Allies to solve the "Hitler mystery." "The Fuehrer hunt is on," he wrote in the *New York Herald Tribune,* "we must have Hitler, dead or alive." Accepting fully the Russian word he was not in Berlin, Eliot suggested that the Allies search Spain and the American and British zones in Germany.

"It would seem," he said, that the Nazi fiend would have chosen to avoid the Russian secret police and "would prefer to take his chances in the west." Spain seemed the best bet, because it lay within airplane radius of Berlin and because "German refugees have been reaching Spain—maybe some to prepare the way for the Fuehrer's escape." Erroneously, he reasoned that Franco still had feelings of gratitude for his fellow dictator.

From Spain, hypothesized the Major, it had been "quite possible" to travel by plane or submarine to Latin America, leaving from a Spanish colony like Rio de Oro for Brazil and then on to Argentina. In Brazil, for example, there might be "some interior airfield which can be hidden from the police." Based on such conjecture, Eliot called for the instant overthrow of Franco, "by force of arms in order to make sure Hitler is not hiding in Spain." This was "sufficient justification" for the ousting of Franco, he advised, and the Americans should not wait to strike. "The trail is still warm," he argued, and America had "ample forces in Europe for the purpose."

While clothing himself in the role of a veracious crusader, Eliot fed the growing maze of rumor and innuendo. He also played into the hands of the Russians, as Moscow radio used his words to call on the Allies to search for and produce Hitler, even at the cost of invading Spain. "If it proved necessary for the British and Americans to use armed force to annihilate Franco's regime, so that Hitler could not hide in Spain," said one broadcast, "such action by the British and the Americans would be fully justified." Nor should the Allies exclude "the possibility of Hitler's escape to Patagonia [Argentina]," acting "without delay, while Hitler's traces were still fresh."

Although fully out of the question, such intervention in Spain could only have delighted the Kremlin.[11] It would have mired the British and Americans in the "Spanish ulcer" (as Napoleon had once called Iberian politics), leaving them open to charges of imperialism and weakening whatever restraints they hoped to place on the Soviets in Europe. It might also have eliminated an old nemesis of European Communism, Franco. The episode provided the Russians with another chance to blast Franco with unfavorable propaganda and to shift part of the burden for finding Hitler away from themselves.

For those persuaded that the Fuehrer had outsmarted the world, the remainder of the summer of 1945 heard a crescendo of stories, each based on the usual speculation and hearsay, that said so. "I think he escaped at the end of the war to a German pocket on the French coast, and was flown there from a makeshift runway through the Tiergarten," voiced many Berliners. Another version had Hitler hiding in tiny Liechtenstein under the alias of "Dr. Brandl." His fleeing, it said, had been prepared during the war and had included the staging of his and Eva Braun's suicide in the Fuehrerbunker. This story had been tied to another rumor that three Swiss bank accounts had been discovered, supposedly belonging to him.

A sensational article in the *Chicago Times,* supporting earlier tales that Hitler and Eva Braun had slipped off to Argentina, received a mountain of publicity. All of the major news services and papers carried it. The "Argentine connection" of the Nazis had been discussed since the 1930s, and the prospect of Hitler seeking refuge among the large German settlements there had been talked about openly during the war. Since the war's end, the Soviets had encouraged the idea, partially to discredit the right wing dictatorship in Argentina and to block that country's membership in the new United Nations. Contributing further to this belief were arrests of prominent Nazis in Paraguay and elsewhere in Latin America. While all this had heretofore rarely been taken seriously, it now found a popular following, as doubt among the public that Hitler had died surged forth. That Hitler was in Argentina would become one of the most celebrated postwar tales of his survival, being resurrected repeatedly in the 1950s and 1960s.

"I am virtually certain," wrote the *Times'* correspondent in Montevideo, Vincent DePascal, "Adolf Hitler and his 'wife,' Eva Braun, the latter dressed in masculine clothes, landed in Argentina and are on an immense, German-owned estate in Patagonia." Quoting "reliable channels," DePascal said Hitler had been living "on one of a number of estates purchased in frozen, desolate Patagonia to provide sanctuaries for the Nazi overlords." How had the pair reached their hideout? "Reportedly," they had "landed on a lonely shore from a German submarine which supposedly returned [to Europe] to surrender to the Allies."

A more appropriate question, which few editors or readers of the *Times* apparently asked, centered on DePascal's evidence. While the paper dazzled its customers with the headline, "Hear Argentina hides Hitler, Eva," it offered no proof. Grounds for the story were empty phrases like "virtually certain," "reliable channels," and "reportedly." Even the effort to associate the Fuehrer with Argentina failed. There "were reasons to believe," said the paper, that the country "may have known Nazi U-boats lurked off its shores." What was definite, it continued, was that there were "enough Nazi sympathizers in Argentina who would jump at the chance to give a haven" to their heroes from Germany. Reaching for the slimmest thread of support, DePascal referred to a pro-Nazi Argentine who had remarked, "I am glad to announce our friends are safe at last." The article represented yellow journalism at its worst.

Nonetheless, in the postwar atmosphere of uncertainty and emotion, the story was reprinted in every major American and European paper. "Hitler Reported Alive," said *The New York Times;* "Hitler and Eva Reported Safe," the *Baltimore Sun* told its readers; "A Hitler Rumour," announced the London *Times.*[12] The excitement even forced formal responses from the Argentine and American governments. Cesar Ameghino, Argentina's Foreign Minister, said his government had been alert to the "possibility" that Hitler had landed in the country, but that "all reports on the matter are suppositions and conjectures without any basis of fact." The United States conceded that it had directed its embassy in Buenos Aires to investigate the story.

What had apparently triggered the *Chicago Times'* article had been the surrender in early July 1945 of the German submarine U-530, at the Argentine port of Mar del Plata. Although the Argentine Navy contended that no one had landed at the port, several Buenos Aires papers reported that witnesses had seen rubber boats go ashore and that other submarines had been spotted.

One paper, *Critica,* offered an even more startling theory about Hitler and the U-boats. The Fuehrer and Eva Braun, it said on July 17, had landed from a U-530 in the Antarctic. The paper suggested that the possible place of debarkation had been Queen Maud Land, a range of mountains deep in the Antarctic region and a few hundred miles east of the South Pole. As proof, *Critica* presented nothing more than had the *Times,* alluding only to a couple of explorations of Antarctica. It mentioned that the Germans had sent an expedition there in 1938 and 1939, from whence "a new Berchtesgaden" for Hitler was "likely to have been built." It argued, furthermore, that the famed American explorer, Richard Byrd, had shown in 1933 that the temperature in the south polar region could support human life.

Despite its preposterous reasoning, the story sold. "Hitler has been at the South Pole," *Le Monde* quoted the Argentine paper. Readers of *The New York Times* were told, "Antarctic Haven Reported."[13] Yet this incredible rush of stories placing Hitler in every corner of the globe was not without a positive effect. Such reports, coupled with the Russian press conferences at the beginning of June, became sufficient embarrassments to the Western Allies that they were forced into investigating the Hitler affair for themselves.

As the Antarctic and Argentine stories sped around the world, Churchill and Truman gathered at the Potsdam Conference with Stalin. Before the meeting, the Prime Minister toured the bunker and ruins in nearby Berlin where Hitler had allegedly died. In the coming months, the British were to formulate their official account of what had happened to him. It would differ radically from what the world had been told by the Russians and the popular press.

5

Death in the Bunker

"Are you convinced Hitler is dead?" the reporter asked the highly decorated and celebrated figure in front of him. It was mid-July 1945, and the occasion was another press conference on the war. But this time the interview took place in Washington, instead of Berlin, and the official being questioned was General Eisenhower, not Marshal Zhukov. Yet, the American leader's response differed little from that of his Russian counterpart a month earlier.

"Well," Eisenhower said carefully, "to tell you the truth, I'm not. I was at first. I thought the evidence was quite clear. But when I actually got to talk to my Russian friends, I found they weren't convinced." The subject, he hinted, had become a Gordian knot for the Allies. But while he expressed public doubts about Hitler's demise, the British and Americans began to accumulate evidence which said the Nazi warlord had not lived through the war.

This effort would stretch into 1946, and include an official British investigation into what had happened to Hitler and interrogations of Nazi war criminals at the Nuremberg trials. It had become important for the Allies to settle the issue, and preferably to prove Hitler would never again endanger the world. Tidying up this loose end from the European war would take from the Soviets one of their propaganda advantages on the rule of Germany and eastern Europe. It would also halt the wild stories that he had survived and lessen apprehension about a future German or Nazi rebirth.

Despite the view of Churchill and the British, and to a similar extent of Truman, that Communism had suddenly become Europe's greatest menace, many in the West were still fearful of Nazism. Contributing to the anxiety were large numbers of arrests in Germany of armed Nazis and their sympathizers. But for most Germans, Hitler's mystique did not survive his defeat, even if he may have been more discredited by his failure than by his crimes. The majority of Germans just wanted to forget the recent past and their own part in it. Allied cares about a resistance movement against them proved unfounded. On the contrary, as the postwar denazification process would show, hardly anyone would admit to having been a Nazi in any meaningful sense.

The rash speculation on Hitler in the summer of 1945 intensified the worldwide search for him. Aside from the contradictory reports of the Russians, the British and Americans held three Nazi prisoners— Goering, Herrgesell, and Morell—who testified they had seen him in the Fuehrerbunker as late as April 22. Throughout their zones in Germany, Anglo-American and French security officers organized door-to-door inspections for Hitler in cities, villages, and farmlands. They screened prisoner of war camps and looked among the millions of the broken German Army. Each report about the Fuehrer, no matter how fantastic it sounded, was checked.

British officers in Germany believed it most likely that if Hitler were alive, he would still be somewhere in the Reich. Possibly, they reasoned, he was hiding in the north German states of Schleswig and Holstein, near the coast, with bogus army papers and awaiting a discharge by the British as a technical or farm worker. He had probably altered his appearance, thought the officers, and would try to slip out of Germany with expertly forged papers. Through their experience with Himmler and other German prisoners, the British had received information that an extensive Nazi program of falsifying military papers had been carried out in the last days of the Third Reich.

The manhunt extended to America, where major seaports and harbors were watched closely. A United States Senator, Theo Bilbo of Mississippi, promised to introduce a measure in Congress offering a million dollar reward for the capture of a live Hitler. "I feel he should be captured, tried and shot as a war criminal," Bilbo proclaimed, doubting the Nazi potentate was dead. "However, if there are any folks who object, if they will let me know I will be glad to pay their share of the million."

The search yielded two more key witnesses from the bunker and other pieces to the Hitler puzzle. A new account of Hitler's death came from Hermann Karnau, a German policeman captured by the Americans. They gave his testimony to the press on June 20, 1945. Karnau had been a policeman in Hitler's detective guard in Berlin since September 1944. His story started on May 1, 1945, as the Russians had drawn near the underground bunker; he saw the bodies of the Fuehrer and Eva Braun burning on the ground above the shelter. Near the corpses were four empty gasoline cans, having apparently been used to pour petrol on them. "I saw the bodies lying a few yards from the entrance to the Chancellery," said Karnau. "I recognized the Fuehrer by his moustache and Eva Braun by her peculiar black shoes. She was wearing a summer dress. I couldn't see the details of their bodies because they were rapidly wrapped in flames."

What had happened to the couple? They had probably died in the bunker at the hands of a Chancellery doctor, Ludwig Stumpfegger, said Karnau. Stumpfegger may have poisoned them, he guessed, because the doctor had poisoned Hitler's favorite Alsatian dog, Blondi, a few days before. The policeman also described for the Americans the bunker below the Chancellery. His recollection of Hitler's last residence was less ornate than the Russian statements earlier, calling it an "underground city." "Sixty feet underground, sixty feet long, and with thick concrete walls," Karnau said, "it had small apartments for the Fuehrer, Eva Braun, Goebbels, Bormann, and other Nazi officials." An emergency exit had led into the garden of the Chancellery.

Hitler had been in the bunker since at least mid-April, Karnau testified, passing the time by sitting on a couch and nervously tapping his fingers. The last words he had heard from the Fuehrer were on the morning of May 1, when Karnau had been standing nearby as the Nazi leader had asked a general, "What's new?" The policeman also confirmed Hitler's marriage. "I first heard rumors among the bunker staff," he said, "and then I was told by one of Hitler's aides." On April 30, he added, he had met a distressed Eva Braun in the bunker. She had been crying. "I'd rather die here," she had sobbed, "I'll not go away." As the sentry tried to calm her, calling her "Fraulein Braun," she had answered, "You may call me Frau Hitler."

From his thorough description of the Fuehrerbunker and its shattered surroundings, little doubt existed that Karnau had been there.[1]

Allied officials and newsmen who finally had been allowed by the Russians to view the Chancellery area in July, verified that gasoline cans (perhaps the ones Karnau had seen beside the bodies) were still there, one or two of them riddled with bullet holes. Fragments of burnt clothing also remained, but evidence of fire on the sandy soil had now gone, possibly washed away by rain. Captured Nazi records also showed Karnau had been one of the bunker personnel.

Another Nazi prisoner, Erich Kempka, corroborated Karnau's account. Hitler's personal chauffeur, Kempka soon became for a time the most important postwar witness of the dictator's last days. Captured in June 1945 by the Americans, his testimony too was given newsmen. Despite the earlier ban on such information, resulting in part from Russian complaints, the Allies believed the evidence of Kempka and Karnau to be a crucial counterweight to the Soviet Union's assertions Hitler had escaped Berlin.

He had been with Hitler to the end in the bunker, Kempka said. The Fuehrer had decided to die, and his wife, refusing to leave him, had joined him in a suicide pact. Shortly before shooting themselves with Walther pistols, explained the chauffeur, the Fuehrer had commanded his SS adjutant, Guensche, to burn their bodies so the remains would not fall to the Russians. Kempka said he had left Berlin on the morning of May 3, and after a series of dramatic escapes through Russian lines, he had reached British occupied territory west of the Elbe River. He was later captured near Berchtesgaden.

Kempka told a fascinating story. The most complete of its kind thus far, it persuaded many British and American officials that Hitler had ended it all in Berlin:

> I last saw Hitler alive on the afternoon of April 29 when I went from my headquarters to the Fuehrer's bunker. I reported to him how we had brought food and other supplies for the various command posts that we had been detailed to defend. Hitler was quiet and normal.
>
> At 2:40 P.M. next day Guensche telephoned me to go to the bunker at once. He told me to get a large supply of gasoline. I ran across the courtyard, reached the bunker through underground passages, and found Bormann carrying the body of Frau Hitler—and I learned later about the wedding two days before. I took the body from Bormann. Blood was trickling from her breast. I carried it to an exit leading into the garden. At the stairs I gave her body to Guensche.

[Heinz] Linge [Hitler's valet] and somebody else had carried Hitler's body, wrapped in a gray blanket, to a spot about six or seven yards from the exit. Both bodies were put in a shallow hole. Men arrived with five cans of gasoline, which were poured on the bodies.

Bormann, Goebbels, Guensche, Linge, I and a couple of others stood at attention and gave a final Hitler salute. The artillery shells were coming in from all sides, quite close. So there was no ceremony but the salute.

Guensche, carrying out Hitler's last order, set the bodies afire. We stayed a couple of minutes and went back to the shelter. We left a single guard to watch the fire. He was a security policeman whom I did not know.

I doubt if anything remained of the bodies. The fire was terrifically intense. Maybe some evidence like bits of bones and teeth could be found, but I doubt it. Shells probably landed there and scattered everything all over.[2]

Why did he believe his chief had shot himself, Kempka was asked? After leaving the flaming corpses, Kempka had descended the stairs in the emergency exit to the bunker, to look a last time at where Hitler had lived and now died. The bunker now vibrated from heavy Russian shelling. He went into the death room:

Opposite the entrance of the room, the dimensions of which are only 3x4 meters, stood a narrow sofa.... Before the right leg of the sofa lay a Walther-Pistol, 6.35 mm. caliber, which, as I knew, belonged to Miss Eva Braun. Also on the floor approximately before the middle of the sofa lay a Walther-Pistol, 7.65 mm. caliber. I supposed that this pistol belonged to the Fuehrer. According to the situation it was clear to me that the Fuehrer and Miss Braun shot themselves. From the location of the two pistols, I concluded that the Fuehrer sat about on the middle of the sofa before firing the shot and that Eva Braun had sat on the right part of the sofa.[3]

Kempka, like Karnau, was considered a reliable witness. His version that Hitler had shot himself and that his body had then been cremated was new, but it would become the crux of the later Allied interpretation of what had happened to the Nazi leader. There were other grounds for believing the chauffeur. The Allies had seen the original of a telegram sent on May 1, 1945, from Goebbels, huddling in the Berlin bunker, to Doenitz, in northern Germany. Hitler, the telegram had informed the Grand Admiral, had died at 3:30 P.M. the day before and chosen Doenitz his successor.

It had also been learned from Karl Brandt, one of Hitler's former doctors seized by the Americans, that the Fuehrer had been in grave health at the last. Brandt, under interrogation, had changed his initial story that there had been nothing physically wrong with the Fuehrer. Hitler suffered from painful gastric troubles, the doctor maintained, and had become a vegetarian and a slave to his private physician, Morell, who had given him strychnine pills to keep up his energy. In the final months, the dictator walked with a stoop, his hands trembled, and he had chronic insomnia. This so weakened him, Brandt suggested, that it had probably prevented him from attempting a perilous escape from the Russians.

Of Hitler's poor health, Count Bernadotte offered more clues while discussing freely his peace negotiations with Himmler that had excited the world at the end of the war. He had seen the SS leader on February 12, April 2, April 21, and April 23-24, said the former Swedish envoy. During their last meeting, Himmler's Gestapo aide, Walter Schellenberg, had told Bernadotte, "Hitler was finished. It was thought that he could not live more than a couple of days at the outset." Himmler had then added "that quite possibly Hitler was already dead, and that, if he were not, he certainly would be within the next few days. The Fuehrer had gone to Berlin to die with the inhabitants of the capital. Berlin was surrounded, and it was only a question of a few days before it would fall."

A bit later, Himmler repeated that Hitler might already be dead. Germany lay defeated, he admitted, and he no longer felt he was breaking his oath of loyalty to the Fuehrer by negotiating with the Allies and trying to save Germany from the Russians. What did Bernadotte think had happened to Hitler? "Adolf Hitler in the spring of 1945," he said, "was a mentally and physically sick man. A heroic act was the last thing of which he was capable." Concluded Bernadotte, he felt "quite certain that he was murdered."[4]

Another part to the Hitler riddle, which lent credibility to Kempka's story that the Fuehrer had perished with Berlin, unfolded. The Allies had learned, partly through Red Army officers in the capital and partly through a Berlin dentist, Feodor Bruck, that dental records had been used by the Soviets to prove that remains they had discovered were Hitler's. Their statements were made public on July 9, 1945. According to the officers, the Russians held two prisoners involved in the identification, who were later found to be Kaethe Heusemann, an assistant to Hitler's dentist, and Fritz Echtmann, a dental mechanic.

Hitler had apparently suffered from pyorrhea, and had been treated at the Chancellery by his dentist, Hugo Blaschke. During the second week of May 1945, a major and a woman officer from the Russian intelligence service, the NKVD, had visited Blaschke's bombed and scarred surgery in Berlin and asked for the dentist or one of his aides. They were told that he had fled several weeks before to Berchtesgaden, but were referred to Heusemann. She had often accompanied the doctor when he had treated Hitler and knew fully the Fuehrer's teeth. There were, it seemed, identifiable bridges on the upper and lower jaws and what was called a "window crown," seldom used in modern dentistry, on one of the incisors.

Heusemann had sought refuge in the Chancellery during the last days of the war. She had seen Hitler several times at the end, and later recounted to Bruck how angry the Fuehrer had been over the lack of military help for Berlin and Himmler's "treason." In the end, said Heusemann, Hitler took poison and shot himself and Eva Braun in the bunker. She had not seen the bodies, but had heard they were burned in the Chancellery garden. Trying to escape to the West, the blond and buxom dental assistant had been seized by the Russians and returned to Berlin. On May 9 the Soviet intelligence officers had visited Blaschke's surgery, which by then had been taken over by Bruck, a Silesian Jewish doctor. Bruck allowed the Russians to search his dental files and told them about Heusemann. She was located and accompanied them to the Chancellery to look for Hitler's dental records, which had probably been placed there by Blaschke when he escaped.

According to Bruck, Heusemann was gone for two days. On returning, she told him that after finding nothing at the Chancellery, the officers had taken her to Russian headquarters in the nearby Berlin suburb of Buch. There she had been shown an upper and lower jawbone, and instantly recognized them as Hitler's. With less certainty, Heusemann identified a bridge made for Eva Braun. A few days later, she disappeared with a dental mechanic, Echtmann; nothing had been heard from them since. At the end of July 1945, Alexander Gorbatov, a Soviet member of the Allied command ruling Berlin, told Western newsmen he had heard "reports" that "Hitler's dentist had taken a human jawbone to Moscow and identified it as Hitler's."[5]

Also suggesting Hitler may have been in ill health and unable to flee Berlin had been a Russian film, completed in July, of the battle for the German capital. The movie interspersed scenes of the actual fighting with flashbacks to Hitler's rise to power, his dreams of a world empire, and his efforts to enslave Russia. The film also showed the interrogation of General Weidling, the Nazi commander who surrendered Berlin to the Russians on May 2. Weidling mentioned his last meeting with Hitler on April 29. "How did he look? What condition was he in?" asked Soviet officers. "I had seen the Fuehrer a year before," was Weidling's reply. "I was shocked at the change in his appearance. He was a ruin." Then the General gave an imitation of the broken Fuehrer, of his hands fumbling over a map, and of his almost inaudible, stammering voice.[6]

That was the extent of Soviet intimations Hitler may not have survived. At the Potsdam Conference in July and August 1945, Stalin again told the Americans he was persuaded the leading Nazi was still around. The subject arose first on July 17, as Stalin and Truman lunched together at American headquarters in Babelsberg, a Berlin suburb. "What are your views of how Hitler died?" the Secretary of State, James Byrnes, asked the Russian Premier. "I believe Hitler is alive," Stalin replied, much to Byrnes' surprise. "Careful research by Soviet investigators has not found any trace of Hitler's remains or any other positive evidence of his death."

Stalin repeated his viewpoint at Potsdam. On July 31, the topic arose during a discussion about which Nazis should be named as war criminals. Clement Attlee, elected Britain's Prime Minister during the Conference and replacing Churchill, said he understood there had been doubt about whether Hitler had died and whether he should be on the list of war criminals to be arrested and brought to trial by the Allies. Stalin, answering Attlee, stressed again that the Nazi leader was "not at our [Russia's] disposal." On the naming of war criminals, he suggested, "Hitler should be added. I quite agree that he should be hanged." The next day the Premier stated he had "no objection to naming Hitler" on the first list of war criminals scheduled for publication in September.

Stalin's motives for insisting that Hitler had cheated the grave had probably not changed in the two months since Zhukov's press conference. With Potsdam considering such crucial issues as Allied administration of Germany, establishing frontiers for Poland, and membership in the United Nations, a "live" Hitler still seemed useful to Moscow. If the Fuehrer were a threat, the Soviets could push harder for larger reparations from Germany, for less food for eastern (i.e., Soviet) Germany, and for the forced transfer to the Reich of millions of Germans living, unwanted by the Russians, in eastern Europe.

To buttress his argument that Hitler might have escaped his armies in Berlin, Stalin appeared especially interested at Potsdam in Allied policy toward Franco and Spain. The Spanish, he stated vigorously, were "feeding semi-fascist regimes in other countries." Franco had "been imposed on the Spanish people by Hitler and Mussolini whose regimes the Allies were in the process of destroying." The Premier admitted that his hatred of Franco went back to the Spanish Civil War, Franco's persecution of leftists and Communists, and Spain's sending of a division of troops to fight against Russia in World War II. Unable to convince Britain and the United States to break off all relations with Spain, Stalin succeeded in urging them not to support Spain's membership in the United Nations. "Franco gives shelter to Nazis," he girded his argument, and for Stalin that included Hitler.

Another interpretation of his behavior at Potsdam has centered on his fear that Hitler might suddenly return and lead a Nazi comeback. Stalin, so one historian has theorized, tried to act in 1945 as Tsar Alexander I had done in 1815, following the Napoleonic Wars. With Napoleon defeated, Alexander had urged his European allies to rigorously suppress France and the principle of revolution. Had the thought of Napoleon's return from Elba and of the Hundred Days crossed Stalin's mind? Since Bonaparte's reappearance restored the unity of the victors at the Congress of Vienna in 1814 and 1815, had Stalin been willing to use Hitler's phantom at Potsdam to recapture something of that Allied unity which had been of the living Hitler's making?

If he intended to revitalize Russia's relations with the Western

Allies, the effort failed.[7] After Potsdam, serious differences between them continued. Soviet propaganda discredited the role of the Allies in winning the war, maintaining instead that Stalin, the Communist party, and the Red Army had been the "liberators of Europe." In meetings of the Allied Control Council, created to administer occupied Germany (but which had hardly achieved even the pretense of such authority), the British and Russians quarreled incessantly. Montgomery complained about poor access for the British across the Soviet zone to Berlin, coal and fuel supplies for the city, and displaced persons from eastern Europe who flooded the British zone.

Zhukov angrily retaliated by asserting that the British were not following the agreement at Potsdam to dismantle completely the German Army. The Russians demanded that discharged personnel of the former German military be prohibited from wearing their uniforms. They protested "the continued existence of German military units in the British zone," producing heated confrontations between Zhukov and Montgomery at Control Council sessions. During one such clash, the Russian commander explained, "I did not entertain any suspicion that the Field Marshal wished to wage war on Russia, but am simply insisting on the disarmament of the Germans."

About the only thing the British and Soviets agreed on had been to exclude Hitler from the list of war criminals to be tried at Nuremberg and elsewhere. The Western Allies believed that by placing him on this dubious role of honor, they would be admitting to the belief he had survived and would only encourage more damaging speculation about him. By the late summer of 1945, they had gathered enough evidence (from Kempka, Karnau, and even the Russians) that strongly suggested Hitler had ended his life in the Berlin bunker. That Moscow never insisted on his being put on the list seemed even more significant.[8] This could have meant that the Kremlin, despite what it had said since April, believed Hitler dead. It might also have been further proof that Stalin's statements had been basically propaganda.

At the beginning of September 1945, President Truman received an official report dealing with the forthcoming trials of Nazi criminals at Nuremberg. The document outlined the evidence assembled by American officials on Hitler's fate and emphasized they were convinced of his death. So were the British, the report said.[9] Not every Allied leader agreed, however. A few weeks later, Dutch radio quoted General

Eisenhower as having told newsmen in the Netherlands that there was "reason to believe" that Hitler had slipped away to freedom.

The remark unleashed an uproar. It especially disturbed the British War Office, and the General was forced to correct what had been said. A week later, he tried to explain what he had meant to say, but failed. "There is every presumption that Hitler is dead," he commented to the press, "but not a bit of positive proof that he is dead." What had prompted such a masterpiece of ambiguity? Why was the supreme American commander, instead of adding to public doubt, not pressing the Soviets for factual information? Was Eisenhower, perhaps like Stalin, genuinely uncertain about the Nazi chief? Or had his respect for and friendship with Marshal Zhukov affected his thinking? His bluntness and willingness to disagree openly with his own side's basic feelings were strangely reminiscent of the behavior of the Marshal four months earlier. Whatever Eisenhower's precise words, the episode played into the hands of the Russians.

Moscow carried its disbelief on Hitler's death even further during August and September 1945. *Pravda,* discussing the initial list of war criminals to be tried at Nuremberg, observed, "It does not include its leader—Hitler. He has saved his skin from the people's wrath for the time being by hiding in some unknown place. That possessed monster, Goebbels, is also missing." Russian officers, interviewed in Berlin by newsmen as the latter toured Hitler's bunker and Chancellery ruins, confidently announced, "Adolf Hitler is still alive."

Another deluge of stories hit the West. One contended that a surgeon had changed Hitler's face in the spring of 1945, enabling the Fuehrer to remain in Germany or Austria with total anonymity. Another tale, published in a London paper, involved Hitler's SS doctor, Stumpfegger, who had reportedly been in the bunker at the end. The doctor had allegedly joined the Fuehrer at the close of 1944, and through a difficult operation had created a "double" for Hitler, thereby helping him escape. Stumpfegger, said the account, had been closely associated with Karl Gebhardt, one of Himmler's doctors responsible for deadly medical experiments on women at the Nazi concentration camp at Ravensbrueck.

Stumpfegger had gone to Ravensbrueck in March 1945, so the story went, to procure instruments necessary for plastic surgery. He had been known for his experiments with paralysis of the brain. Just as Nazi Berlin neared its end on May 1, several women in the bunker were allowed to bid Hitler good-bye. During the brief audience, wherein the dictator supposedly stood next to Stumpfegger, he never answered the women. The man thought to be the Fuehrer moved only slightly and held the ladies' hands. "I am sure it was the Fuehrer," one of the women later testified, "but he had changed a great deal."[10] Stumpfegger's "double" was a new twist to an old story; moreover, none of the female witnesses were identified.

Then came the bold Soviet accusation at the beginning of September 1945. The British had been harboring Hitler and Eva Braun in their zone of Germany, said Moscow, presumably for eventual use against their Russian allies. "The heavily sought after couple are alive and well, and living in a moated castle in Westphalia," said a story in the government paper, *Izvestia.* Wincing and chafing at such a blunt, unsubstantiated charge, the British government ordered an immediate inquiry into what had happened to Hitler and two months later issued an official statement on the results.[11]

With this investigation, the Western Allies hoped to formalize what they already suspected and offset the Russian version, widely accepted by the western public, that Hitler had survived. At the end of September, an opinion poll in the United States showed that almost 70 percent of the nation did not believe him deceased.[12] The British, as they conducted their special inquiry, kept silent on the matter. But shortly before they announced their findings, the French paper, *Le Monde,* without explaining its source, published an article on Hitler that paralleled closely what the British soon concluded. "Hitler and Eva Braun," the paper said, "had been cremated at the Chancellery in the presence of Bormann, who the Fuehrer had, in a testament, designated as his successor."

On November 1, 1945, the British intelligence service issued a report determining "that Hitler and Eva Braun died shortly after 2:30 on April 30, 1945, in a bunker of the Reich Chancellery, their bodies being burned just outside the bunker." Hitler had shot himself through the mouth and his wife had taken poison. The report, said the British, was "based largely on eyewitnesses' accounts" and would not be altered materially by other witnesses who might yet be found. It was also as authoritative "as possible without bodies."

The statement, telling a bizarre story, but one fully in character with the evil and fanatical persons involved in it, became the official Anglo-American view of the death. Chronicling Hitler's last days from April 20, his birthday, the British constructed the following sequence of events. He had intended to fly from Berlin to Berchtesgaden that day, and to continue the hopeless struggle from there. Influenced by Eva Braun, who he married on April 29 and who wished for the "peculiar glory" of dying with him, he postponed his departure. Two days later, at a staff conference, he informed his advisers that he considered the war lost and desired to stay in Berlin to the last. If the city fell, he would die there.

When his generals and Admiral Doenitz moved to new headquarters in northern Germany, said the British report, Hitler had spurned all advice to leave, as did his faithful Goebbels. From April 22 he had stayed in his deep concrete refuge with Eva Braun, the Goebbels family, Stumpfegger, Bormann, and a host of adjutants and servants. He turned night into day, rising at 1:30 P.M. and going to bed about 5:30 in the morning. Although he appeared calmer following his decision to remain in Berlin, he burst into periodic tantrums, storming he had been betrayed by the Army and by even his closest advisers.

He suffered from poor physical health, the British statement continued, aggravated by the nervous strain, unhealthy living conditions in the cramped bunker, and the eccentric hours he kept. Visited on the night of April 23-24 by his Minister of Armaments, Albert Speer, Hitler had disclosed to him that he had made plans for suicide and the complete destruction of his body by burning. He had repeated his suicide plans to Field Marshal von Greim, after the latter had flown into the Russian-encircled Berlin to report to the Fuehrer on the evening of April 26. Greim, accompanied by a female pilot, Hanna Reitsch, was made Commander-in-Chief of the German Air Force (or what was left of it) in place of Goering, accused of trying to take over power from Hitler a few days earlier. The dictator had given Greim and Reitsch poison capsules such as already had been passed around to everyone in the shelter. After the war had ended, Greim would swallow his.

News had suddenly arrived at the Fuehrerbunker on April 28 of Himmler's negotiations with the Allies, and early the next day Soviet tanks broke into the nearby Potsdamer Platz. Hitler ordered Greim to mount a Luftwaffe attack to support the German Twelfth Army, which had been erroneously reported to the bunker to be within shelling distance and possibly able to mount an offensive against the Russians. But this was pure fantasy, the British investigation determined, as no one could save Berlin from the Red Army.[13] Later that day, Hitler had sent telegrams to Doenitz that were full of despair and hysterical recriminations against the Army and his aides.

That evening he had married Eva Braun, the only person he believed had remained totally loyal to him. After the ceremony the pair had retired to their apartments, with Hitler's secretary, for a marriage feast. It had been a strange wedding breakfast, for according to Eva Braun the talk was solely about suicide, so much that she had to leave. Hitler then had his Alsatian dog destroyed, and some hours thereafter—about 2:30 A.M. on April 30—said good-bye to about twenty people, half of them women, whom he had called from other bunkers and cellars nearby. Twelve hours later, his chauffeur, Kempka, had been directed to send 200 liters of gasoline to the underground fortress. Between 160 and 180 liters were soon collected and placed in the Chancellery garden just outside the emergency exit of the shelter.

At about the same time, Hitler and Eva Braun had made their last appearance alive, said the British report. It explained the couple's self-murder which had followed:

> They went around the bunker and shook hands with their immediate entourage, and retired to their own apartments, where they both committed suicide, Hitler by shooting himself, apparently through the mouth, Eva Braun apparently by taking poison, though she was supplied with a revolver.
>
> After the suicide the bodies were taken into the garden just outside the bunker by Goebbels, Bormann, perhaps Stumpfegger and one or two others, Hitler wrapped in a blanket, presumably because he was bloody. The bodies were placed side by side in the garden about three yards from the emergency exit of the bunker, and drenched with petrol.
>
> Because of the shelling the party withdrew under the shelter of the emergency exit, and a petrol-soaked and lighted rag was thrown on the bodies, which at once caught fire. The party then stood at attention, gave the Hitler salute and retired.
>
> From then on the evidence is less circumstantial. How often the

bodies were resoaked or how long they burned is not known. One witness was informed that they burned until nothing was left; more probably they were charred until they were unrecognizable and the bodies broken up and probably buried.[14]

To bolster its case, British intelligence cited telegrams sent on the evening of May 1 from Bormann and Goebbels to Doenitz. These informed the Admiral that the Fuehrer's will, having named Doenitz as his successor, was in force and that Hitler had died at 3:30 P.M. the previous day. The report concluded that while the proof was not complete, it was "positive, circumstantial, consistent, and independent." Furthermore, there existed "no evidence whatever to support any of the theories which have been circulated and which presuppose that Hitler is still alive."

A mixed reaction greeted the report. Overcoming six months of feverish speculation had been impossible. *The Times* (London) accepted the version, calling it a "careful and exhaustive investigation" based on "a mass of first-hand evidence." The text of the study, however, left unclear precisely which facts had been collected from where, and this omission seemed to be its key weakness. Except for the mention of Speer and Hanna Reitsch, it said nothing of the eyewitnesses who had been interrogated. It even failed to acknowledge Kempka, one of the principals in the story. Nor did it note the Russians. Had they supplied documents or witnesses?

As hard evidence, the report cited only telegrams from the bunker to Doenitz on May 1, which had been seized with other papers and his government at Flensburg on May 23. These messages, and especially the one from Goebbels, corrected a significant misconception. Hitler had not died on May 1, as Doenitz had announced that evening over Hamburg radio, but the day before. The report gave no explanation of why the new Nazi leader had changed the date in his broadcast. An American magazine commented that "the proof was no more positive than any proof could be 'without bodies.' Adolf Hitler was probably dead, but the legend of a living Fuehrer was still alive."[15]

Others expressed skepticism. The Russian press never mentioned the British report; Moscow had not cooperated in the investigation. The inquiry may have been responsible, however, for the Soviet agreement on December 3, 1945, for the Western Allies to dig for whatever might remain of Hitler and Eva Braun in the Chancellery garden. A week later Allied representatives met in the garden and watched eight German laborers excavate the ground near the bunker. The digging lasted all day. It uncovered two hats (which some argued belonged to Hitler), an undergarment with Eva Braun's initials, and several documents written by Goebbels. The group agreed to reassemble the next morning, but when they arrived at the shelter a Russian guard refused to admit them. The Soviets charged that records had been removed from the Chancellery by the investigators. Despite repeated denials and lengthy arguments and negotiations, the Soviets refused to allow further Allied inspection of the bunker site.

Although the French claimed later that they had been invited back to witness another excavation, following the episode Russian soldiers guarding the Chancellery area refused to permit visitors into the underground sanctum. British pilots touring the ruins in 1946 were told by a Russian officer that nothing could be seen in the shelter, because "Hitler never died." When pressed for further details, the officer explained, "The fascist leader escaped in an airplane and is hiding in Argentina."

Aside from the Soviets, there were many resourceful "Hitler hunters" in the West who had been pursuing the Fuehrer's ghost around the world and who found the British verdict unacceptable. Germans still reportedly asked, "Is he really dead?" The subject elicited hushed talk in bread lines and the subway in Berlin. Rarely using Hitler's name and referring only to "him" or "he," Berliners based their judgments on intuition. "Hitler was much too cowardly to have been around where it was dangerous," said a matronly Hausfrau, "and far too selfish to have taken his own life." At least a few Germans believed the theory that shortly before the close of the war, the Fuehrer had undergone facial surgery, making him unrecognizable and giving him markedly "Jewish" features. Such changes, they guessed, ensured that he would live the remainder of his life unsuspected, possibly even in the Reich.

The British report especially revitalized the "double" theory. The body which the report said had been set aflame had not been Hitler's, contended some independent investigators, but that of a look alike brought into the Fuehrerbunker at the last moment. Several tried experiments to show that it was impossible to destroy a human body with 180 liters of gasoline. They used a pig in one test, but it only roasted and its fat melted. Kempka later revealed that the 180 liters were not the only gasoline available and that the remains of Hitler and his wife had smoldered for a long time. There had been enough petrol, he said, to ignite the bodies of Goebbels and his wife, who had killed themselves the next day, and for one of Hitler's security officers, Rattenhuber, to set afire parts of the bunker before the Russians arrived.

One disbeliever, a rabid French Nazi pursuer, Ray Petitfrère, maintained Hitler had several former doubles ready to die and be cremated in his place. But the substitution, Petitfrère claimed, had not occurred during the last hours as the Red Army had nearly reached the bunker. Such an exchange, he said, would have been witnessed by too many persons to have remained a secret. Instead, the Fuehrer double incinerated in the Chancellery garden had been dead, embalmed, and hidden for weeks in a corner of the shelter. If Hitler had planned to escape, Petitfrère reasoned further, he would not have given his followers or the world such a shocking example of cowardice. Nor would Eva Braun have killed herself alongside a "mummy" or a man who had not been her lover.[16]

Some who denounced the British report did so by renewing attention on what now rapidly became a standard theme in the saga of Hitler's survival—the sex life of Eva Braun and the Fuehrer. The belief seemed to be that if it could be determined the couple had given birth to a child, which had never been seriously considered by the public since it had only recently learned of Eva Braun's existence, there might also be a chance to prove them alive. Whatever enhanced the aura of mystery around Hitler, such as his sexual activity, both popular and serious Hitler hunters exploited. Photographs, having been discovered by American intelligence officers and showing Hitler holding a small child called Uschi, appeared in European and American papers.

"Is she Hitler's daughter?" the London *Sunday Express* asked the obvious. "Many people have claimed she is." Others asserted the pictures definitely answered the earlier conjecture about whether Adolf and Eva had ever produced children and the prewar speculation about whether he had been impotent. But American intelligence promptly spoiled the story. It said that the small girl in Hitler's arms had been the daughter of Eva Braun's friend, a Frau Schneider. Fritz Braun, Eva's father, also denied that she had ever been pregnant. He denounced theories that Hitler might have had children by another woman; the Fuehrer had been, he said, "strictly a one-woman man." Another report, without proof, said Hitler and Eva Braun had become the parents of a son on New Year's night in 1938. The birth had occurred in San Remo, Italy, and the baby had later been given secret automobile rides through Berlin.

Even some Allied leaders appeared uncertain about what the British had concluded. Washington kept as silent on the report as Moscow. General Eisenhower, in his story of the war published a year later, did not mention what had happened to Hitler and left the impression the tyrant may not have met his end. One of the officials involved in the American intelligence service's inquiry into the affair, W. F. Heimlich, admitted publicly in October 1946 that he doubted the German leader had died.[17] But like so many others, Heimlich offered no explanation or facts.

Thus, while critics of the British findings did not deny the evidence, they contended there still existed a possibility of evading the final judgment that Hitler was no more. Some insisted that witnesses like Kempka, Karnau, and Bruck had been carefully briefed for interrogators and that their testimonies were deliberate cover-stories. In the absence of total proof, especially the missing *corpus delicti,* those persons who remained fascinated with Hitler, either because of hate or a desire to see the excitement of the war continue, found room for any idea that might seem attractive. Of his actual demise, however, further evidence would soon be uncovered, including more witnesses to the final days and several key documents.

6

The Last Days

"As we entered, we saw the Fuehrer sitting on a small divan," the prisoner explained to American and British interrogators. "Eva Braun was at his side, with her head resting on his shoulders. The Fuehrer was only slightly slumped forward and everyone recognized that he was dead." It was December 1945. The captive, Artur Axmann, former head of the Hitler Youth, had just been arrested in the Bavarian Alps after a lengthy Anglo-American intelligence operation. He had been in the Fuehrerbunker during Hitler's last days.

Axmann testified that he had arrived in Hitler's "death room" only minutes after the suicide. "The Fuehrer's jaw hung somewhat loosely down and a pistol lay on the floor," he continued, adding especially to Kempka's story. "Blood was dripping from both temples, and his mouth was bloody and smeared, but there was not much blood spattered around." "What had happened?" he was asked. "I believe Hitler took poison first and then shot himself through the mouth," came the reply, "and that the concussion of such a blast resulted in the blood on the Fuehrer's temples."

Axmann's statement generally backed the British report, which said Hitler had shot himself through the mouth.[1] So did other testimony of Nazi prisoners and the discovery at the end of December of Hitler's last will and testament. They seemed to confirm that he had taken his life in his underground hiding-place. At the time of Axmann's arrest, the story of Hanna Reitsch, the daring Nazi pilot who had been one of the last visitors to the Fuehrerbunker, and had been captured by the Allies in the summer of 1945, became known.

The petite, blond flyer had accompanied General of the Luftwaffe, Ritter von Greim, into Berlin on the night of April 26, 1945, amidst the furious Russian assault on the city. A Nazi zealot who worshipped Hitler and saw in him the model of German honor, she was the only woman during World War II to win the Iron Cross military decoration. She told a harrowing account, highly colored by bias and rhetoric, of her eleventh-hour visit to the Fuehrerbunker.

After having landed among heavy Russian fire at Gatow Airport in West Berlin, she and Greim had changed planes and flown toward the heart of the city. Moving at tree top level toward the Brandenburg Gate, they had found themselves sandwiched between the street fighting below and German-Soviet dogfights in the air above. Greim had been wounded severely, but the plane landed safely on the East-West Axis, the wide boulevard running alongside the Tiergarten, and a car sped them to Hitler.

He had been pleased to see them. In a dramatic welcoming scene, recalled Reitsch, he had denounced Goering for having sent him a telegram offering to assume power as his successor and rule from Berchtesgaden. The Fuehrer had spoken of the treasonous Goering with tears in his eyes, his head bowed, and his hands shaking uncontrollably. "His words," said the pilot, "were full of remorse and self-pity." He had then named the injured Greim the new head of the Luftwaffe, stripping Goering of his offices and ordering his arrest.

To save the "honor" of the Luftwaffe, Greim and Reitsch had begged to remain in the shelter and die with the Fuehrer. Later, Hitler had called Reitsch to his apartment. His face was deeply lined, constant moisture in his eyes. In a small voice, he had said, "Hanna, you belong to those who will die with me. Each of us has a vial of poison such as this." He handed her one for herself and one for Greim. Then he had told her of his suicide plan. "I do not wish that one of us falls to the Russians, nor do I wish our bodies to be found by them. Eva and I will have our bodies burned."

Reitsch began to sob. She knew that her beloved Fuehrer had now admitted that the cause was lost; she begged him to save himself. But he refused, arguing that he had hoped to die with "honor" and to "defend Berlin to the last." Besides, he had said, he might still be rescued by the German Twelfth Army under General Wenck, which was advancing from the south. Later that night, April 26-27, the first heavy Russian artillery barrage hit the Chancellery.

Reitsch also discussed those she had met in the shelter who were among Hitler's inner circle: Goebbels and his family, Bormann, Naumann, Voss, Krebs, Stumpfegger, Baur, Heinz Lorenz, and General Wilhelm Burgdorf. She had especially observed the tiny Goebbels, who strode about the bunker "like an animal, muttering vile accusations" against Goering and charging him with having lost the war for Germany. When not ranting against his enemies, the hobbling and club-footed Propaganda Minister had talked of the example those in the bunker had set. "We are teaching the world how men die for their 'honor,'" he had preached. "One day the whole world will acknowledge that we did right, that we sought to protect the world against Bolshevism with our lives." As though he were on a stage or before a legion·of historians waiting to record his every word, he would hold forth at any moment of the day. Always he had talked of "honor," of "how to die," of "standing true to the Fuehrer to the last," and of "setting an example that will long blaze as a holy thing from the pages of history."

Eva Braun, said Reitsch, had remained to the end the "showpiece" of the Fuehrer's doomed party. Pretty, always polishing her nails and changing clothes, she had been charming and thoughtful in Hitler's presence. She seemed to accept the prospect of dying easily. Her frequent remark had been, "Poor, poor Adolf, deserted by everyone, betrayed by all." Reitsch also described Bormann. He had moved about very little, documenting Hitler's every word and action for posterity. His record, he had said immodestly, would be smuggled out of the bunker "to take its place among the greatest chapters of German history."

About Hitler, Reitsch had heard from the others that he had apparently collapsed during the last major military conference on April 20.[2] Finally seeing the situation as hopeless, with Berlin about to be encircled and Germany nearly overrun by the enemy, he had broken down. Nevertheless, he talked incessantly of Wenck freeing Berlin and saving him. Walking about the bunker, grasping a map that had disintegrated from sweat, he planned Wenck's campaign. He had become a pathetic sight, said Reitsch, directing armies that never existed and talking with anyone who would listen to him.

Could he have escaped? Hitler never left the Fuehrerbunker alive, the pilot answered confidently, because he was physically unable to do so. "Had a path been cleared for him from the bunker to freedom," she said, adding to the testimony of Brandt and Himmler (as related by Bernadotte), "he would not have had the strength to use it." Nor had he the will to live; only his hope for Wenck's arrival kept him from going through with the mass suicide he had planned. "Hitler is dead!" Reitsch exclaimed to her Allied captors. "The man I saw in the shelter could not have lived."

As the Russian shelling of the Chancellery intensified during the night of April 27-28, Hitler had reviewed the plans for the mass suicides and destruction of the bodies. When the Soviets reached the Chancellery grounds, he had decided, the self-murders would begin. Then came "the worst blow of all," said Reitsch, "Himmler's betrayal." When Hitler learned on April 29 of Himmler's peace negotiations, he had raged like a madman, his face red and nearly unrecognizable.[3] After his tantrum, he had sunk into a stupor, and the bunker fell silent. News came that the Russians would attempt to take the Chancellery on April 30.

Early that morning, Greim and Reitsch left the bunker and the ruined capital at Hitler's order. They were to rally the Luftwaffe in support of Wenck, he had commanded, and Greim was to arrest the "traitor" Himmler. Armed with visions of freeing Berlin and their leader and with letters from the Goebbels' to their eldest son, they fled the bunker. In what Reitsch testified had been the last plane available (a tiny two-seater, hidden near the Brandenburg Gate), they had flown out of the city in a hail of artillery fire and explosions that had tossed the craft like a feather. Below, she described the unforgettable scene, "Berlin was a sea of flames."

Only a few days after the capture of Axmann and the release of Reitsch's story, another piece of the puzzle was found. It too affirmed Hitler's death and the version put forth by the British. This was the discovery and identification by British and American intelligence of his personal and political testaments and the certificate of his marriage to Eva Braun. The documents had been known to the British from Goebbels' telegram to Doenitz on May 1, 1945, mentioning the Fuehrer's "Testament of April 29." Three copies of the testament, indicated the telegram, had been "sent out of Berlin." One was to Doenitz, one to Field Marshal Ferdinand Schoerner (then commanding a German Army Group in Bohemia), and one "for preservation and publication" in the Nazi party archive in Munich.

The set of papers Hitler had intended for Munich fell into the hands of the Allies first. They were found in Hanover in November 1945 on Heinz Lorenz, a German posing as a Luxemburg citizen and requesting work from the British Military Government. Lorenz seemed too well-versed on the last days in Hitler's bunker, so the British arrested and quickly identified him. While being searched, papers discovered sewn into the lining of his clothes were seized and found to be copies of Hitler's personal and political testaments and a document signed by Goebbels, an "Appendix to the Fuehrer's Political Testament." "I was in the Fuehrerbunker at the end," Lorenz admitted under interrogation, "working as Goebbels' press liaison to the Fuehrer." He had been given the papers to take to Munich, he said, and he confirmed that three copies had been made.

"I was accompanied out of Berlin," Lorenz told the British, "by Major Willi Johannmeier, who carried the testaments to Schoerner, and an SS officer, Wilhelm Zander, who took them to Doenitz." Johannmeier was found easily at his parents' home in Iserlohn in the Ruhr. A soldier of total loyalty, he denied any knowledge of the testament and said he had only been a guard for Zander and Lorenz. American and British authorities tracked Zander, a former adviser to Bormann, from Munich to the tiny Bavarian villages of Tegernsee and Aidenbach, near the Austrian border. Despite a plausible story by his wife that he had died, Zander was caught and arrested on December 28, 1945. He spoke freely and as a disillusioned Nazi idealist whose world had been forever shattered.

His story agreed with Lorenz's. "I took my documents to Hanover," he said, "and when I saw that delivery of them to Doenitz was impossible, I walked to Munich and hid them in a trunk." Within hours, the British and Americans recovered them. Then Allied intelligence returned to Johannmeier. But he persisted in arguing that he did not have a copy of the Hitler papers. Motivated by loyalty and indifferent to fear or reward, he had been ordered never to allow his cache to fall to the enemy. Only after lengthy British questioning had he confessed, "I have the papers." He had buried them in the backyard garden at his home in Iserlohn.

Did the testaments contribute to explaining what had happened to their infamous author? "There is no possible doubt now about authenticity [of the papers]," a senior British intelligence officer announced to the press shortly after their discovery. "Apart from any eye-witness account of the actual burning of the bodies of Hitler and Eva Braun, their last hours are known." What had the documents said? The personal testament had announced the Fuehrer's marriage and impending death:

> Although during the years of struggle I believed that I could not undertake the responsibility of marriage, now, before the end of my life, I have decided to take as my wife the woman who, after many years of true friendship, came to this town, already besieged, of her own free will, in order to share my fate. She will go to her death with me at her own wish, as my wife. . . . My wife and I chose to die in order to escape the shame of overthrow or capitulation. It is our wish that our bodies be burnt immediately in the place where I have performed the greater part of my daily work during the course of my twelve years' service to my people.[4]

Before ending it all, Hitler had added in his political testament a final blast at his enemies. He warned of a rebirth of Nazism, proclaimed once more that he had never wanted war, and blamed the latter on "international politicians who either came of Jewish stock, or worked for Jewish interests." Commented *Der Morgen,* a postwar Berlin paper supervised by the Allies, "This scourge of humanity, not to mention of the Germans, spreads further lies from the grave."

Authenticating the testaments posed no problem. Experts and other evidence identified Hitler's signature. One of the signatories of the personal testament, Lieutenant-Colonel Nicolaus von Below, who admitted having been the last to leave the bunker before Hitler's death, surfaced in January 1946 as a law student at the University of Bonn. Several months later, the Allies announced the arrest of two of the dictator's secretaries, Frau Gerda Christian and Frau Gertrude Junge. Junge had typed the testaments, and since both had been in the shelter until May 1, after the suicides of Hitler and Eva Braun, they added details and color to the death story recounted by the British, but did not change it. Christian had learned of the self-murders from Hitler's valet, Heinz Linge, and Junge from Guensche. "Hitler's ashes," Junge claimed she had been told by Guensche, "were collected into a box which was given to Reich Youth Leader Axmann."[5]

These and other witnesses provided testimony for the major trial of Nazi war criminals at Nuremberg, which lasted from November 1945 to October 1946. First in a series of trials, it condemned to death such Nazi bigwigs as Goering, Bormann, Keitel, and Jodl. It tried Bormann in absentia. He had not been captured, but several witnesses, including Axmann and Kempka, said that the man closest to Hitler during the war had died in a tank explosion in Berlin as he fled the Fuehrerbunker on the night of May 1–2, 1945. The trials, in addition to producing a mass of information about the Third Reich, gave worldwide publicity to the incredible crimes of the Nazis. They had murdered nearly six million Jews, the Nuremberg court estimated, plus another six million European civilians. Nazi terror had also been aimed at fellow Germans who resisted Hitler; over 200,000 of them had suffered in the concentration camps.

Because of the British investigation and because Hitler had not been included on the list of war criminals at Nuremberg, the major trial dealt only briefly with his demise. The judges questioned Kempka, and as before, he stated he had seen no more than Hitler's legs protruding from the short blanket in which his body had been rolled after he had shot himself on April 30. But this glimpse of the Fuehrer's boots, Kempka assured interrogators, had been sufficient for him to declare, "that Hitler is dead is something I can say with certainty." He added that he had himself carried the body of Eva Braun into the grounds of the Chancellery to be burned. Curiously, *The Times* (London), which had earlier accepted the British intelligence report, observed that the chauffeur's statement "left the mystery of Hitler's end as undecided as before."

Hans Fritsche, head of the radio department of Goebbels' Propaganda Ministry and captured by the Russians on May 2, 1945, also appeared before the judges at Nuremberg. One of the first Soviet announcements on Hitler's fate had been to say that Fritsche had declared the Fuehrer a suicide. Acquitted at Nuremberg, he later told what he knew about the deaths in the bunker, the last phase of the battle of Berlin, and the life of Nazi captives in Soviet prisons.

He had spent the last days in a cellar of the Propaganda Ministry, said Fritsche, one of the many such hiding places in the heart of besieged Berlin. As early as April 20, Goebbels had informed Fritsche that "Hitler had promised him personally that he [Hitler] would not leave Berlin." Although he had seen Goebbels for the last time the next day, Fritsche had learned through messengers from Hitler's bunker that the Fuehrer had held his final military conference and given up in despair on the war. Backed by Goebbels and Bormann, who had promised to stay with him to the end, he had decided to commit suicide.

Then on April 30, as the Red Army drove into the Wilhelmstrasse and to within yards of the Chancellery, rumors spread along the nearby street cellars that Hitler had sent his testament to Doenitz and that he had died. As Fritsche prepared to surrender his staff to the Russians on May 1, the Ministry cellar was visited by Werner Naumann, Goebbels' assistant who came from the Fuehrerbunker. Hitler had killed himself the previous afternoon (April 30), Naumann had said, and Goebbels had done likewise. Those left in the Chancellery and bunker planned a mass escape for nine o'clock that evening, led by Bormann and available German tanks. As the action began, Fritsche had met briefly with Bormann and promised to hold off surrendering until the exodus could be completed.

On the morning of May 2, Fritsche said, he and the others hiding in the Propaganda Ministry had capitulated to the Russians. "Hitler did not fall in battle," he quickly told his captors, "but took his own life." "Where does your information come from?" he was questioned repeatedly. He had heard of the death from several sources, Fritsche answered, including Naumann. Another was Wilfried Bade, a Ministry official called to the Fuehrerbunker for several hours on April 30 and informed of Hitler's marriage, suicide, and apparent cremation. Several SS men from Hitler's bodyguard, shortly before their attempted escape from the bunker with Bormann, told Fritsche that the body had been burned.

He had heard a similar story later from Werner Haase, an ailing Berlin surgeon who had once been Hitler's personal physician. Haase had worked at the end of April in the underground Chancellery hospital near the bunker. Haase and Fritsche met several times in Soviet prisons. According to Haase, whose source had allegedly been another of Hitler's doctors, Stumpfegger, the Fuehrer had retired to his room with Eva Braun about four o'clock on the afternoon of April 30. He had directed Stumpfegger to enter the room in two hours and burn his body and that of his wife. "Stumpfegger found Hitler shot and Eva Braun poisoned when he opened the door," Haase had explained to Fritsche.

The corpses had then been taken by Bormann and Goebbels into the Chancellery garden and set afire, Fritsche had learned. He had also seen Fritz Echtmann, the Berlin dental mechanic, in a Soviet prison. Echtmann had X-rays of Hitler's teeth and had identified for the Russians a half-burned jaw as Hitler's. An assistant (probably Heusemann) had done the same, Echtmann confided to his prison-mate. At Nuremberg Fritsche related how the Russians had taken him to a small village between Berlin and Bernau on May 4, 1945 and shown him the bodies of Goebbels, his skull badly burned, and his six children. "Hitler found escape in death," Fritsche testified, "leaving behind him the order to keep on fighting. He also left behind the official report that he had died in battle."[6]

Except to corroborate his suicide, the Nuremberg tribunal shed no light on what had happened to Hitler. While the Allied-controlled German press covered the trials extensively, the Germans were per-mitted to read little about their former dictator. Only at the beginning of May 1946 did papers in Berlin, celebrating the first anniversary of the Nazi defeat, discuss his death. *Der Tagesspiegel* published a portion of Doenitz's announcement on German radio, General Weidling's order to the Berlin garrison to surrender, and the rumors of Hitler's death which had swept through the capital on May 1-2, 1945.

By the beginning of 1947, more evidence had accumulated that strongly suggested that Hitler had ended his life in his underground headquarters. The papers of Rudolf Semmler, another of Goebbels' aides remaining with his boss during the final days, revealed that as early as March 1945, the Propaganda Minister had planned his and Hitler's deaths. Goebbels spent March 4, Semmler recorded in his diary, "thinking out the most dramatic way of finishing." "At one time he talks of suicide at the last moment," wrote the aide, "at another he plays with the idea of blowing up the shelter." Three weeks later, Semmler had noted:

Goebbels has persuaded Hitler not to leave Berlin. He has reminded him of his oath taken on January 30th, 1933. That evening Hitler said to Goebbels in the Reich Chancellery: "We will never leave this building

again of our own free will. No power in the world can ever force us to
abandon our position."

Now all preparations are being made for a real "Twilight of the gods"
scene.[7]

Semmler added details about Hitler's failing health and his continued refusal in the last months to appear in public or on radio.
Goebbels, said his subordinate, had become frustrated by the
Fuehrer's silence. It undermined the morale of the German people,
Goebbels had claimed. The Minister had told a press conference in
December 1944 that he had purposely "spread the rumor abroad
through German agents that Hitler was dead." "By these rumors,"
continued Goebbels, "the general assumption that we could not stage
a comeback was strengthened. Now imagine the immense surprise
they have had in the British and American headquarters [from the
Ardennes Offensive of the Germans that had just begun in the West]."

Others even closer to Hitler came forward. Fraulein Elizabeth
Schroeder had been one of his secretaries. She had left the bunker on
April 22, 1945, and been captured by the Americans at Berchtesgaden. "In 1945, Hitler's physical decline became more and more
obvious," she said. His left hand had trembled continuously, and he
had pulled his right leg after him as he walked. "When he wanted to lie
down on the sofa during tea," she remembered, "he had to have a
servant put his legs up for him because he was not capable of doing it
himself anymore." His eyes were also failing. At the end, said
Schroeder, "he presented the picture of a completely broken man who
could not see a way out anymore."

An American psychiatrist, Douglas Kelley, who studied the
Nuremberg war criminals, substantiated this analysis. Hitler, Kelley
concluded from interviews with Goering, one of the Fuehrer's doctors
(Brandt), and his secretaries, probably committed suicide. His personality, contended Kelley, had been "of the paranoid hysterical type"
in which the pressures of the war had pushed him toward "actual
culminated suicide as an end." Hitler's left leg and arm had started
trembling at the close of 1943, asserted Kelley, who diagnosed the
tremors as a hysterical reaction. By the next year the shaking had
become so pronounced that he could not use his hand and held it still
with the opposite arm. He had also suffered from neurotic obsessions,

said the psychiatrist, fearing death and, until 1944 and 1945 as the military disasters piled up, suicide. His gastric pains, moreover, convinced him he had stomach cancer. Continually calling in new physicians, Kelley said, Hitler had taken "amazing amounts of medicines" and "received constant injections at the rate of one every two hours or so."[8]

Gerhard Boldt, an aide-de-camp to General Krebs, had been another witness to Hitler's last days. Stationed in the Fuehrerbunker till the day before Hitler's suicide, he had escaped from Berlin on April 29, 1945, with two other officers and gone to Luebeck. There the British arrested him ten months later. When meeting Hitler for the first time in February 1945, Boldt recalled for interrogators, he had been shocked by the Fuehrer's weakened and sickly appearance. "This was not the powerful Hitler the German people knew in previous years," he had thought to himself. The Nazi chief walked "heavily stooping," his "left arm hangs slackly and his hand trembles a good deal," Boldt observed.

The officer also portrayed how the final military staff meetings in the bunker had been adapted to Hitler's moods; "the ceaseless intrigues" for power among Hitler's leaders; the Fuehrer's dismissal of generals who gave him unpleasant news; his refusal to leave the bunker and visit the "destruction wrought by bombing" and other "horrors of the war"; and his becoming increasingly "hesitant and undecided." Of the evil and power-hungry Bormann, Boldt said, he "became the filter for all who tried to approach Hitler or had anything to say about any matter whatever. In the whole surroundings of Hitler, Bormann had not one friend, but he was feared."

As the Soviet avalanche had converged on Berlin on April 21, 1945, Hitler had announced at a military conference that he would remain in the city. "The war has been lost," he confessed. "I am going to shoot myself." Two days later, when the Supreme Command of the German military evacuated Berlin to the north, Boldt had been assigned to the bunker. The latter, Boldt said, formed "a maze of shelter rooms" and corridors under the Chancellery; dark and crowded, filled with soldiers and SS men, the air was musty and stale. One could listen "at leisure" from this seemingly impregnable sanctum to "the crash of the Russian shells somewhere in the center of the city."

At his military conference on April 24, added Boldt, Hitler had furiously denounced "the incapacity of the German military leaders" on the Russian front and the "arrogant, dull, undecided SS leaders." The next day, during the heaviest Russian artillery attack thus far on the middle of Berlin, the Fuehrer had talked of a war possibly breaking out "between the Bolsheviks and the Anglo-Saxons over their prey, Germany." He had ordered the German Twelfth Army, led by Wenck, to attack toward Berlin from the south and west. The military situation deteriorated rapidly throughout the city, news that spread like wildfire in the bunker. Of Goering's treachery, Hitler "wept like a child, then raved like a maniac," Boldt said. Goebbels, too, "was boiling with fury and expressed his feelings in a theatrical manner."

Boldt confirmed the heroic flight of Reitsch and Greim into the shelter. By April 27, he continued with his grim account, "hell was let loose, shell burst upon shell burst hit the area of the Reich Chancellery. The shelter shook every time as if under an earthquake." About Hitler's wedding to Eva Braun, Boldt conceded "that up to that moment I had known nothing whatever about the existence of this woman, let alone seen her." Outside the Fuehrerbunker, as Boldt vividly described, thousands of Berliners hid in cellars, suffering from thirst, hunger, fire, smoke, and exhaustion. Wounded soldiers and civilians were everywhere. Then Hitler had issued "the most inhuman of all his orders." Since the Russians had broken into subway tunnels, he had directed that the locks of the river Spree be opened and the tunnels flooded. Thousands of wounded, looking for refuge in the subways, were "drowned mercilessly."

Axmann and General Weidling, on separate occasions during April 28, had offered Hitler safe passage out of the imperiled city. Axmann had pledged to use every Hitler Youth boy fighting in the streets to ensure the Fuehrer's escape. "No," Hitler said again, determined to remain in his mole-like hiding place. As the news reached the bunker that Wenck could not rescue Berlin and that Hitler still refused to flee, Boldt recounted that "a real end-of-the-world mood began to spread" through the shelter. The Russians had pushed into the Wilhelmstrasse, about a thousand yards away. "A tornado of fire and steel rained down upon the Reich Chancellery and the neighbouring area," said Boldt. The next afternoon, he and two other officers had left the Chancellery with Hitler's permission, to reach Wenck.[9]

Less than twenty-four hours later, the Fuehrer had reportedly ended his life.

If further proof were needed, aside from a corpse, that Hitler had not survived, the publication in the spring of 1947 of an authoritative book, *The Last Days of Hitler,* provided it. Its author, a young Oxford University historian, Hugh Trevor-Roper, had guided the investigation by British intelligence into Hitler's death two years earlier and authenticated Hitler's last will and testament. Blessed with a brilliant and inquisitive mind, Trevor-Roper marshaled his facts as well as any talented lawyer to show that Hitler had ended his own life on the afternoon of April 30, 1945, as the British report had said.

Reflecting the ongoing public interest in the question, the book soon became a Book-of-the-Month Club selection in the United States. Part of the popular appeal of *The Last Days of Hitler* was the result of Trevor-Roper's skillful writing. "It is more readable than a novel," the *Manchester Guardian* said of the study. The author offered a masterful analysis of the character and actions of Hitler and the base creatures who had served him. The first effort by a trained scholar to explain the Nazi Goetterdaemmerung, it rested on captured German records and interviews of those who had witnessed the last days. The standard work on its subject, *The Last Days of Hitler* became a model of scholarship for future research on Nazi Germany.

Hitler's goal to the end, said Trevor-Roper, had been "world power or ruin." He discussed not only the question of Hitler's death, but the plot of July 20, 1944, Hitler's routine, health, and personality, his relations with the generals, Goebbels' program of universal destruction in Germany, Himmler's fantastic character and last-ditch peace maneuvers, Goering's fall from power, and Bormann's intrigues. Across Bormann's desk had passed all the top-secret orders from Hitler—the directives leading to the annihilation of the Jews and other "inferior" races, the persecution of the churches, the mass murders in euthanasia institutes and concentration camps. After the July conspiracy, this "evil genius of the Fuehrer" never left Hitler's side.[10]

"There is perhaps no period of Hitler's life with which we are more familiar," revealed Trevor-Roper, than his final months. Until November 20, 1944, Hitler had been at his headquarters in East Prussia, where the July plot had occurred; then till December 10 at

Berlin; from December 11 till January 15 at Bad Nauheim, from where he had directed the Ardennes offensive; and finally, from January 16 till the end at Berlin, in the Chancellery bunker, "which he never left." *The Last Days of Hitler* described how hopeless the Nazi military situation became in Berlin, prompting the notorious outburst of the Fuehrer on April 22, where he had denounced everyone as traitors and vowed to stay in the capital. When Wenck's Twelfth Army and other forces failed to rescue him, as he had ordered repeatedly, he sent hysterical telegrams to his Supreme Command, withdrawing further northward each day from Berlin. Against this background of military collapse and desperation, judged Trevor-Roper, Hitler had chosen suicide.

The Last Days of Hitler, except for one minor point, the time of the Fuehrer's marriage to Eva Braun (now placed in the small hours of the morning of April 29, instead of the evening of the twenty-ninth), recounted and expanded the British intelligence report. The key events in the Fuehrerbunker, Trevor-Roper assured his readers, "can be ascribed with certainty to days and hours": the coming and going of Greim, the news of Himmler's treachery, the signing of Hitler's testament, the suicide of the Fuehrer and Eva Braun, the telegrams to Doenitz, and the mass escape, of which Bormann had been suspected of being a part, from the underground fortress.

Of the suicides on April 30, 1945, the book described their elaborate planning by Hitler and Goebbels, Kempka's collecting of the gasoline for the cremation of the bodies, and the orders to the Chancellery guards to leave the garden area and stay away. After lunch, Hitler and his wife said their last farewells to the bunker elite:

> Hitler and Eva Braun shook hands with them all, and then returned to their suite. The others were dismissed, all but the high priests and those few others whose services would be necessary. These waited in the passage. A single shot was heard. After an interval they entered the suite. Hitler was lying on the sofa, which was soaked with blood. He had shot himself through the mouth. Eva Braun was also on the sofa, also dead. A revolver was by her side, but she had not used it; she had swallowed poison. The time was half-past three.[11]

Shortly thereafter, Axmann had arrived and was allowed to see the dead bodies. Outside the bunker, another ceremony had been prepared, "the Viking funeral" for Hitler. Kempka had sent the gasoline to the garden and gone into the bunker. Guensche greeted him with the words, "The Chief is dead." At that moment, the door of Hitler's suite had opened, and Kempka too had become a part of the funeral scene.

As Axmann stood among the corpses, two SS men, one of them Hitler's servant, Linge, entered the room. They readied the bodies for the funeral.

> They wrapped Hitler's body in a blanket, concealing the bloodstained and shattered head, and carried it out into the passage, where the other observers easily recognised it by the familiar black trousers. Then two other SS officers carried the body up the four flights of stairs to the emergency exit, and so out into the garden. After this, Bormann entered the room, and took up the body of Eva Braun. Her death had been tidier, and no blanket was needed to conceal the evidence of it. Bormann carried the body into the passage, and then handed it to Kempka, who took it to the foot of the stairs. There it was taken from him by Guensche; and Guensche in turn gave it to a third SS officer, who carried it too upstairs to the garden. . . .
>
> The two corpses were placed side by side, a few feet from the porch, and petrol from the cans was poured over them. A Russian bombardment added to the strangeness and danger of the ceremony, and the mourners withdrew for some protection under the shelter of the porch. There Guensche dipped a rag in petrol, set it alight, and flung it out upon the corpses. They were at once enveloped in a sheet of flame. The mourners stood to attention, gave the Hitler salute, and withdrew again into the Bunker, where they dispersed. Guensche afterwards described the spectacle to those who had missed it. The burning of Hitler's body, he said, was the most terrible experience in his life.[12]

What had then happened to the bodies? Set alight about 4 P.M. and still burning two hours later, noted Trevor-Roper, they were buried late that night by SS and police guards in a bomb crater in the garden. Linge afterwards told a secretary that the corpses had been burned, as Hitler had directed, "till nothing remained." This did not convince Trevor-Roper. He doubted whether "such total combustion could have taken place." About 180 liters of gasoline had been used, proba-bly having charred the flesh, drained the moisture from the bodies, and left them "only an unrecognisable and fragile remainder." The bones, Trevor-Roper concluded, would have withstood the heat; but they had never been found. Perhaps they had mixed and been lost among the bodies of the many soldiers who had died in the garden defending the Chancellery, he speculated. The Russians had dug throughout the garden, unearthing mutilated carcasses by the score. Or, as Guensche stated, possibly Axmann had collected the ashes in a box and taken them out of the Chancellery.

The Fuehrer, said *The Last Days of Hitler,* had been physically unable to escape the bunker. He had not been hurt, as many imagined, by the explosion of July 20, 1944. Instead, contended Trevor-Roper, Hitler became a "physical wreck" by the end of the war because of "his manner of life" and "his doctors." Morell, the British historian asserted, had been at best a "quack," a "gross but deflated old man, of cringing manners, inarticulate speech, and the hygienic habits of a pig." Interested only in "quick drugs and fancy nostrums" for the money they could bring him, he had given Hitler pills and injections by the dozens—morphine, hypnotics, dextrose, hormones, and vitamins. For the crass Morell, Hitler served as the perfect guinea pig.

The Fuehrer's physical decline had become apparent in 1943. His left arm and leg trembled, his left foot dragged as he walked, he had developed a stoop, and he suffered from stomachaches. Some had diagnosed the shaking as Parkinson's disease, others called it the result of hysteria. For the gastric pains, Morell, said Trevor-Roper, had fed Hitler endless anti-gas pills, compounded of strychnine and belladonna. When other doctors, like Brandt and Giesing, criticized Morell, Hitler would not listen to reason or logic. Morell's control over the Fuehrer's person was unchallenged, till they argued at the end of April 1945 and Morell left the bunker.[13]

More significant than describing Hitler's end, *The Last Days of Hitler* provided what the British report had not. Trevor-Roper explained which facts and evidence had been collected and from where. In the book and in later publications, he disclosed how he had pursued his investigation for British intelligence in the autumn of 1945. He had been guided, he said, by the following questions, which face every historian seeking the facts: who first said so, and what opportunities did he have of knowing?

When subjected to this test, much of the evidence had crumbled. So the claim of a Stuttgart doctor to Trevor-Roper that he had personally attended Hitler when the Fuehrer had been wounded near his bunker on May 1, and had pronounced him dead. Another supposed authority, a Swiss journalist, Carmen Mory, had testified that to her knowledge, Hitler was living on an estate in Bavaria with Eva Braun and her sister. But she too had no opportunity of knowing whether Hitler had escaped Berlin, particularly since she had been in a Nazi concentration camp at the end of the war.

Another instance was a story spread by the SS leader and one of Himmler's closest advisers, Schellenberg, after his surrender in Sweden. He maintained that Himmler had poisoned Hitler. "But how did he know?" asked Trevor-Roper. Schellenberg had not seen Hitler since 1942. His sole evidence was his own wishful thinking: he wanted to believe Himmler had accepted his [Schellenberg's] advice and by a selective interpretation of Himmler's remarks, he had persuaded himself that the chief of the SS and police had done that. Trevor-Roper had interrogated Schellenberg and others among Hitler's staff, plus using the reports of Count Bernadotte (the Swedish emissary who had talked with Himmler and Schellenberg at the close of the war), "and Schellenberg's legend dissolved."

At the beginning of his investigation, the Soviet Union permitted Trevor-Roper to visit the ruins of the Chancellery and bunker. The bunker, he learned with astonishment, had been utterly neglected. Poorly guarded outside, its dark and dank interior smelled of decay; two or three inches of water covered the floor. Broken furniture and moldering papers littered each room. Books on opera-house architecture lay soaked and ruined. Trevor-Roper discovered that Hitler's last days had been spent in part designing a new opera house for his home town in Austria. The British investigator found even more shocking the apparent Russian failure to examine the premises thoroughly, and their missing several key documents. "There had been no search [by the Russians]," Trevor-Roper later recalled, "only casual pilfering."

Having perused the bunker, he began studying the documents he had collected and looking for witnesses. He also had the series of telegrams seized along with Doenitz and the Flensburg government in May 1945 and that had passed between Doenitz and Hitler's headquarters. Goebbels had sent the last telegram on May 1, informing Doenitz that Hitler had died "yesterday" (i.e., April 30). It soon became apparent that Doenitz's statement on German radio the evening of May 1, saying Hitler died that day fighting at the head of his troops, had been pure invention. Except for Goebbels' telegram, Doenitz had no other proof. And Goebbels could not be questioned because he was dead.

Doenitz and Hitler's other principal advisers, Keitel, Jodl, and Speer, Trevor-Roper learned, had been with Hitler until April 22. That day a mass exodus from the Fuehrerbunker had occurred following Hitler's military conference, where he declared the war lost and uttered his resolve to die in Berlin. Thus, Hitler's life had not been accounted for during the period from April 22 to May 1. Who and where were the witnesses from those murky days?

To find them, Trevor-Roper cross-examined the officials who had left on April 22 (most having been caught at Flensburg or Berchtesgaden) about who they had left behind in Berlin. He interviewed prisoners like Speer, Keitel, Jodl, Doenitz, and two of Hitler's secretaries, Schroeder and Johanna Wolff. He also interrogated several of Hitler's detective and SS guards who had been evacuated to Berchtesgaden. Each recalled people they had left in the bunker after April 22 and who would be possible witnesses to Hitler's final moments.

Eventually, Trevor-Roper had found seven of the witnesses and interrogated them: Karnau, a policeman from the detective guard; Eric Mansfield and Hilco Poppen, two other policemen; Fraulein Else Krueger, Bormann's secretary; Kempka, the chauffeur; .Reitsch, the pilot; and Baronness von Varo, a casual visitor to the Fuehrerbunker, discovered by British journalists in Berlin. Added to Karnau and Kempka, Mansfield had testified that he had been on sentry duty in the bunker tower on the afternoon of April 30 and had watched the burning of the bodies of Hitler and Eva Braun. Some time afterwards he and Karnau went together to catch a closer glimpse of the corpses.

Altogether, Trevor-Roper questioned forty-two witnesses. He carefully checked their testimony against other material, like the diary of Luftwaffe General, Karl Koller, who had been in touch with the bunker as late as April 27, and that of Graf Schwerin von Krosigk, who became Foreign Minister in Doenitz's brief government. Also valuable had been a diary kept for Hitler by his personal servant, Linge, from October 1944 till the end of February 1945.

A British officer had picked up this diary in September 1945 in the ruins of the Chancellery. Written by hand in the form of an appointment book, it had been overlooked by the Russians. Events which it summarized were inscribed, hour by hour, on the left-hand page. The right-hand page had contained the address of the Fuehrer's headquarters, such as East Prussia or Berlin, and Linge's signature. Concise and factual, its entries consisted only of interviews, meals, and meetings; but the diary revealed much about Hitler. It illustrated clearly the routine of his daily life, the nature of his court and visitors, the deviations of his health, and the increasing regularity of his engagements.

Based on these sources, Trevor-Roper had submitted his intelligence report of November 1945 to the British government. Other evidence, he suggested in the document, might be forthcoming from Hitler's pilot, Baur, and Rattenhuber, head of Hitler's detective guard who had ordered the burial of the Fuehrer's body. These had been reported captured by the Russians in an official communique. Also, Trevor-Roper criticized the Soviet Union for not having allowed the British to use the diaries of Hitler's adjutants, allegedly held by the Russians.[14] Zhukov had cited the diaries in his press conference of June 9, 1945, as proof for Hitler's wedding. Subsequent evidence (e.g., Hitler's will and testament), except for Axmann's testimony that Hitler had both poisoned and shot himself, agreed with Trevor-Roper's findings, and he added this to his book.

The Last Days of Hitler earned its author a mountain of praise. "From exhaustive research," said one reviewer, "[Trevor-Roper] has put together a carefully documented, irrefutable and unforgettable reconstruction" of Hitler's end. The American historian, Arthur Schlesinger, Jr., called the book "an astounding and resounding success," and compared Trevor-Roper with Edward Gibbon. Commented *Le Monde,* "For us to see how Hitler died is to understand why he died. There is now a book that should be read by the Germans." The London *Evening Standard,* reviewing the second edition of the study three years later, said it had established "beyond any possibility of doubt that Hitler committed suicide."

Time, the American news magazine, seemed less sure. "Pretty convincing," it admitted of the evidence. "But since no body has ever been found," it cautioned, "the question of Hitler's death is still a topic that haunts historians." Not historians alone, however. The subject fascinated the press and the man on the street. Colonel W. F. Heimlich, former American military intelligence officer in postwar Berlin, totally discounted Trevor-Roper's findings in a book, *Who Killed Hitler?*, and put forth his own "American private intelligence report." "Astounded" by the Oxford don's writing of his account "without consulting his American colleagues," Heimlich contended that Hitler's death had been a homicide. The Fuehrer had been murdered by Himmler, he said, who had the motive of hoping to succeed the Fuehrer. Himmler's doctor, Stumpfegger, had slowly poisoned Hitler till one of the SS officers in the bunker and the Fuehrer's adjutant, Guensche, had shot him through the head. And Heimlich's proof? Schellenberg, Bernadotte, and Karnau, whom he accused Trevor-Roper of misquoting and ignoring.

Later on, Trevor-Roper would have little patience with those who persisted, despite his book, in thinking Hitler had survived. "Mythopoeia," he said, far outdistanced "veracity" as a feature of the human race. Offended by the many stories continuing after his book, saying Hitler had escaped miraculously to Argentina or elsewhere, he argued, "Reason is powerless against the obstinate love of fiction."[15] He was probably right. There is much evidence that legend is both enjoyed and needed by the public.

But this dedicated historian himself may have inadvertently contributed to an important piece of Hitler hero worship. Ironically, while undermining the myths that Hitler had died "fighting to the last breath against Bolshevism" or that he had lived, Trevor-Roper had found that the Fuehrer had enough courage left to shoot himself and had received a funeral worthy of an ancient Germanic chieftain. The Nazi warlord, implied *The Last Days of Hitler,* had set a final and parting example for his generals, whom he had distrusted and despised. He had chosen the formal and correct death of a true German soldier—with a revolver.

the service he has rendered, but because we
is preëminently the best qualified man in the
for the place.

Is Hitler Dead?

Over the week-end of November 12, th
world was speculating about Hitler. He had
public appearance for about four months; th
reports that he would speak on Sunday, bu
Himmler read a long speech purporting to co
Hitler, and offering the nonsensical excuse
though he was not too busy to write this speec
unable to take a few minutes more and bro

From *The New Republic,* November 1944

with high explosives.
Four of today's targets were hit
Mingkiang. The capture of Szeic
widened to 175 miles the breach in

Continued on Page 4, Column 1 · Continued on Page 3, Column 8

Zhukoff Says Hitler Wed Actress In Berlin, May Be Alive in Europe

By The Associated Press.

BERLIN, June 9—Adolf Hitler married two days before Berlin's fall, and the lovers may have escaped from the German capital by plane, Marshal Gregory K. Zhukoff, Russian conqueror of the city, said today.

"We have found no corpse that could be Hitler's," he said in the first authoritative report on the Hitler mystery.

Marshal Zhukoff said that Hitler and his bride, Eva Braun, had had good opportunities to get away from Berlin after one of history's most macabre marriages. "He could have taken off at the very last moment, for there was an air-

not yet found Hitler's body. "My personal opinion is that he has disappeared somewhere into Europe," General Berzarin said. "Perhaps he is in Spain with Franco. He had the possibility of taking off and getting away."

[Robert Magidoff of the National Broadcasting Company attributed to Marshal Zhukoff the statement that Hitler might be hiding in Europe and said that the Soviet Marshal had added, "Now it is up to you British and Americans to find him."]

General Berzarin said that the Russians had found several bodies in the Reich Chancellery with Hit-

From *The New York Times,* June 1945

DID ADOLF AND
EVA DIE HERE?

This is the evidence in Hitler's room

by PERCY KNAUTH

From *Life*, July 1945

The parade was sponsored by the Queens County Council of the American Legion, commanded by Aloysius J. Maickel.

HITLER SOUGHT IN BOSTON

Ships at Other Ports Are Being Carefully Watched

Special to The New York Times.

BOSTON, Aug. 16—Adolph Hitler is being sought here and at other seaports on incoming ships, it was declared today.

Processing of passengers and crew members of the Swedish freighter Travancore, first to reach this port since the news of the Japanese surrender, led to the disclosure that all such ship complements have undergone this procedure for some time in a search for identifying marks of Hitler and other Nazi war lords who may have escaped from Europe.

Maine Ship Slip Collapses

HARPSWELL, Me., Aug. 16 (AP)—A section of the Casco Bay lines steamer slip at Bailey Island collapsed today, plunging eleven per-

From *The New York Times*, August 1945

THE FUEHRER'S DOUBLE GETS A CAREFUL CHECK

Henrich Noll, 38-year-old German male nurse, having his identity papers looked over by Corp. Edward J. Kulick of the Military Police on a street in Frankfort, Germany, last Saturday. Mr. Noll, who has been frequently stopped, has kept his toothbrush mustache on the chance of portraying Hitler in a planned Austrian movie.

Associated Press

BRITAIN TO REDU(UNREQUITED TRA(

Cripps Says He Will Cut D(on the Sterling Balances— Deficit Is £110,000,000

By RAYMOND DANIELL
Special to The New York Times

LONDON, Jan. 9—Altho Britain is producing half again much as in 1938 and selling m to North America, she is earn fewer dollars than prior to dev ation last Sept. 18, Sir Staff Cripps, Chancellor of the chequer, reported today in a view of the nation's econo achievements in 1949.

Sales to the United States Canada for the October-Novem period, he said, were running the rate of £161,000,000 a y This, he added, compared wit rate of £120,000,000 in the tl quarter of 1949 and £143,000,00 the first quarter. Because pound had been devalued fr $4.03 to $2.80, he estimated t Britain's exports were now ea ing 7 per cent less dollars than the third quarter and 22 per c less than in the first quarter last year.

The Chancellor estimated B ain's over-all trade deficit for year at about £110,000,000 and, the clearest language he has used, asserted his intention slowing down the rate at wh Britain's sterling area credit could draw on their blocked counts. It is essential that th balances, which are being liquid ed through exports that br Britain no actual revenue in turn, be released more slowly order that exports can be diver to markets where they earn h currency, Sir Stafford said.

"But there is another very i portant side to this picture" added. "These resources have b made available, many of them, countries urgently in need of sistance in their post-war rec struction. Unless we had provid this help, we should undoubte have made an even greater spre of communism. What are un quited exports to us are immen ly valuable supporting imports

---

RED TALY

ers and Worst alf

O RISE

irearms Used tion

ESI

persons sixty in a today. lash ba ers that eighteen

d to in wounded cal con nded in t in the by both were re nd gre

vas still a stated ntrol by nds of brought amunist r move upon to the city e police ed by

ccurred. bor de general w. The e Com General e hours ty-four-

IS HITLER REALLY DEAD?

A Historian Examines the Evidence

H. R. TREVOR-ROPER

ER 1945 the circumstances
eath or disappearance had
e months dark and mys-
sions of his death or escape
ent. Some stated that he
fighting in Berlin, others

the facts, had they wishe
ferred to perpetuate the
time they declared Hitler
they doubted their decla
announced that they had
corpses of both Hitler an

From *Commentary*, February 1951

From *The Times* (London), October 1954

ss Administration's handling of Alaska's
p- tions to full statehood.
he
ie,
nd
as

COURT RULING SOUGH
ON HITLER'S DEATH

er
nd
he
he ### REQUEST FOR CERTIFIC
m BERCHTESGADEN, Oct. 14.—The distric
to here, which is dealing with a request
is. Austrian court to issue an official
er certificate for Hitler, announced t
a " According to all investigations carri
on so far there can be no doubt that Hitle
k- mitted suicide on April 30, 1945, in his
ce bunker chancellery."
rt The Austrian court and relatives of
and Eva Braun have asked for the cer
to enable settlement of property clan
i Berlin dentist, Fritz Echtmann, who
ly false teeth for Hitler and Eva Braun
as give further evidence here to-morrow.
as earlier that he had seen their dentures, t
er with a Nazi Party badge and an Iro
military decoration, in a cigar box sh
him by Soviet Army officers. Echtn
former prisoner of war in Russia, ha
recalled by the district court to clarif
points of his earlier evidence.—*Reuter*
er
ed

From *Police Gazette*, January 1977
reprint of a 1950s headline

by The U.S. Army Intelligence Officer who m... investigation in Berlin for Gen. Eisenhower's

EXPOSED

Hitler's Fake Suicide

by COL W.F. HEIMLICH
Former Chief, U.S. Intelligence, Berlin

From *Police Gazette,* January 1977, reprint of a 1950s headline

HITLER'S ARGENTINE CONNECTION

Nazi loyalist.

...nderground had infiltrated the
...rican country so completely it
...oversea suburb of the Third Reich.
...me time for Hitler's aides to flee
...y knew just where to go...

...o the Police
...hat established

From *Police Gazette,* January 1977, reprint of a 1950s headline

Lest Hitler Reappear, Murder Case Is Filed

Special to The New York Times

BERLIN, Feb. 19 — The West Berlin Attorney General has opened proceedings charging Hitler with mass murder between 1933 and 1945.

Attorney General Hans Günther said today that he considered the move necessary in case Hitler reappeared. It is presumed that he died April 30, 1945.

The legal step was taken to insure that any prosecution can continue beyond next May 8, the date after which no new case involving Nazi crimes can be opened under German law.

Mr. Günther said he expected the Bundestag to lift the controversial 20-year statute of limitations on murder. But he decided to act anyway to make sure that no necessary step was left untaken.

According to all available evidence, Hitler and his bride of one day, Eva Braun, committed suicide in Berlin April 30, 1945. His valet, Heinz Linge, has declared that he and a chauffeur poured gasoline over the bodies and set them afire.

Cover of *Police Gazette,* January 1977

7

Officially Dead

The cartoon in 1946 depicted a sad and weary Hitler, standing amidst everlasting fire and gazing at gutted buildings and destruction. He was "crying from hell," said the humorous drawing in Berlin's *Der Tagesspiegel,* and wondering to himself, "When will the Germans finally realize what I have done for them?" For many Germans, their one-time Fuehrer was a shameful thing of the past. He had left them in defeat and ruin, living under armies of occupation, condemned by the world as mass murderers, and facing the postwar task of reconstructing their country. Although Germans rarely discussed him, and then only in hushed tones, his death still keenly interested them.

One heard frequent whispers that, despite the British investigation and other proof saying he died in the Fuehrerbunker, he had succeeded in getting to Argentina. Some Germans imagined him living as a monk in Italy or a herdsman in the Swiss Alps. One Frau insisted she had seen him in Magdeburg in July 1947, posing as a Polish Army lieutenant and speaking fluent Polish and Russian. For his sympathizers and the romantics, Hitler still lived. Other Germans, having been lied to so many times by Nazi propaganda, found it hard to believe Doenitz's original statement of May 1, 1945, that the Fuehrer had departed this life. Occasionally the Allied authorities would uncover Germans who looked remarkably like the dictator. American military police stopped one repeatedly (even as late as January 1950), a mustachioed male nurse in Frankfurt, Heinrich Noll, but always released him.

Despite the usual postwar rumors and allegations, the Germans did much in the decade after the publication of Trevor-Roper's book that added to the evidence that Hitler had perished in the bunker. A court at Berchtesgaden, aided by testimony from several former Nazis freed from Russian prisons, officially declared him dead in October 1956. Although sporadic fear reigned in some foreign circles about a Nazi rebirth in the German Socialist Reich party, formed partially in opposition to the new Bonn Republic in 1949, and other small right wing groups, Germany seemed more eager than other nations to settle this issue of its immediate past. Only with Hitler dead, both literally and figuratively, most Germans were convinced, could they begin returning to a normal life.

As the Western Allies broke further with the Russians over the administration of Germany and helped to create the Federal Republic in the western half, press and political restrictions there were relaxed. Even before the formation of the Bonn government, the controversy surrounding Hitler's death spilled into the German courts. Since he had not been tried at Nuremberg (for example, in absentia) or been declared officially dead, many legal questions involving his estate and property rose after the war. Nor had the British investigation of 1945 and the opinion of the American Military Governor in Germany, Lucius Clay, both stating Hitler had ended his life, satisfied the law.[1]

Because of the unusual circumstances of the Hitler case and because he had held a few scattered properties in Bavaria, a court in Munich opened denazification proceedings against him in the autumn of 1947. According to the denazification law, a former Nazi, if convicted as a "major offender" (i.e., an active supporter of Hitler and his regime), could lose his estate to confiscation. "Was Hitler an Active Nazi?" queried a cynical headline in *World Jewish Affairs.*

Hitler's holdings included an apartment house in Munich, royalties from a publishing company for sales of his book *Mein Kampf,* and the ruins of his villa at Berchtesgaden, which, although it had been registered in Bormann's name, actually belonged to Hitler. After deliberating for several weeks, the court pronounced invalid his last will and testament, which had bequeathed his "possessions" to the Nazi party, the state, his relatives, and "faithful fellow workers" chosen by Bormann.

In the spring of 1948 the court postponed a final decision on what should happen to Hitler's estate, because his death had never been legally established. For that purpose, the court borrowed from the Nuremberg records documents dealing with his end in the bunker. Confronted with the testimony of Kempka, Fritsche, and other witnesses, and telegrams from the bunker mentioning his death, the court ordered the confiscation of the fortune of both Hitler and Eva Braun. It also directed that their property be given to the state of Bavaria and a fund for the benefit of the victims of Nazism.

To no one's surprise, the judges said Hitler would have been classified a "major Nazi offender," if he had lived. But the court stopped short of proclaiming him dead. It said only that the available evidence indicated he had committed suicide in Berlin in 1945 with his wife of a few hours, Eva Braun. As the court delivered its decision, the presence (or lack thereof) of the Hitlers was symbolized by empty chairs placed before the judges.

Denazification did not end the German courts' entanglement with the Nazi Fuehrer.[2] Despite what had happened, the Munich police informed a lawyer that the city still considered Hitler a "legal resident." The police, furthermore, seized several items belonging to his estate in a raid on a Munich merchant's home in December 1950. German and French publishers waged a royal battle in the courts over the rights to print Hitler's *Tischgespraeche,* his "table talk" and secret conversations during the war, as recorded by Bormann and others.

His sister, Paula Hitler-Wolf, who lived in Bavaria and who had earlier tried unsuccessfully through the courts to receive a part of her brother's fortune, also claimed the publication rights. She embarked on a new effort in October 1952 to seek proof of his death which, she argued, would entitle her to an inheritance payment from Bavaria. Frau Anni Winter, Hitler's former housekeeper who had been mentioned in his personal testament, filed a suit against the Bavarian government to recover gifts she had once received from her boss.

Such legal questions even involved the Austrian courts.[3] When Austria produced a painting by the Dutch master, Jan Vermeer, and showed that it had belonged to Hitler, the Vienna government confiscated it on the basis that the government viewed all former members of the Nazi regime "automatically as war criminals." But Hitler's sister and several Jewish businessmen, who had lost property in Austria following the Nazi seizure of the country in 1938, challenged the claim. Faced with a legal dilemma, Austria asked the Bonn government in 1952 for a formal announcement of Hitler's death (i.e., a death certificate) to complete its title to the painting.[4] This unleashed a major legal struggle in the Federal Republic, taking four years to resolve and engaging courts in Berlin and Berchtesgaden.

Meanwhile, as the lawyers and judges pondered the Hitler question, so did the German press and many one-time Nazis. The first of several postwar outpourings of books, memoirs, diaries, reminiscences, and magazine articles appeared on the dictator. Most of this "Hitler wave" (or *Hitler Welle,* as the Germans have named a more recent upsurge in interest in the Fuehrer) resulted from publications by former Nazi officials and his advisers who hoped for headlines and royalties. A few had significantly purer motives: they wished to speak their conscience and contribute to an understanding of why the Nazi debacle had occurred.

Popular German magazines like *Quick* and *Revue* competed in a furious bidding war for the most sensational stories. In the summer of 1949 *Revue* published a scandalous piece by one of Hitler's cronies from the early days of the Nazi party, Hermann Esser, titled "The Great Lover, Adolf Hitler." Other magazines, like *Der Spiegel,* and newspapers, published stories on Eva Braun and women (especially movie actresses) who claimed to have been intimate with the Fuehrer. There was no end to the curiosity about the Nazi leader's sex life. Schellenberg, Himmler's former Gestapo henchman, said he had seen secret SS reports proving "Hitler was so ruled by daemonic forces driving him that he ceased to have thoughts of normal cohabitation with a woman." "Not so," said Karl Wilhelm Krause, Hitler's personal servant. "Hitler was in no way an enemy of the women," he contended. At Berchtesgaden, he said, the Fuehrer and Eva Braun had "a connecting door between both of their bedrooms." One German editor, repulsed by such "tell all" musings, ran a satirical article headlined "I was Hitler's toothbrush."[5]

While the venerating of Hitler's sex life and the rash of publications about him disturbed the American occupation authorities, a large number of ex-Nazis agreed that the Fuehrer had died, a sick and ruined man, in his bunker. None, except Kempka, had any opportunity of knowing for certain. But few things attracted attention like a picture or story of the tyrant. Schellenberg asserted that during 1943 the Fuehrer had exhibited symptoms of Parkinson's disease and, according to SS doctors, "a chronic degeneration of the nervous system." His appearance in the spring of 1945 "as seen in the newsreels," Schellenberg said, "confirmed my impression." Hardly more reliable were the accounts of Krause and one of Hitler's press chiefs, Otto Dietrich. Krause had been removed as Hitler's servant in 1943, and Dietrich dismissed from his office in March 1945. Both accused Morell's pills and drugs of having destroyed Hitler's health, and each maintained the Fuehrer had been too sick to have survived the war.

Dietrich, who wrote his memoir in prison in 1946 and still worshipped Hitler, reasoned that the Fuehrer's nature and his "flying only in perfect weather" proved that he had not left Berlin at the end, but stayed there to die. Had he escaped by plane to Japan or Spain? "Only persons completely ignorant of Hitler's nature," answered Dietrich, "can imagine him guilty of personal cowardice. As for having any intentions to flee, that shameful idea never entered his mind, let alone crossed his lips." Moreover, Dietrich maintained, Hitler's pilot, Baur, had been captured by the Russians.[6]

Several more modest and trustworthy accounts appeared. Karl Koller, a former Luftwaffe general, noted in his diary that he had talked by telephone to the Fuehrerbunker and his new commander, Greim, on April 27, 1945. Hitler still lived, Greim had said, and he no longer condemned the entire Luftwaffe. Koller described his visit with Greim and Reitsch on May 8, the day after the German surrender. Both had said that no one would ever find Hitler's corpse: he had carefully arranged for it to be burned.

Two other officers working in the German Supreme Command stationed near Berlin until April 20, 1945, Joachim Schultz and Walter Luedde-Neurath, confirmed Hitler's outburst at the military conference on April 22, his decision to remain in Berlin, and his failing health. Moments before the Supreme Command evacuated to northern Germany on April 20 (with Keitel and Jodl to follow three days later), Luedde-Neurath had seen the Fuehrer personally for the final time. "Hitler's speech and eyes were as expressive as ever," he recorded in his diary. "His spiritual elasticity appeared preserved. He was in no way insane—at least in the customary sense of the word. Yet physically he gave the impression of being a beaten and broken man: exhausted, stooped, powerless, and nervous."

Schultz discussed Doenitz's investigation into Hitler's death, which had been reported to his headquarters in Schleswig-Holstein on May 1, by telegrams from Goebbels and Bormann in the Fuehrer-bunker. Doenitz, through a rigorous interrogation of witnesses, including personnel at his headquarters and in the Chancellery who had transmitted and received the messages, confirmed the authenticity of the telegrams and that Hitler was no more. "After what has happened in Berlin and in the Chancellery bunker," Schultz had entered in his diary on May 1, "there cannot be any doubt that Hitler is no longer living."[7]

Countless others commented on Hitler's declining health in the war. "From my view," testified Karl Wahl, a former Nazi party leader who had seen the Fuehrer for the last time on February 25, 1945, at a meeting of party officials in Berlin, "Hitler was in this hour a very sick man." General Heinz Guderian, Hitler's Chief of the Army General Staff till his forced resignation in March 1945, maintained that it had been the German defeat at Stalingrad in 1943 and the July plot a year later that worsened Hitler's health. After the Russian disaster, Guderian said he noticed the Fuehrer's "right hand [this was probably his left hand] trembled, he stooped, he stared fixedly, his eyes had a tendency to bulge and were dull and lustreless, there were hectic red spots on his cheeks. He was more excitable than ever." Hitler, the General concluded, had suffered from paralysis agitans, Parkinson's disease.

In the best position to know the Fuehrer's physical state was one of his secretaries, who had left him on April 21, 1945, and who published her memoir anonymously in 1949.[8] Hitler had become a "human wreck," she said, "existing only through the injections of his private doctor, Morell." He had lost "control over his nervous system," and tried to hide from those around him the trembling of the left side of his body. She also described a jungle of intrigue among his doctors for his favor. According to Morell, she said, the root of the Fuehrer's poor health had been the lining of his intestines, which gave him stomach and intestinal pains. After the July plot, an ear specialist (probably Giesing) who had examined Hitler observed that he had been taking as many as sixteen anti-gas tablets per day, all prescribed by Morell. Several doctors, including Brandt, had tried in September 1944 to oust Morell from Hitler's court by claiming to the Fuehrer and Bormann that Morell's pills contained poisonous substances. But Hitler had defended Morell, arguing that the latter kept him healthy.

"I have simply no time to be sick," he once told his secretaries. Shortly thereafter, Himmler had begun a close surveillance of Morell and Hitler's condition through Stumpfegger.

The secretary also provided one of the strongest testimonies that "Hitler knew everything" about the Nazi concentration camps and mass murders. "I am very certain," she said, discounting the feeling of some Germans that he had been ignorant of the atrocities, "that Hitler was informed precisely on the concentration camps by Himmler." Hitler's talks with his "loyal Heinrich" during the war had been strictly private, except for Bormann's occasional attendance. "When discussion at military conferences arose about the rumors of mass murder and persecution in the camps," she added, "Hitler said nothing or quickly changed the subject." In one instance, Himmler had been questioned by several generals about SS barbarism in Poland. "To my surprise," recalled the secretary, "he defended himself by assuring his listeners that he carried out only the directives of the 'Fuehrer.' But, he added: 'The person of the Fuehrer must in no way be connected with this. I accept complete responsibility.'"[9]

Only two former Nazis who published their accounts had been present in the Fuehrerbunker at the end. One was Guenter Schwaegermann, Goebbels' adjutant. He told *Der Spiegel* in 1951 of the intricately planned suicides on May 1, 1945, of Goebbels and his wife, and of the murder of their six children. Hitler had already died, said the adjutant, his charred body buried in a shallow bomb crater in the Chancellery garden. After Goebbels' command, Schwaegermann had tried to burn the corpses of the Minister and his wife, but fled from the approaching Russians before the job could be completed.

The other was Kempka, the chauffeur, whose reminiscences of *Der Chef* (as he and other servants called Hitler) were published with the startling title, *Ich habe Adolf Hitler verbrannt.** He told what he knew of the last days, often exaggerating, like his assertion that Eva Braun had informed him of Hitler's intention to remove Bormann after the war. Hitler's adjutant, Guensche, said Kempka, had instructed him on what had happened to the Fuehrer. Guensche had received the order from Hitler to burn his and Eva Braun's bodies. "I do not wish to be exhibited in a Russian sanitarium after my death," Hitler had explained to Guensche.

I Burned Up Adolf Hitler.

As Kempka had entered the bunker on the afternoon of April 30, 1945, after having sent gasoline to the Chancellery garden, he had met a deathly pale and disturbed Guensche. "The Chief is dead," he whispered to the chauffeur. Then, finding it difficult to express what had happened in words, he had raised his right arm and pointed his finger like a gun into his mouth. Kempka eventually learned the details:

> In his apartment, the Chief had shot himself with his pistol through the mouth.
> Eva Hitler sat next to him, slumped against the arm of the sofa. She had poisoned herself. She had also held a pistol. The right arm hung over the side of the sofa and on the floor lay her revolver.[10]

Guensche explained to Kempka that he, Bormann, and Linge had heard the shot and burst into Hitler's room. They found the couple dead. Moments later, Kempka, Bormann, and Guensche, with the others acting as pallbearers, carried the bodies into the garden. The corpses, set afire and saluted by the small funeral party, burned till the early evening. Many in the Fuehrerbunker had gone a final time to view the historic remains. Even battle-hardened SS guards like Rattenhuber and Mohnke had wept, Kempka recalled. Several hours later, Rattenhuber had told Kempka that he, Linge, and several policemen had "buried together the charred remains" in "a small grave." In melodramatic fashion, Kempka related what he had seen on re-entering the bunker and the suicide room:

> A feeling of total emptiness overcame us. The traces of death were easy to see. The pistols of Eva and Adolf Hitler lay on the red carpet. On the table as well as on the floor were distinct traces of blood from the death of the "Fuehrer." An overturned vase lay on the table. Slumped before us was a small childhood portrait of Hitler's mother. Above the writing table hung the picture of Frederick the Great.[11]

Other evidence, mainly of a documentary nature, appeared soon after the war and hinted, albeit in a circumstantial way, that Hitler had not survived. In 1948 a portion of the diary of Goebbels, ignored by the Russians in 1945 but salvaged by the Allies from the wrecked courtyard of the Propaganda Ministry in Berlin, was published. It revealed Goebbels' concern already in March 1942 for Hitler's "ailing" physical condition and his "severe attacks of giddiness."[12] Additional documents, such as the secret records of the Fuehrer's daily military conferences, disclosed Hitler's obsession with suicide. A defeated military leader, he had said repeatedly, must perform the most honorable and logical act in his moment of failure—shooting himself. He had also feared being seized by the Russians (as he would tell many in the Fuehrerbunker at the end) and "put into the Lubianka," a Moscow prison, "to be 'worked over.'"

For the Germans, the issue of Hitler's fate would not be settled officially in the press or among the recollections of former Nazis. This fell to the West German courts of law, which began meeting in 1952 at the request of an Austrian tribunal to issue an official death certificate for the Fuehrer. This widely publicized process, which would take four years to complete, unfolded with a lengthy dispute over which court, one in Berlin-Schoeneberg or one in Berchtesgaden, had the right to hear the case. The gradual release of Nazi prisoners from the Soviet Union delayed decisions on both the question of jurisdiction and of producing a death certificate. Several had been in the Fuehrerbunker in the final days in 1945, captured by the Russians, and involved in the Soviet investigation into what had happened to Hitler.

The Soviet Union, since its confusing statements of June 9, 1945, saying he was both dead and alive, had released nothing official on Hitler. It had demolished the bunker in 1947 and begun dismantling the Chancellery, using remnants of its materials to construct a memorial in east Berlin to the Soviet dead in the war. Moscow had never mentioned the British report or Trevor-Roper's book. Nor did it permit the book behind the Iron Curtain, except in Czechoslovakia before the Communist coup there in 1948 and in Yugoslavia, after Tito declared his country's freedom from Russia later that year. But aside from the formal silence and a periodic Soviet guard in Berlin discussing Hitler's "mysterious disappearance," other Russian moves since the war had hinted that Moscow believed Hitler had not really escaped the grave after all. Although this had later been branded by Trevor-Roper and others as a *volte face* on the part of the Russians, it seemed more a continuation of Moscow's unfortunate policy of duplicity, begun in 1945. The Kremlin maintained an authoritative silence, thereby sustaining the foreign rumors of Hitler's survival perpetuated by Zhukov's press conference. At the same time, it conceded the opposite in both film and the press.

It showed a new documentary movie, titled *The Fall of Berlin,* in the Russian sector of the former German capital in June 1950. Much to the surprise of Western observers, the film deviated sharply in one respect from Stalin's orthodox view of the war. Hitler and Eva Braun were shown not as fleeing to Spain or Argentina, but dying by their own hands in the Fuehrerbunker. After having first tested the reliability of poison on Hitler's dog, the film revealed, they had swallowed poison themselves. It also exhibited an unmistakable picture of Goebbels' body, blackened and charred.

Equally dramatic, a statement in the 1952 edition of the *Soviet Encyclopedia* discussed the Nazi leader's career and death. Briefly and bluntly, it explained his demise: "Out of fear of the rightful judgment of the peoples, Hitler ended his life through suicide, as was reported by the Headquarters of the German Supreme Command on 1 May 1945." Except for a French historian, who mistranslated the sentence to read that Hitler had "committed suicide on May 1, 1945," it went unnoticed in the West.[13]

Given Moscow's curious history in treating the subject, why had Stalin permitted such a blatant concession? Trevor-Roper suggested that only after several years of rigorous cross-examining by the Russians of captured Nazis who had been in or near the Fuehrerbunker at the end, had the Kremlin ruled Hitler deceased. There were undoubtedly other reasons, especially dealing with propaganda. The chief feature of the film on Berlin, for example, aside from its portrayal of Hitler's suicide by poisoning, was its fulsome worship of Stalin.

By 1948 and 1949, as the Russians prepared the film, the orthodox Stalinist interpretation of the war had been completed. The heroic conflict, it said, had not been won by the Red Army, its leaders, and the people, who Stalin had toasted in 1945, but by the Premier's military genius. In claiming the accolades for the victory, Stalin gave himself what he had denied his generals in 1945: credit for having ensured Hitler's death. The Kremlin may also have wished to deflate publicity given in the United States and Britain to the tiny neo-Nazi movements in the Federal Republic and the periodic dismissal of ex-Nazis from political posts.

A further *de facto* admission by the Soviet Union of Hitler's demise resulted from the freeing of the German prisoners still in Russia, especially those who had been with Hitler in the Fuehrerbunker or were able to recognize his remains. After Stalin's death in March 1953, changing the path of Soviet foreign policy, and because of the personal efforts of the West German Chancellor, Konrad Adenauer, to achieve the reunification of West and East Germany, the Russians liberated the prisoners. During Adenauer's visit to Moscow in August 1955, he made no progress on unification, but obtained the release of the captives by establishing diplomatic relations with the Soviet Union. But even before the breakthrough regarding those in Soviet custody, one had returned earlier and another had told her story to a fellow prisoner who had been freed.

Frau Lieslott Spalcke arrived back in Germany in December 1953, and Fritz Echtmann, the dental mechanic reported as having identi-fied Hitler's jaw for the Russians in May 1945, returned the following year. Spalcke had shared a cell at Butyrka, a Moscow prison, with Kaethe Heusemann, the assistant to Hitler's dentist who, like Echt-mann, had been rumored to have authenticated Hitler's jawbone found by the Russians. For nearly a year, Heusemann had regaled her prisonmates with stories *ad nauseum* of her last days in the Chan-cellery in 1945. As the Russians had seized the remnants of Berlin and Hitler's bunker, Heusemann said, she had escaped to her home. Two weeks later, the Soviets had called her to the Chancellery. Once there, a Polish doctor and a Russian officer showed her a cigar box. Inside had been a picture of Hitler's mother, a Nazi party badge, and several dental fittings. Asked if she recognized the fittings, she had replied "yes," and identified them positively as Hitler's and, though these were less certain, Eva Braun's. Echtmann had also been called to the Chancellery, and he had confirmed Heusemann's observation. The Russians had then flown her to Moscow.[14]

Echtmann, in testimony before the Berchtesgaden court consider-ing whether to declare Hitler legally dead or not, supported Heuse-mann's story to Frau Spalcke. He had actually made false teeth for Hitler in 1944, as well as certain other fittings for Eva Braun. Summoned by the Russians at the beginning of May 1945, he said, he too had been shown the mysterious cigar box. It held, as Heusemann had discovered, the dentures of Hitler and Eva Braun, along with a Nazi party badge and an Iron Cross military decoration. For his troubles, Echtmann too was shipped to Russia—to the Lubianka prison in Moscow.[15] Later he had shared a cell with Harry Mengershausen, an officer in Hitler's bodyguard who had helped with Hitler's burial, and exchanged reminiscences with him.

In July 1955 the Berchtesgaden court finally received the job of deciding whether Hitler should be pronounced dead. This came just in time to hear testimony from the other German prisoners, who soon returned from Russia and who had knowledge of what had happened to the dictator. Arriving in Germany during the next year were Hitler's valet, Linge; the pilot, Baur; Mengershausen; the chief of the detective bodyguard, Rattenhuber; the adjutant, Guensche; the SS commandant of the Chancellery, Mohnke; Heusemann; and several lesser officials. The Russians kept behind bars another key figure, Weidling, commander of the Berlin garrison who had surrendered the city.

This so-called "Reich Chancellery group" of prisoners substantiated what had been strongly suspected by the world since 1945: that the Russians had found Hitler's mangled carcass and conducted an extensive investigation into the circumstances of his death. From the returning prisoners, the world learned that the evidence and witnesses captured by the Soviets, including the charred and moldering body of the Fuehrer, had been removed from Germany to Russia by the end of August 1945. The witnesses, originally captives of the Red Army, had then become political prisoners and placed in the Lubianka jail. Separately and methodically re-examined, they had been made to write down the full history of their experiences in the final days of Nazi Berlin. Wearily they repeated the facts they had already stated in Germany.

The Russians did not believe them at first. They accused Baur of having flown the Fuehrer out of Berlin to safety, and Rattenhuber of having arranged his secret escape by U-boat to Argentina. Nevertheless, after almost a year of interrogation, the refusal of their captors to believe them started to wane. This may have been responsible for what had followed in the summer of 1946. The Russians suddenly assembled and flew the Reich Chancellery group, much to their surprise, to Berlin. There they were taken to the Chancellery and forced to re-enact, on its original site, the whole episode of Hitler's death, burial, and cremation.

Apparently satisfied with the conclusions, the Russians had returned the witnesses to the Soviet Union and sent them to different prisons, some to the Arctic, others to the Ural Mountains. What had the Russians done with Hitler's remains? Having identified them, they had sought to hide them from the Germans to make certain the body would never be discovered and revered. They asked one German prisoner, transferred from the Urals to the Lubianka prison in 1949, if he could identify a photograph of the charred bodies of Hitler and Eva Braun. Unless he could see the bodies himself, he had answered, he could not be positive. Hitler's body, he then learned, lay somewhere in Moscow, "in better keeping with us," said a Russian official, "than under the Brandenburg Gate in Berlin."[16] The Germans must have nothing for relic worship or martyrdom.

Baur and Linge arrived in Germany in October 1955. Initial confusion reigned in the press about Baur's remarks as he disembarked from the train that had brought him to freedom. In the rush to interview him, reporters had incorrectly quoted him as saying he had actually witnessed Hitler's suicide. But this soon straightened itself out, and both men testified at Berchtesgaden and published their stories. Their accounts tallied closely with the statements of Kempka and Axmann to the Allies a decade earlier, that Hitler had shot himself with a revolver.

Linge serialized his story in newspapers around the world. Still referring to Hitler as "the Chief," "the Fuehrer," or "my Master," he boasted erroneously that "I was nearer to the Fuehrer than any other man." He recalled Hitler's relations with Eva Braun, contending "they were lovers" and that once he had walked in on the Fuehrer while "Eva [was] in his arms." Linge's version of the dictator's death began with Hitler's dramatic order to his valet and others in the Fuehrerbunker on April 25, 1945, to destroy his body after he had ended it all.

"There is no way out anymore Linge," Hitler had said. "I have decided with Fraulein Braun that we will die together." The thought of being captured and executed terrified him, and he believed the Russians would even try to infiltrate someone into the bunker among

German refugees wanting to be hidden there. "That person will have orders to get me dead or alive," he had told Linge. "If they get hold of me dead or alive, they'll take me to Moscow. They'll put me on public exhibition. I shall be like a dummy in a waxworks." Then his voice had risen hysterically, as he shouted, "It must never happen, I tell you. It must never, never happen."

Hitler, after his midnight marriage ceremony on April 29, had prepared for his death. He visited the Goebbels family a final time and rejected the plea of his Propaganda Minister that he leave Berlin with the aid of the Hitler Youth. It was now the afternoon of April 30. Linge maintained that he had been the last to see the Fuehrer alive, Hitler reminding him again of his duty to do away with the body. The servant "did not want to hear the fatal and final shot," so he turned and ran from the death room. Regaining his composure, he had gone back to the scene where he "noticed the whiff of smoke" and slowly "pushed the door open."

Pausing as he had entered the room, and hearing "the ominous rumble of the Russian bombardment" outside, Linge feared what he would see. "There almost upright in a sitting position on a couch," he recalled, "was the body of Adolf Hitler. A small hole the size of a German silver mark showed on his right temple and a trickle of blood ran slowly down over his cheek." A pistol, a 7.65 caliber Walther, lay on the floor "where it had dropped from his right hand." A few feet away lay a 6.35 caliber pistol. "Death," concluded the servant, "must have come in an instant."

Eva Braun's body sat next to Hitler's. "I believe she had died a few minutes before the Fuehrer," Linge testified. "No mark showed on her face, it was as though she had fallen asleep. She had swallowed a capsule of poison, one of a dozen Hitler had got from an army doctor for just such a circumstance as this." With much concern, Linge had helped wrap the bodies in thick blankets, "very carefully so that no one could look on the face of the dead Hitler." Two "Hitler commandos" then carried the Fuehrer's limp body into the Chancellery garden. Guensche had carried Eva Braun's.

As they heard Russian artillery and the chatter of machine guns nearby, Linge, Guensche and others "poured tin after tin of gasoline on the bodies." Linge said he ignited the corpses with matches and a newspaper, producing instantly "a blinding funeral pyre." But because of the wind and rapidly burning gasoline, the fire "died as quickly as it flared." Although the flame ate away Hitler's uniform and Eva's dress, "the Fuehrer and his bride still were recognizable," recalled Linge.

At the orders of Bormann and Goebbels, the bodies had been set afire again and again. Linge returned to the bunker, meanwhile, and spent hours destroying Hitler's personal papers and possessions. What did he think had finally happened to the bodies? The valet was uncertain. Someone later told him that "Hitler commandos had taken them to a spot nearby and buried them there." Had the Russians found them? He doubted it:

> So closely and so frequently was I questioned subsequently that I am satisfied the body was never found.
>
> I have a theory—but it can never be more than a theory—that the commandos buried Hitler and his bride in a common grave near the Chancellery where they probably lie to this day.
>
> But I do not know.[17]

Linge likewise confirmed the demise of Bormann and Goebbels. "After Hitler's death," he said, "I accompanied the Reich Leader [Bormann] to the Weidendammer Bridge. Then he jumped on a tank. A few minutes later, after he had mounted the tank, it was hit by an anti-tank shell. The fighting machine burned completely." Goebbels and his wife had shot themselves, said Linge, after having their children murdered with poisonous injections administered by an SS doctor.[18]

Baur, even though he had been in the Fuehrerbunker at the end, had not been involved in the suicides and barbaric funeral. Hitler had acquired his personal pilot in 1932. Although Baur described Hitler's physical decline by 1945, and added a few new details to Goering's infidelity and Himmler's belated efforts to convince Hitler to leave Berlin, he repeated the stories of the others. He had been called several times to the Fuehrerbunker on April 30. In his last meeting with Hitler that day, the Fuehrer had taken both of Baur's hands and said, "Baur, I want to say good-bye to you." The pilot protested: "I tried to persuade him that there were still planes available, and that I could get him away to Japan or the Argentine, or to one of the Sheiks, who were all very friendly to him on account of his attitude to the Jews."

Hitler had balked, and instead ordered Baur to make certain the bodies of himself and Eva Braun did not survive. He thanked the pilot for his many years of faithful service and presented him with a gift, his portrait of Frederick the Great that hung in his apartment. An hour later, Baur learned of the suicides. As he entered the bunker, he met Goebbels, Rattenhuber, and Bormann, plus several SS men, "all very obviously on edge." Goebbels informed him that Hitler had finished his life and that the body was "already being burned." Hitler had shot himself "in the temple," noted Goebbels. "Eva Braun took poison, and she was sitting on the sofa as though she were asleep." Rattenhuber had later said, observing the differences in the self-murders, "that during the burning Eva Braun's body had twitched violently" while "Hitler's body had shrunk in on itself." Although Baur never went into the garden to see for himself what had happened to the bodies, early on the morning of May 1 a policeman had appeared in the Fuehrerbunker and reported to Rattenhuber that the corpses had been consumed, apart from "negligible remains," and buried in shell-holes.

Baur gave an equally fascinating account of life for the Germans in Soviet prisons. The Russians wounded and captured him on the morning of May 2, as he fled with Bormann and the others from the Chancellery. After the initial interrogations in Berlin about what had happened to Hitler, they sent Baur to Poland, where he lost his badly injured leg to amputation. Then it had been on to Butyrka prison in Moscow in November 1945, where "the interrogations went on, and on and on." A Soviet agent assigned specially to Baur, said the pilot, "stuck to me like a leech for years." The official cross-examined Baur daily for two months about the final hours at the Chancellery, and made him write down what he remembered.

After transfer to the Lubianka prison at the beginning of 1946 and back to Butyrka, his interrogator had demanded to know where Baur had flown Hitler. Baur described the ordeal:

> What he wanted me to tell him was that Hitler wasn't really dead at all, and that I had flown him away to some place of safety. According to him this was also what the Americans believed. Now where had I flown

him? You might wonder why—if I had flown Hitler to safety—I had returned to the Reich Chancellery and let myself be taken prisoner. But that was just the devilish ingenuity of it all—it was to put them off the scent. . . .

However, if I only told them where Hitler was now, everything would be alright. In fact, I would be liberally rewarded and given a good job in Chile—or if I felt I wouldn't be safe abroad after that, I could stay in Russia.[19]

The Russians also included Baur among those in the Reich Chancellery group taken to Berlin in the summer of 1946, to act out Hitler's final days. Once there, they beat and threatened him, arguing "that the bodies of Hitler and his wife had not been burnt at all, but preserved, and that I had been brought to Berlin to identify them." Baur never inspected any corpse, however. Having been made to sign a statement certifying that the man who had said good-bye to him in the bunker "actually was Hitler," he and the others in the Reich Chancellery group were returned to Russia.

He spent the next several years in various prisons and labor camps. A Soviet court finally convicted him in May 1950 for having helped Hitler plan the war and for committing crimes against Russian citizens. He had received a twenty-five year sentence in a labor camp. This saw him again shipped around the Soviet prison system: in July 1950 to Krasnogorsk; then to Borovitchi, between Moscow and Leningrad; in July 1951 to Pervo-Uralsk; and in February 1954 to Volkovo near Ivanovo, northeast of Moscow.[20] His liberation, which he thought would never happen, came the following year.

Others, like Mengershausen, the bodyguard reported as having buried Hitler and Eva Braun, testified before the court at Berchtesgaden, but chose not to publish their stories. Mengershausen stated that he had actually dug the Fuehrer's grave on the evening of April 30, 1945, and although he had poured several cans of gasoline on them, the bodies were not consumed by the fire or even left unrecognizable. Together with a colleague, later killed in the fighting in Berlin, he had buried the remains on three wooden boards several feet deep in the ground.

Having been seized shortly thereafter by the Russians and made to admit his role in the macabre funeral, he had shown his captors on

May 13 where he had buried Hitler in the garden. But Mengershausen saw immediately, he said, that the grave had been dug up and bodies removed. Several days before, as known from the experience of the dental assistants, Echtmann and Heusemann, the Soviets had already discovered and exhumed the bodies. A month later the Russians took Mengershausen by car to a small grove of trees outside Berlin. There he had positively identified the carcasses of Hitler and the Goebbels', lying in wooden crates. While viewing them, he had noticed (like Linge) a small hole in Hitler's right temple, leading him to conclude that the Fuehrer had shot himself there. Although Hitler's body appeared in a far worse state than the Goebbels', said Mengershausen, one could clearly recognize his facial structure, and his jaws were intact. The feet had been completely destroyed, the skin and flesh blackened and burned.

As Mengershausen testified at Berchtesgaden, the German paper, *Das Bild,* published an additional piece of evidence regarding the Soviet disinternment of the corpses. The work had apparently been the job of a special detachment of the Russian intelligence service, the NKVD. A member of the unit, Fjedor Pavlovich Vassilki, had later told an East Berlin police officer on whom he had been billeted, how the bodies were discovered. "Hitler's skull," Vassilki had said, "was almost intact, as were the cranium and the upper and lower jaws." Vassilki had also affirmed that its identity had been "indisputably proved by the teeth."[21]

The other prisoners returning from Russia contributed little to the stories of their colleagues. Rattenhuber said that although he had not seen Hitler buried, he had been told that evening that the body had been placed in a bomb crater in the Chancellery garden. Guensche, released in April 1956, confirmed in several statements to the press that he had seen Hitler dead and had taken part in the cremation of the corpse. Karl Schneider, another who had been near the ghastly death scene and an SS major in Hitler's bodyguard, asserted that the Russians had dug up Hitler's remains at the beginning of May 1945 and transported the skull to Moscow for study. Heusemann related to the court what she had said to Frau Spalcke in prison—that she had identified Hitler's teeth for the Russians. Her version would not be published till her interview in 1963 with Cornelius Ryan, the American writer. Helmut Kunz, a dentist called to the Chancellery in April

1945 when Hitler's dentist, Blaschke, had left Berlin, claimed Eva Braun had told him of her suicide the day before it became a reality.

What was notable about the Reich Chancellery group was their testimony, made independent of the statements of Hitler's aides captured a decade earlier. The Fuehrer's self-destruction and funeral on April 30, 1945, amid the thunder of Russian guns, had now been described by a multitude of those who had observed it from varying perspectives. They generally agreed on what they had seen. This testimony alone, on top of the documents found in 1945 (i.e., the telegrams and Hitler's testaments), provided sufficient grounds for the Berchtesgaden court to close its case.

It was the morning of October 25, 1956. A throng of newsmen, photographers, and television cameramen from Europe and the United States crowded around a bulletin board in the office of the Munich Palace of Justice, where the landmark decision was posted. The Bavarian Ministry of Justice issued a short summary of the court's findings, barely four and a half pages. "There can no longer exist even the smallest doubt," the court had concluded, "that Hitler took his own life on 30 April 1945 in the 'Fuehrerbunker' of the Reich Chancellery in Berlin, by shooting himself in the right temple." To arrive at its judgment, the court said, it had questioned forty-two witnesses, including thirteen recently liberated from Soviet prisons. Moreover, the judge had studied intensively both the German and foreign literature on the subject. He had even examined similar historical cases, such as the mysterious circumstances of the death of the Russian tsar, Alexander I, who had died in 1825 but, according to legend, had lived as a hermit for another thirty-five years.

Otherwise, just as with the British investigation earlier, the court gave little explanation of which sources had yielded what evidence. The verdict told a familiar story. Hitler had first uttered on April 22, 1945, to those in the Fuehrerbunker, his intention to take his own life. Under the pressure of the worsening military situation, he had explained with great excitement to his advisers, who had begged him to leave Berlin, that he would stay in the capital and shoot himself if his battered Army could not liberate it. The thought of being caught alive by the Russians and imprisoned obsessed him.

Already by April 26, the court continued, Soviet troops had overrun most of the city. Three days later Hitler had married Eva Braun, and the two had decided on their method of suicide. He would shoot himself, she would take poison. Meanwhile, cyanide capsules had been supplied to everyone in the Fuehrerbunker by Himmler. But Hitler had by then lost confidence in his SS and police leader, suspecting him of treason and believing that Himmler may have given him harmless pellets to ensure that he would fall into the hands of the enemy. Not wishing to take any chances, Hitler ordered the poison be tried on his dog, Blondi, which died immediately.

He had said good-bye to his aides and servants on April 29 and 30. The Russians had now pushed into the nearby Wilhelmstrasse; flames engulfed the Reich Chancellery. Thus, said the court, "with the Russians about to enter the bunker at any moment," Hitler had shot himself. It was 3:30 P.M. on April 30:

> Those waiting in neighboring rooms of the bunker, including Goebbels and Bormann, found him in a sitting position, dead, while Eva Braun's body was lying next to him on a sofa. In Hitler's right temple, a bullet hole was visible, from which blood was dripping. At his feet lay his personal weapons, two pistols of 7.65 and 6.35 caliber. A shot had been fired from the larger one, whose smell of gunpowder was still noticeable. . . . No injuries were present on the body of Eva Braun.[22]

While the court offered no hard evidence, it maintained that the "different other versions" of Hitler's death—e.g., his shooting himself in the mouth—"may be completely excluded." His body and that of his wife were partially cremated in the Chancellery garden, it said, in view of Goebbels, Bormann, Krebs, and an adjutant, General Wilhelm Burgdorf. Later in the evening, "after burning for a long time," the remains were buried in a crater. The Russians, proclaimed the court, had definitely found the makeshift grave, dug up what was left of the bodies, and identified them:

> On 9–11 May 1945, the assistant and the technician of Hitler's dentist—both having returned from the Soviet Union in 1953 and 1955—had been shown false teeth in Berlin by a Russian Commission, and each identified them independently as those of Adolf Hitler and Eva Braun. This dealt especially with a gold bridge which was inserted in Hitler's upper jaw in 1933 and had been reduced in 1944 from 11 to 9

parts by the inflammation of the gums. Also shown with this bridge had been a human lower jaw, whose parts had matched exactly with the gold bridge as well as other features (2 small bridges), and been recognized undeniably as belonging to Hitler.[23]

In a parting comment, the court said its work had proven that the many stories of Hitler's survival and escape from Berlin to faraway lands were "no longer worth considering." Ironically, in the room where the decision had been posted hung a calendar with the saying for October 25, "Each dies as he lives."[24] For some, the court's judgment offered an opportunity to discuss the politics of the moment. In a bitter attack on the armed Soviet suppression of the Hungarian revolt, *The New York Times* observed, "Hitler is dead, but the evil of his deeds lives after him." The chaos Hitler had created in central and eastern Europe, the paper insisted, had "enabled Stalin and the Soviets to press their world-conquering ambitions by force of arms until they have imposed Communist tyranny on one-third of the human race."

The use of Hitler's fate in Cold War rhetoric notwithstanding, the death certificate of the Nazi despot had now been issued. It was eleven years, five months, and twenty-five days after the fact. For the serious student of history, both in Germany and abroad, the evidence uncovered since 1945 appeared overwhelming, if not conclusive. Former President Truman, having never made an official statement on Hitler's death while in office, admitted a decade later his conviction that the German leader had been a suicide. Michael Musmanno, a judge at the Nuremberg trials and a member of the Pennsylvania Supreme Court, said in a book on Hitler's demise, *Ten Days to Die,* that he had both swallowed poison and shot himself in the mouth. How did one therefore account for the blood allegedly found on his temples? "The blast of the pistol-shot's explosion in Hitler's mouth," reasoned Musmanno, "ruptured the veins on either side of his forehead."

Musmanno had interviewed two hundred of "Hitler's intimates" in three years of research, and the judge marvelled at the spell which Hitler's personality had cast on his closest minions. He had visited Hugo Blaschke, Hitler's dentist and a graduate of the University of Pennsylvania, at a prison camp near Nuremberg in 1947. Musmanno reminded Blaschke that if he had stayed in the United States he would have been living after the war in ease and comfort, not behind barbed wire. "Yes, that was a big mistake," the dentist had replied. Then he paused, his eyes taking on a misty shine. "But, on the other hand," he continued, "if I had not returned, I would never have been Hitler's dentist."

By publishing several letters written in the final days by Eva Braun and the Goebbels', Musmanno contributed to the documentation on the Fuehrer's death. Each had been carried out of the Fuehrerbunker by Greim and Reitsch on April 29, 1945; each confirmed Hitler's impending death. A fearful and worried Frau Goebbels wrote to her eldest son, Harald Quandt, the previous day, "We have only one mind left to us: To be true unto death to the Fuehrer; that we be allowed to end our lives together with him is a merciful fate upon which we could hardly have counted." In this connection, a French historian, Georges Blond, theorized that Goebbels and his wife "could never have committed the atrocious massacre of their children if they had not known that Hitler was dead." For the parents, Blond said, there was no reason to go on living after the tragedy had reached its climax with the end of the Fuehrer.

A film in 1955 by the renowned German novelist, Erich Maria Remarque, whose German citizenship had been stripped from him by the Nazis, dramatized Hitler's death, as envisioned by Musmanno. Titled *The Last Ten Days*, it showed a sobering scene where General Jodl hopelessly discussed a hero's death with Hitler in the Fuehrerbunker. "My Fuehrer," suggested his military adviser, "place yourself at the head of the troops and escape to freedom in a historic way." "And if I am wounded," answered a pale and feeble Hitler, "if I fall alive to the violence of my enemies? People would lead me around the whole world in a cage." The movie played to enthusiastic audiences in Germany, England, and the United States, yet another reminder of the enduring appeal of its subject.[25] The press discussed it at length. Munich's *Sueddeutsche Zeitung,* encountering "the lively interest of a surprisingly large number of readers," published the reaction of Kempka to the film, plus a series of documents and reports portraying Germany's final months in the war.

It had also become a subject for novelists. *The Mad Dictator* offered the following scenario. Hitler, covering himself with Doenitz's announcement to the world on May 1, 1945, that he had died a "hero's death," had tried to flee Berlin at the last moment. But as the Fuehrer, his chauffeur, and doctor, Morell, arrived at a Berlin airport for the desperate flight to freedom, Hitler was recognized and shot by a despairing workman, embittered by the loss of his family in the war. In a final spectacle, Hitler was returned nearly dead to the Fuehrer-bunker. There he married Eva Braun, who agreed to commit suicide to repay her lover for the marriage. After he had died in her arms, however, she had refused to kill herself in a shocking display of dishonor and logic, arguing "The Fuehrer was a madman."

With less imagination, but with a careful consideration of the facts, the first major postwar biographies of Hitler appeared. Based on Trevor-Roper, Semmler, Reitsch, Kempka, the testimony of Speer and Keitel at Nuremberg, and Goebbels' telegram to Doenitz on May 1, 1945, they determined that Hitler had shot himself the day before, and that his body had been burned outside the bunker.[26] The British historian, Alan Bullock, whose *Hitler: A Study in Tyranny* would become a classic analysis of the dictator's career and personality, had no doubts about what had happened.

"The weight of circumstantial evidence set out in Trevor-Roper's book," he wrote, "when added to the state of Hitler's health at the time and the psychological probability that this was the end he would choose, make a sufficiently strong case to convince all but the constitutionally incredulous—or those who have not bothered to study the evidence."[27] But there were still plenty of both, the disbelievers and those who ignored the facts. To them the Fuehrer had not gone to the grave in 1945. He had fooled the world a last time; he had somehow survived.

8

The Scenario of Survival

"Hitler Seen Alive," "Hitler's Fake Suicide," "Hitler in Argentina." With these headlines, the *Police Gazette* dazzled its readers in barber shops and at drug-store newsstands throughout the United States. It was on the trail of the former Nazi Fuehrer, proclaimed the magazine in the 1950s and 1960. A book by a Hungarian refugee in Buenos Aires bore the eye-raising title, *Je sais que Hitler est vivant.** A weekly newspaper for American high school students carried the title line in 1955, "Clear Up Hitler's Death." The dictator seemed almost as popular and marketable as he had been in 1945.

But not with the German magazine, *Heim und Welt.* "Always new, always different, always sensational assertions and representations are made," it complained in June 1952, "that Hitler is not dead, but is alive somewhere." And the origin of such reports? "Foreign countries," it deplored, "deal as always with Hitler's ghost." The Hannover publication had a point. In the decade and a half after World War II, the American and Western European press used as much ink to allege the Fuehrer alive as dead.

Despite the powerful case that had been built since 1945 for his eleventh-hour suicide in the Berlin bunker, in the imagination of the faithful (as well as his enemies) Hitler still turned up periodically in remote corners of the world. The maze of popular books and magazines that purported to have tracked him had inherited a wealth of stories from the war. When pieced together by the press, these tales produced a basic scenario: that a "double" had died in Hitler's place; that the Fuehrer had escaped to the Argentine or the Antarctic; that

I Know that Hitler Is Alive.

126

he had sired several children or successors; and that Goebbels and Bormann had also survived, aiding him in secretly planning the future comeback of Nazism.

Such popular stories may not have convinced the world that Hitler still lived. But they kept astir a popular belief that he might not have met his end, an uncertainty that stemmed from the final days of the war and from no announcement from the Russians that his body had been found. As late as May 1947, two years after the war had ended and one year after the conclusion of the major Nuremberg trial, nearly half of America believed he was still around—somewhere.[1]

This lingering fascination reflected several things about the postwar world. Since it crossed national borders and social classes, it illustrated again the dramatic and worldwide impact of the war. While few fans of the Hitler chase desired a return to the war, some may have wished to relive its excitement and adventure through the "Fuehrer is alive" stories. But the true believers rarely pictured the fugitive hero or villain as a sixty- or seventy-year-old man, probably ill with palsy and other ailments. Instead, they saw him as the dynamic personality they had remembered from newsreels and radio during the war. Many recalled his hypnotic and charismatic effect on the German masses, which now stood in sharp contrast to the lackluster presence of postwar leaders like Adenauer, Eisenhower, Attlee, and even Nikita Khrushchev.

Such tales were also a tribute to the unmatched hatred Hitler had inspired around the globe. They may have been an unconscious effort to belittle and bring dishonor to him by suggesting he had turned and run, and to hurl venomous insults at him. Even if posthumous, these could be felt by his enemies as a bit of well-deserved revenge. His murder of millions of Jews and others, as forcefully demonstrated at Nuremberg, had left the world aghast and questioning seriously whether man was really more angel than animal. "A demonic personality obsessed by racial delusions," said a former Nazi leader in describing Hitler. Another German called him "the motorized Attila, the modern Anti-Christ," whose barbarism might have signaled the end of the world. The modern era had never been confronted with such sheer evil, and there were many intrigued by it.[2]

Postwar skepticism and distrust of the German people also made the stories popular. Instinctively militaristic and racist, so the argument went, they would never be content without ruling Europe. By unconsciously keeping Hitler "alive," one could continue to fight this nascent German impulse toward fascism—an attitude not unlike that of the Soviet Union in the summer of 1945. Hitler was also a convenient *bete noir* for the "Cold War." Whenever the Soviet Union and the United States clashed in the United Nations, their delegates charged that the opposing side acted like Hitler.

His survival had become by 1950 a part of popular mythology. Such stories attempted to explain why the tyrant had died, leaving a radically changed and uncertain world, and to explain why his body had never been found. These accounts may even have resulted from the fanaticism and religious fervor with which the world had fought him. Almost singlehandedly, Hitler had been responsible for the war. From the Western viewpoint, the war had been a death struggle against the human incarnation of Satan, Good against Evil, Right against Wrong. As his Nazi followers had zealously worshipped him as their godlike Fuehrer, so his enemies had attributed to him demonic and superhuman powers. Might not such qualities, so the reasoning went, have ensured his survival?

Postwar myths of a live Hitler, moreover, possibly mirrored in a minor way the Western world's hopes for the future, its relations with Russia and Communism, and one of the bonds that tied it together and gave it a sense of purpose. The war had created a new world order which, like the old, required a new mythology to bind people to it and to provide support for its institutions. In the thinking of the man on the street, who enchanted himself with tales of Hitler's survival, they perhaps unconsciously helped persuade him of the need for the continued Anglo-American and French presence in Western Germany and Europe.

It may have subconsciously contributed, therefore, to a much greater postwar myth, the menace of a monolithic and global Communism and the necessity of the West to contain the danger. The constant reappearance of accounts of Hitler, alive or dead, legitimized what the war had done. It had divided the earth into forces of Good and Evil (i.e., Democracy versus Communism), buttressed Anglo-American authority in Western Europe, and provided justification not to appease the other side (as the West had done with Hitler in the 1930s). Similarly, the Soviet Union had exploited the Hitler mystery since 1945 as one means (among many) to explain its rule over East Germany and the rest of Eastern Europe.

What evidence did the postwar Hitler hunters offer to gird their exciting claims? They relied on supposition and insinuation, no documents and no testimony from actual witnesses. When subjected to Trevor-Roper's test—i.e., who first said so, and what opportunities did he have of knowing?—their proof crumbled quickly. The survival theorists paid little attention to who had said what or to the chances a witness had of knowing what had happened in the bunker. An Austrian writer described the reasoning of the skeptic and disbeliever:

> In any case—as with the investigation of the most trusted officials—there exists an eighty percent probability that Hitler met his end in one form or another.
>
> And for the remaining twenty percent, vigilance must be the order of the day!
>
> As is well known, one should be very careful in politics and love in using the words "never" and "eternal." Despite this, it can probably be asserted with one hundred percent accuracy that Adolf Hitler—if he really should be living—will never have another chance![3]

One of the most ardent doubters, the French magazine *Bonjour*, published in 1952 a series of articles disputing that the Fuehrer had died. The magazine said nothing of Trevor-Roper or the British investigation pronouncing Hitler a suicide. Instead, *Bonjour* quoted General Koller, the last Luftwaffe Chief of Staff, who stayed in the Fuehrerbunker till April 23, 1945, as saying Hitler had "deserted" his people. The magazine accused witnesses like Kempka and Axmann of "contradicting themselves" and questioned the evidence that Hitler and Eva Braun had died in the bunker:

> Where are in fact the bodies? Were they buried in any bomb crater? Were the ashes scattered to the wind? The answers, which the (still surviving) witnesses give to these questions, are not convincing. Of Hitler and Eva there is, however, nothing left. There is much that speaks against Hitler's suicide. All who had known Hitler and are able to give an objective judgment of him, do not believe that he was capable of suicide by shooting. Hitler believed firmly as a rock in his invincibility.[4]

Other events, argued *Bonjour,* had indicated Hitler probably survived. It recalled for its readers Zhukov's press conference on June 9, 1945, and cited from the memoirs of the American Secretary of State, James Byrnes, Stalin's remark to him that Hitler most likely had "flown away" to Spain or Argentina. Further, when the Soviets had allowed the Allies to dig in the Chancellery garden six months later, nothing had been unearthed that resembled a body, and only a few pieces of clothing with the initials "E.B." and a scattering of Goebbels' records were found. The next day Moscow had stopped the excavation, accusing the Allies of pilfering important documents from the area.

Bonjour and other French sources quickly pointed out that Commissioner Guillaume, a renowned French criminologist sent to Berlin in October 1945 to investigate the Hitler mystery, had returned to Paris empty-handed. Even more suspicious had been the Soviet invitation to the French Military Government in Berlin on January 17, 1946, to participate in further digging in the garden. Allegedly, the exhumation by German prisoners and Russian officers had produced the remains of two badly burned and decayed bodies, identified immediately by doctors as "probably" those of Hitler and Eva Braun. But the French representatives had come away from the excavation bewildered. Not only had there been two graves unearthed, thus contradicting the testimony of Kempka and others that the Fuehrer and his wife had been enclosed together in a shallow bomb crater, but the French official had been kept a lengthy distance from the burial places.[5] Why had the Russians apparently staged the digging, asked the Paris press, and only for the French?

The American magazine, *Police Gazette,* seized on remarks by public figures to add credibility to its popular series of articles, "Hitler is Alive," published in the early 1950s. As the *Gazette* proudly announced, General Eisenhower, soon to become President of the United States, even responded to its "revelations about Hitler's disappearance." "I cannot disprove any of the facts in the *Police Gazette* articles," Eisenhower replied, when asked if the magazine had a well-founded viewpoint. "We have been unable to unearth one bit of tangible evidence of Hitler's death, [and] many people are of the opinion that Hitler escaped from Berlin."

Comments by other public figures encouraged the press. *The New York Times* carried a headline in November 1951, "Doubts Theory Hitler was a Suicide," whose story told of the skepticism of the retiring American Commissioner for Bavaria, George Shuster, that Hitler had died in the Fuehrerbunker. "I have no substitute theory," Shuster had said in Munich, "but I do not believe that one. I think we must simply resign ourselves to mystery. I am convinced, however, that Hitler is dead, else he would have appeared on the scene long ago." The Central Registrar's Office in West Berlin, which kept German death certificate records, also reminded the world in January 1954 that Hitler was "not officially dead yet."[6]

Since no formal announcement had been forthcoming from the Soviet Union that it had discovered Hitler's carcass in the Berlin ruins, the *Gazette, Bonjour,* and other popular publications stressed that the Fuehrer had disappeared from the bunker in the last days of the war. He had left one or several "doubles" to perish in his place, which the Russians had admitted finding, and then made his way out of his wrecked capital and country to freedom. While most of those in eager pursuit of the Nazi leader agreed he had outlived his regime, their accounts of how he had achieved such a miracle varied. Usually based on rumors that had risen in the summer and fall of 1945, they said Hitler's face had been lifted and a look-alike slipped into the Fuehrerbunker to sacrifice himself for the real Fuehrer.

A story prominent in Vienna in 1951 said that Hitler had been so seriously injured in the bomb blast in July 1944 that he had died two months later. But before his demise, the report said, Bormann had produced an excellent stand-in for the Fuehrer (whose pseudonym was Strasser) who employed a large array of disguises to fulfill his role. Totally under Bormann's control, Strasser had functioned as the German chief of state throughout the last months of the war. He had fled the bunker with Bormann in the late hours of May 1, 1945, the Vienna story added, and probably died with Hitler's ruthless secretary as they tried to break through the Russian lines in a tank.

Another version had Hitler remaining safely hidden from the Russians in a super-secret Berlin cellar (not his bunker) through the end of the war and into the first months of 1946. Then with the aid of former Nazi friends, he had been smuggled out of Germany.[7] To give an air of plausibility to such tales, the *Police Gazette* ran an article in June 1952 by W. F. Heimlich on "Hitler's fake suicide." The *Gazette* advertised Heimlich, a former postwar official of American intelligence in Berlin, to its readers as an expert on what happened to Hitler.

To lend weight to his theory that the Nazis had feigned Hitler's suicide, Heimlich recalled the Allied discovery in September 1945 near Travemuende, a town northwest of Luebeck, of a large transport plane. Its flight crew claimed to have volunteered to fly Hitler out of Germany. Heimlich further asserted that the bloodstains on the sofa where the dictator had "reportedly killed himself" in the bunker were "not of the blood type of Hitler or Eva Braun." American intelligence, he continued, which had excavated the Chancellery garden in December 1945, had "found no signs of any bodies and more significantly no evidences of burning or of fire."

Armed with this information, Heimlich said, he had written a report to Allied headquarters in Frankfurt, noting, "On the basis of present evidence, no insurance company in America would pay a death claim on Adolf Hitler." Why had his story been suppressed by the American government, which had issued no report (as had the British) on the Hitler mystery? "Because," charged Heimlich, "of the fear that it might give credence to the rumors rampant throughout the world that Hitler was indeed alive." He also suggested that his viewpoint, if made public, might have affected significantly the Nazis who had fled to Latin America. They would have been encouraged to believe that their Fuehrer had outlived his enemies and now "awaited a chance to return as did Napoleon from Elba." The American government, alleged Heimlich, could not accept his political dynamite because Washington seriously feared a Nazi revival in 1945 and 1946.

Heimlich suffered from wounded pride. He had most likely embarrassed his government with poor reasoning and his complete ignoring of the British investigation in the autumn of 1945. As for his recollections in the *Gazette* seven years later, the plane at Travemuende had been found in mid-June, not September, and the British never proved it had waited to whisk Hitler out of the country. Furthermore, the Russians had carefully controlled the Allied search of both the bunker (including Hitler's couch) and the Chancellery garden. But years later, such conclusions excited casual readers of the *Gazette* and other magazines.

Still another reason for believing the Hitler double thesis, said *Bonjour* and the French, centered on the story of a former Russian war correspondent, Lew Slawin. He had supposedly been with the first Soviet troops storming Berlin and been present when the city had capitulated. After the war he had published a short pamphlet titled "The Last Days of the Fascist Empire." Despite warnings from his commanders, Slawin had talked with ranking officers of the German army and Hitler's personal SS guard, seized by the Red Army.

The reporter had even interviewed General Weidling, who had surrendered the Berlin garrison to the Russians. Weidling had told the correspondent that he had seen Hitler for the first time in a year on April 24, 1945, when the Fuehrer had appointed him commander of the Berlin forces. "As I now saw the Fuehrer," Slawin had quoted him as saying, "I was astonished at his appearance." Weidling stood before "a human wreck" whose "head shook, hands trembled, and speech was hardly distinguishable." There existed in the Fuehrerbunker, the General continued, an "atmosphere of mistrust, and there were likewise rumors abounding that proclaimed Hitler was no longer Hitler, but his double."

Slawin and later *Bonjour* had jumped on this last phrase. They accepted it literally, when in fact—if indeed Weidling had uttered such words—it was a figure of speech to describe Hitler's poor physical condition at the end. Five days later Weidling had again appeared in the bunker before Hitler, reporting to him the hopelessness of further resistance. "My commands," the Fuehrer had mumbled and stammered, "are never followed." Such few words, so uncharacteristic of the talkative leader, had amazed Weidling. As Russian artillery smashed into the Chancellery walls above, several of Hitler's guards had entered the shelter on April 30 and encountered their chief. "Hitler's swollen leg stamped increasingly on the floor, without bending the knee," they had told Slawin, "but his right hand, raised to give the Nazi salute, trembled noticeably."

Hitler's near total silence had surprised his guards. It especially aroused *Bonjour*'s suspicion. "Did he fear the betrayal of his shaking voice?" it asked. "Or did he fail to speak because he was not Hitler, but his double, and had therefore been forbidden to use his voice?" As the day had worn on, Weidling received a letter from the Fuehrer granting him freedom in commanding the Berlin troops to escape the

Russian net closing in on the heart of the city. Three hours later, however, another letter had arrived at his headquarters from the Fuehrerbunker, signed by Hitler's adjutants, countermanding Hitler's directive.

Wondering what had happened, Weidling traveled with great risk through the burning and smoking ruins to reach the Chancellery and inquire about the sudden reversal. He had found only Goebbels, Bormann, and Krebs—no Hitler. The Fuehrer and Eva Braun, they instructed him, had poisoned themselves and were then shot to ensure their death. After Hitler's wish, their bodies had been burned in the Chancellery garden. Weidling, reported Slawin, had found the suicides hard to believe, but had no time to investigate for himself.

The Russians, Slawin had learned in the days after the city had surrendered, had uncovered six bodies in and near the Chancellery. Each apparently resembled Hitler and each had been shot in the head. When questioned about the Fuehrer look-alikes, Weidling had told the Russians, "These jokes about the doubles are the silliest and most disastrous fraud of which the National Socialists have been accused. Silly and disastrous because such deceit will be accepted as part of the proof that will speak against Hitler's suicide." *Bonjour* interpreted Weidling's remark, which clearly illustrated his disdain for the hypothesis that a double had died for Hitler, as meaning the General had accepted it. Although this testimony of Weidling, as reported by Slawin and *Bonjour,* would agree with that published by the Soviet Union in 1961, the French magazine used it to back its contention that Hitler had disappeared.[8] It had also borrowed heavily from Ladislas Szabo, a Hungarian refugee living in Argentina, who had published in 1947 his book *Je sais que Hitler est vivant.*

Szabo had in turn made use of a story from the London *Evening Standard* in 1945, quoting the Russians as saying that one of Hitler's physicians had killed his famous patient with poison. With a bit of imagination, the *Standard* had identified the doctor as Stumpfegger, who had joined the Fuehrer's staff in the fall of 1944. Stumpfegger had been an associate of one of Himmler's doctors, Gebhardt, notorious for his ghastly medical experiments on inmates at the Ravensbrueck concentration camp, said the *Standard.* Szabo and *Bonjour* added that Stumpfegger had arranged for the "phony" Hitler and for his apparent suicide in the bunker, while the "authentic" Fuehrer escaped. Stumpfegger, they assumed, had performed plastic surgery and a hair transplant to create Hitler's stand-in. Further, he had drugged the latter heavily, paralyzed his mind, and thereby ensured his obedience.

In support of his tale, Szabo noted that Hitler had said good-bye to a group of women during the final hours in the bunker. At the farewell, however, the Fuehrer had said almost nothing. He had barely moved, in fact, and only shaken hands with his guests. "Was that Adolf Hitler or one of his 'doubles,' changed into a semi-paralytic by Stumpfegger's operation?" queried Szabo. One of the women, asserted the writer, had later said with certainty that she had seen Hitler, "but he had changed a great deal."

That had been enough for Szabo. He determined that the "real" Hitler, after signing his last will and testament, had abandoned the bunker. "He took off from the Gatow Airport or from the long Charlottenburg highway in a fast plane," he surmised, "leaving Bormann, Goebbels, and Stumpfegger to care for the macabre scene of cremating his assassinated 'double.'" He wound up his story by recalling that a mysterious voice had interrupted German radio at the end of June 1945, promising that Hitler still lived. Bormann had been responsible, guessed Szabo.[9]

With a substitute having died in the bunker, so said the basic postwar version of Hitler's survival, the tyrant had fled safely from embattled Berlin. *Bonjour* and Szabo agreed that he had been on the last plane to leave Gatow airport on April 27, 1945. Hitler had another chance to leave two days later with Hanna Reitsch, added *Bonjour*. One of his self-proclaimed friends from his days in Vienna prior to World War I, Josef Greiner, claimed that Hitler had flown out of Tempelhof airport on the afternoon of April 30. It mattered little to Greiner or the others that both Berlin airfields—Tempelhof and Gatow—had by then been totally overrun by the Russians and that Reitsch and Greim had barely gotten out of the city the previous day by taking off from the East-West Axis.

Greiner insisted in 1947 that one of his acquaintances, a certain "Engineer B," had seen Hitler at Tempelhof on April 30. He stood near a new Messerschmidt fighter plane, dressed in his "field gray uniform and motioning feverishly to a few [Nazi] party functionaries." "There is not one iota of proof present that Hitler is dead," assumed Greiner, whose story resembled a fairy tale. Greiner, it seems, had a political motive. Despising what the Nazis had done to his native Austria, he tried to discredit Hitler further by arguing that the dictator had fled and had therefore "struck himself finally from the book of heroes."[10] But it was preposterous to think that Hitler could have been standing at Tempelhof on April 30, 1945, inasmuch as the entire airfield and all of Berlin, except a few square miles in the center of the city, lay firmly in Russian clutches.

An even more ridiculous idea, attributed to an Austrian member of Hitler's guard (who was never identified), said that about 2:30 P.M. on April 30, Hitler had left the Chancellery and disappeared in the direction of a launching area for V-rockets.[11] These destructive weapons used by the Nazis to bomb London at the end of the war, could hardly have been Hitler's ticket to freedom. The rockets had no way of carrying humans, nor did the Germans have the technology to land them in a pre-determined place without exploding.

After leaving his doomed capital, said the survival scenario, Hitler most likely had gone to Denmark or Norway, both held by the German armies till the beginning of May 1945. Or, it was speculated, he may have gone to one of the French ports. This part of the story had originated with several Nazi pilots who had declared in the summer of 1945 that they had personally winged Hitler to safety in Denmark. One, an ex-lieutenant Mackensen, told the press again in March 1948 of his alleged flight with the Fuehrer, Eva Braun, and Bormann on May 5, 1945, amid crashing bombs and other artillery fire, out of Tempelhof Airport to the Danish coast. From there, the pilot outlined in detail, a vibrant Hitler had said good-bye to a handful of admirers and disappeared.[12] Musmanno, the former Nuremberg judge and author of a book on Hitler's death, later interrogated Mackensen. While *Bonjour* and other Fuehrer hunters eagerly accepted the pilot's statement, its gross inaccuracies (e.g., Berlin had surrendered three days before Mackensen said he had spirited Hitler out of the city) convinced Musmanno of Mackensen's "utter worthlessness as a Hitler witness."

Even *The Times* of London, one of the world's most sophisticated and reserved newspapers, found such nonsense worth printing. Proclaiming the headline, "Hitler's Last Pilot," it carried the story of Peter Baumgart, a German airman also alleging to have taken Hitler and Eva Braun to Denmark. They had departed from Berlin on April 28, said Baumgart, landing overnight in Magdeburg to avoid Allied bombers and arriving in Denmark the next day. Psychiatrists examined the pilot as he went to trial in Poland for war crimes. Most disappointing, *The Times* seemed to dignify the episode with the dubious comment that Hitler "was reported to have committed suicide" in Berlin.

Assuming Hitler had made it to Denmark, where had he gone from there? *Bonjour* quoted Mackensen as saying the Fuehrer had boarded a ship. This and other reports spawned the popular idea that he had left Europe by submarine and spent several months hiding in a U-boat before secretly disembarking in Latin America, the Antarctic, or elsewhere. Szabo reasoned that Allied air and radar superiority, plus Hitler's choice of a German admiral, Doenitz, as his successor, had made the U-boat the "sole means" of the Fuehrer's departure. A note found in a bottle, which had washed ashore on the Danish coast in 1946, especially intrigued the Hitler chasers. It contained writing on a page torn from the logbook of the German U-boat *Naueclus* and dated a year earlier. Hitler had not died in the bunker, said the paper, but aboard the *Naueclus,* which had sunk on November 15, 1945, while en route from Finland to Spain.

The postwar assertions that a submarine had taken Hitler and Eva Braun to Latin America or the Antarctic had another source. A story had appeared in the summer of 1945 that two German U-boats, the U-530 and U-977, had surrendered at the seaport of Mar del Plata in Argentina.[13] According to *Bonjour,* Szabo, the *Police Gazette,* and similar publications, a third U-boat had given itself up at Leixoes, on the Portuguese coast. Each boat, they said, had originally left the coast of Norway in the spring of 1945 and moved south. They had formed a sort of "phantom convoy," whose mission had been to transport Hitler, Eva Braun, and possibly Bormann and others, to their postwar hideout. Wishing to appear highly scientific to their readers, *Bonjour* and the others offered the boats' logbooks and the testimony of the ships' captains as evidence. The first submarine had surrendered at Leixoes on June 4; U-530 had gone ashore in Argentina in mid-July.

A search of the U-530 had produced nothing, except a large cache of cigarettes whose use on the boat had been forbidden. *Bonjour* saw this as a key discovery, suggesting that the cigarettes had been for a "secret cargo" that had once been aboard. Perhaps Hitler and the remnants of his court? Hitler, of course, did not smoke nor did he permit others to do so in his presence. Testimony from the U-530's former captain, Kurt Langer, had made the ship even more suspect. The U-530 that he had once known, stated Langer, had been incapable of extended trips across oceans. But the vessel seized in Argentina was nearly new. There could only be one explanation, said *Bonjour* and its fellow Hitler hounds. The Nazis had purposely "attempted to confuse the Allied authorities by falsely naming the U-boat."

Meanwhile, another U-boat surfaced at Mar del Plata, the U-977, commanded by Heinz Schaeffer. He explained that the boat had sailed to Argentina to avoid surrendering directly to the British. Schaeffer, in the hope of acquitting himself of the "scurrilous charges" in the press that he had helped the worst criminal in history to escape, later published a book, portraying the course of his trip across the Atlantic. It had taken the U-977 several months, he said, because it had been low on fuel and forced to move more slowly by electric generator. But it had not been involved in transporting Hitler.

Schaeffer could not persuade the avid Hitler sleuths.[14] The imagination of Szabo, the Montevideo paper *El Dia, Bonjour,* and the *Police Gazette* proved relentless. Obviously, they guessed, the captive U-boats had been part of a ghost fleet of submarines that had passed near the Argentine coast. The U-530 and U-977 had probably lost contact with the others and been forced to surrender. Had Hitler been on one of the ships? Certainly, the story went, and aboard the lead boat in the convoy, the "Admiral's U-boat," whose existence had only been known to the Fuehrer, his successor Doenitz, and the boat's commander. Many German submarines had been unaccounted for after the war, argued the Hitler buffs, and it would have been easy to issue the entire fleet bogus identification numbers to fool the Allies.

They saved the best for last. "Where did the Fuehrer go?" asked the *Police Gazette.* He had sailed past South America to the Antarctic where, the magazine maintained, the Germans had been busy since 1938 constructing a "new Berchtesgaden" (in Szabo's words) for their beloved Fuehrer. The *Gazette* and its counterparts in Europe and Latin America based their fantasy on a German South Pole expedition in 1938 and 1939, which had allegedly been ordered by Hitler and

Goering. One of the prizes of the exploration had been Hitler's "intimate friendship," according to *Bonjour,* with the captain of the mission, Alfred Ritscher.

Bonjour and its allies also cited Doenitz as a reason Hitler had gone to the South Pole. At the end of 1943, the Admiral, recently appointed Supreme Commander of the Navy, had allegedly said in a speech, "The German submarine fleet has even now established an earthly paradise, an impregnable fortress, for the Fuehrer, in whatever part of the world." *Bonjour* inferred from this nebulous statement and Doenitz's new appointment that Hitler had already been thinking of escaping, especially as his military failure in Russia had unfolded. The magazine added to its speculation the assertion that German engineers had been ordered in August 1940 to prepare for building purposes a metal base that could withstand temperatures to 60° below zero. "Where was such construction to be done," queried *Bonjour,* "if not in the Antarctic?"

Even the American government, it said, had suspected that the former chief Nazi might be living at the South Pole. Why else would the American explorer, Admiral Richard Byrd, for example, have guided his most extensive expedition into the Antarctic during 1946 and 1947? It mattered little to those pursuing Hitler that this Byrd adventure was little more than another in a series to establish America's claims to the polar continent. "All of this," concluded *Bonjour,* "forces us to consider the hypothesis of Hitler's flight to the sixth continent as thoroughly probable and valid."

It appeared that Szabo and the popular magazines, plus the leading Paris newspaper *Le Monde,* which placed Hitler in Argentina in December 1947, saw themselves partly as inheritors of the crusade against Nazism begun by the Western press in 1945. Szabo warned of a return of German fascism and its diabolical Fuehrer. "It is a fact," he argued, "that Nazism is not dead in Europe. The world is in danger. Its peace is newly menaced by Adolf Hitler." Like the Austrian anti-Nazi, Greiner, Szabo and serials like *Bonjour* mixed a fanatical devotion to their cause with a flair for yellow journalism (not to mention a thirst for money). This combination blinded them to the simplest of facts and warped their judgment.

The "Argentine connection," of which it had been said since 1945 that Hitler and Eva Braun had landed by U-boat and settled comfortably among Germans on the plains of Patagonia, flourished in other circles. The dictatorship of Juan Peron encouraged it by offering ex-Nazis protection, allowing them to form political organizations and publish nationalist and anti-Semitic propaganda. Out of Buenos Aires came Nazi publications like the *Freie Presse* and *Der Weg,* which gained popularity among radical right wing Germans in central Europe. Even the popular biographer Emil Ludwig, just before he died in September 1948, fell prey to the myth. He contended that Hitler had not really expired in the Fuehrerbunker, but had made his way by U-boat to Argentina.

Others attracted to the view that Hitler had fled to Argentina included the American evangelist preacher, Herbert W. Armstrong, and his son Garner Ted, whose Worldwide Church of God eventually became the wealthiest religious organization of its kind. Soliciting money through a gloom-and-doom message and prophecy of a coming utopia, the elder Armstrong preached that the British had been the descendants of the ten lost tribes of Israel, while the Germans had descended from the warlike Assyrians. He proclaimed that a huge Nazi underground movement existed in Allied- and Russian-occupied Germany, and that it would return to bring World War III.

"I doubt seriously," Armstrong said in 1948, "that Hitler committed suicide. He may have escaped, alive." Soon, predicted the preacher, "Hitler may pull a fake resurrection." He would be aided by the Pope, a false prophet according to Armstrong, "who will then claim power to perform miracles, resurrecting the Roman Empire, by uniting ten nations in Europe." War would again be declared by Hitler on the United States and Britain, and out of the ensuing chaos Christ would come a second time and save the world. At the latest, Armstrong told his faithful, the world could reckon with Hitler's return by 1972.[15]

Stories of the Fuehrer in Argentina found an avid audience in the United States. Few news counters, taverns, and barber shops failed to provide their customers with the *Police Gazette* or other sensational sheets that contained the latest "scoop" on where Hitler had supposedly been spotted. The *Gazette,* pleased with its series in the early 1950s, ran it again in 1956 and 1960. A German newspaper in Canada responded to one of its issues by noting, "Our wish is to leave Hitler where he is, otherwise enroll him as a corporal in the German Bundeswehr." But its plot had a familiar ring. The magazine only intensified its criticism of the Argentine government for protecting ex-Nazis, and it discussed the dramatic capture in Argentina earlier in the year of Adolf Eichmann, an SS officer charged with the destruction of millions of Jews.

Eichmann's subsequent trial and execution in Israel briefly revived serious thoughts that Hitler might still be around. Musmanno, testifying in Jerusalem against the coldblooded Nazi bureaucrat, recalled about the trial, "I was asked by many persons in Israel, and in the United States when I returned, if it were not possible that Hitler might still be alive. They argued to me that if Eichmann could evade detection since the end of the war, why couldn't Hitler have similarly concealed himself?" The proceedings against Eichmann also kindled thoughts of what would have occurred had Hitler been brought to trial. A cartoon in the Vienna *Arbeiter-Zeitung* showed the dictator in a frenzy, defending himself in the courtroom. "First I have followed the command of Providence," the caption imagined Hitler saying, "second I knew nothing of the gas chambers, and third I once helped a Jew put out a cigarette at the Landsberg prison."

Publicity that unfolded in the 1960s about ODESSA, a secret postwar escape organization of the SS underground, further sparked the "Hitler in Argentina" stories. A clandestine agency set up in 1947, it had aided SS members and other high Nazi officials to leave Germany and avoid arrest by the Allies. ODESSA had two main routes of escape, from Bremen in northern Germany to Rome and from Bremen to Genoa. The key route for ODESSA outside Europe ended in Buenos Aires, and one of its most prominent travelers had been Eichmann. Some asked, why not Hitler?

For a moment in February 1960, the world received a scare that the wild rumors of Hitler in Argentina might suddenly prove true. In the waters off the Argentina coast, the latter's navy attacked what it first officially described as an "unidentified undersea object." But many Argentines thought it a foreign submarine. Ships had been tracking the thing for three weeks, said reports out of Buenos Aires. What was it? When it came to guessing, nothing seemed too fantastic. Some thought it a German U-boat that had been cruising since the surrender in 1945 and looking for a safe haven. Eager Argentine newsmen figured they had the story of the century if the vessel docked and

Hitler strolled down the gangplank with Eva Braun on his arm. But, alas, the few days of excitement came to nothing—only more speculation for those who had followed the subject faithfully since the war.[16]

Argentina and the Antarctic by no means monopolized the mythical place to where Hitler had escaped. At one time or another, he was allegedly seen in nearly every country of the world, except for Russia. Even *Bonjour* discounted the reports of Swedish diplomats at the end of the war which had said that the Fuehrer had surrendered to Stalin and been locked in a prison in the Urals. Another Austrian version had him smuggled from Berlin in 1946 to Arabia, where he had joined his former ally, the Sultan of Jerusalem, in leading an anti-Western and anti-Israel policy.

Other stories said he had been spotted living as a disguised merchant in Bavaria or Austria. Letters continually arrived at the Bavarian Ministry of Justice, some from Hitler's admirers, purporting to know his hiding place. Information in August 1956 from the Austrian Press Agency said that jewels and gold thought to be Hitler's had been dug up in northern Austria by former members of the Fuehrer's guard. This set off a minor wave of conjecture: might he be hiding in his native country? His dedicated enemies found equally disconcerting a story that placed him in a monastery high in the Himalayan mountains of Tibet.

An openly pro-Nazi magazine in West Germany, *Tempo Der Welt,* declared in May 1950 that Hitler had escaped to Tibet at the end of the war, that he would soon return to Germany, and that such plans were being cared for by his still loyal (and alive) secretary, Bormann. Karl Heinz Kaerner, owner of the gutter periodical, maintained that he had talked to Bormann the previous summer in Spanish Morocco. Bormann, said Kaerner, had told him that "Hitler is alive in a Tibetan monastery" and that "one day we will be back" in power in Germany. An immediate best seller on newsstands, the magazine cover carried the title "May 8, 1945," the day on which the Nazis had surrendered. It pictured a black American soldier, bayonet in one hand and gun in the other, gloating over a shot-down German fighter plane. Not unexpectedly, the publication earned the careful scrutiny of the American authorities in West Germany.[17]

Such stories, especially that Bormann had lived through the war and gone into hiding, became popular among the postwar Hitler pursuers to buttress their arguments that the Fuehrer had lived. Some enthusiasts even believed Goebbels had made it safely out of the Fuehrerbunker and had ensconced himself somewhere. The body found by the Russians in May 1945 and announced as Goebbels', they said, had been a double. Some thought he had slipped off to Bavaria or Spain, others that he had taken a submarine to Argentina. A few even said the former Roman Catholic had withdrawn to the seclusion of a distant monastery. "He was considered too clever not to have taken steps to save his life," said one of his biographers. "The people were so accustomed to regard him as a liar that they did not believe in his own proven death."[18]

But it appeared more vogue to think that Bormann had escaped. Like Hitler, Bormann too had become at the end of the war a mystery for the world. During the final days of the Third Reich, he had exerted almost total power. As others had deserted the hopeless cause, this arch-Machiavellian had remained faithful to the Fuehrer. He had signed Hitler's political testament and been a witness to his wedding. As one of his last acts, Hitler had named him Minister of the Nazi party in Doenitz's government. Bormann had also been one of those who had watched the flames devour Hitler's body in the Chancellery garden, as Russian shells landed nearby. He and Goebbels had then sought unsuccessfully to negotiate with the Russians.

Suddenly Bormann had vanished from the bunker. Even though several witnesses testified they had seen him leave the Chancellery and die in a tank explosion in Berlin on the morning of May 2, 1945, it took the Allies nearly thirty years to confirm his demise.[19] The Nuremberg tribunal had sentenced him *in absentia* to death. The search for him continued. A former SS major who had escaped with him, Joachim Tiburtius, told reporters in Munich in 1953 that "Bormann had the same chances for escape as I did." When he had last seen the ambitious secretary, said Tiburtius, Bormann had reached an area where he had "relative security."

Reports sighted Bormann in Morocco, Spain, China, Russia, and as a businessman in various countries of Latin America. The seizure of Eichmann in Argentina by the Israeli secret police in 1960 raised anew the belief he had escaped. Those chasing Hitler after the war often alleged that Bormann had been responsible for the Fuehrer's escape and that he carefully planned for the return of Hitler and

Nazism to Germany. For example, the Berlin paper, *Der Telegraf,* announced that Eberhard Stern, allegedly a German neo-Nazi leader, had found Bormann disguised as a monk in an Italian monastery.

Bormann had fled from Berlin to Spain in 1945, Stern had told the paper, and with the assumed name of Father Martini Bormagione (others said he used the name Carlos Vincenti) he had made his way to Rome. The exploding tank in which Bormann had reportedly died, said Stern, only knocked the Nazi leader unconscious. When he had awakened, he found that the others in his group that fled the Chancellery had gone, thinking him dead. Although Stern had not met Bormann, he claimed to have photographed the monk from outside the monastery grounds. *Der Telegraf* eagerly published the picture.

A few people, mostly political and social misfits, genuinely believed that Bormann was alive and preparing Hitler's comeback. The Hitler Legion, a tiny Nazi cell in England, proclaimed in 1951 "that Adolf Hitler, like Jesus Christ, could never die. Hitler was the reincarnated Spirit of Christ, at the Second Coming." The Legion, citing the biblical books of Isaiah, Luke, and Revelations, prophesied the return of Hitler and Germany to power, the shattering of the "Britannic-Jewish-American imperialism," and the rise of a new world order based on "Aryan socialism."

A German publisher in Lueneberg also forecast Hitler's return. In a pro-Nazi pamphlet he distributed in 1954 titled *We Acquit Hitler,* he described a fictional trial of the Fuehrer before a war crimes tribunal, wherein the charges against him were given a few lines and his uninterrupted reply twenty-five pages. "The Jewish question," said the infamous defendant, "was not a German invention. I killed 1,500,000 Jews, not 6,000,000; the latter is a propaganda figure for the purpose of restitution claims." The loss of Jewish lives, he maintained, had been insignificant compared to war losses suffered by other peoples, particularly Germany. Not guilty was the verdict, concluded the pamphlet, spoken in the name of "public opinion."

That Hitler would eventually reappear also attracted a black man in Kentucky, Will Johnson, who was sentenced to prison in 1957 for fraud. A court convicted him of collecting thousands of dollars with letters he had sent that contained the signature "Adolf Hitler" and promised a "new Revolution" in America. Johnson had asserted that Hitler still lived and wished to create in the United States "a new imperial regime." Those who supported the cause financially would be given lucrative positions after the "seizure of power," vowed Johnson.[20]

Such illusions that Hitler would re-emerge naturally rested on the premise that he had outlasted the war. An opinion poll taken among its German readers by *Heim und Welt,* showed many of them persuaded that their one-time Fuehrer had escaped to freedom. "Hitler's flight was either successful or his death resulted on 3 May on the island of Ruegen," one reader in Zwingenberg wrote the magazine, "where Goering had hunted every year from 1933-1939." "Yes, Hitler lived," another noted boldly, adding that Bormann and other Nazis had been flown out of Berlin to northern Italy, and from there to unknown destinations. Still another from Wiesbaden claimed he had been a Chancellery guard at the end, and on April 28, 1945, he had seen Hitler leave the building with a detachment of SS men and head by automobile toward the airport. Readers from Berlin had similar fantasies. Either they had "personally" seen Hitler leave the city or had spoken with German soldiers who had witnessed it.[21]

Despite the host of melodramatic tales that Hitler had outlived the war and would soon return, the world saw no such phenomenon occur. As each year passed, without his reappearance, the wild stories began to wane. In their place, the "Hitler is alive" press made an abortive attempt in the 1950s and beginning of the 1960s to attract new converts by combining their theory with rumors about Hitler's sex life and health. Such efforts, however, drowned in a new tide of attention on the Fuehrer in West Germany and in a sobering realization on the part of both his enemies and followers that he had indeed breathed his last in the Fuehrerbunker. Simon Wiesenthal, the most renowned of the Nazi hunters and chiefly responsible for the capture of Eichmann and other SS butchers, observed that "the biggest unsolved Nazi mystery" now concerned the fate of Bormann, not Hitler.

9

A Hitler Wave

"Adolf Hitler, Anatomy of a Dictator," flashed the headline in *Der Spiegel*. "The Man Called Adolf Hitler," another German magazine titled a similar article which pretended to "give the facts" to its readers about its subject who, it confessed, "has been dead for nineteen years." *The Times* of London, commenting on these and a flood of other publications appearing in West Germany in the spring of 1964, noted that "eighteen or so years after Hitler's death, he is being discussed again in Germany, especially by the young. Their interest is reduced to one basic question—how to understand this man and why the German people, between 1933 and 1945, followed him."

The *Koelnische Rundschau* called this outburst of curiosity about Germany's recent past, and especially the deluge of books, newspaper and magazine articles, television shows, and movies about Hitler, the "Hitler wave" (*Hitler Welle*). Following in the steps of the first outpouring of attention on the Fuehrer shortly after World War II, this "wave" of interest began in the late 1950s and has continued to the present. Its scope would be much wider and include more than merely the impossible survival tales that had characterized the immediate postwar years. Producing both sensationalism and works of historical value, such an eruption contributed significantly to the nearly universal acceptance that Hitler had died in the bunker.

This inquisitiveness resulted from the capture of Eichmann, the trial of SS officers who had administered the Nazi death camp at Auschwitz, the twentieth anniversary of the bomb attempt on Hitler's life, and the desire of younger Germans to learn more about him.

Most youths had been told little by their parents, teachers, and the older generation. History classes at the German secondary schools had stopped with Bismarck, totally ignoring the World Wars and Hitler. The "wave" may also have been heightened by the building of the Berlin Wall, whose concrete and barbed wire became a brutal reminder to the world of the "Cold War" and of the Russian and Allied division of Germany, both consquences of Hitler's defeat.

The vast material that appeared on Hitler took varied forms. Books and press articles swept newsstands and bookstores, not only in West Germany but in the United States and England. Some had a scholarly nature, such as Shirer's *The Rise and Fall of the Third Reich*. A best seller that sold 102,000 copies in three months, the book generated ample controversy in Germany for its view (in the words of *Der Spiegel*) "that the Third Reich was an exclusively German phenomenon" and "nothing more than a logical continuation of German history." *Hitler's Second Book* also appeared, whose publisher described it as a companion to *Mein Kampf* and written (but never published) by Hitler in 1928.

Other Hitler documents, including tons of captured Nazi records held by the Allies, were made public. The London *Sunday Express*, advertising "Hitler's last words, just as they were spoken in the bunker under Berlin," printed excerpts from the Fuehrer's final table talk, which he had dictated to Bormann from February through April 1945. This lengthier "testament" revealed Hitler's maniac hatred of the Jews, even in the last days of his life. On February 13, 1945, he had talked about using the war to wipe out the Jews:

> I have always been absolutely fair in my dealings with the Jews. On the eve of war, I gave them one final warning. I told them that, if they precipitated another war, they would not be spared and that I would exterminate the vermin throughout Europe, and this time once and for all. To this warning they retorted with a declaration of war. . . .
>
> Well, we have lanced the Jewish abcess; and the world of the future will be eternally grateful to us.[1]

The new Hitler "wave" spilled into television and theaters. *Der Spiegel* moaned that Hitler had become a "cinema hero." British television interviewed his sister, Paula Wolf, who provided fond recollections of her brother for a documentary film called *Tyranny*. Hollywood movies at the beginning of the 1960s, such as one starring Richard Basehart, portrayed Hitler as a raging dictator consumed with sex. An exception was the widely acclaimed *Judgment at Nuremberg*. Others, produced in Europe, dealt with the German concentration camps, using captured Nazi film. The growing Hitler mania even touched the phonograph industry. A storm of protest accompanied the appearance in the Federal Republic of phonograph records with his voice and Nazi marching songs.[2]

Some stories in this media blitz related, in one way or another, to Hitler's fate at the end of the war. Noticeably fewer accounts on the subject earnestly believed he had survived. An American encyclopedia, for example, said "it is fairly certain that he died." A West Berlin lawyer opened proceedings in February 1965 charging Hitler with mass murder, should he suddenly reappear or the West German Parliament fail to extend the statute of limitations on punishing Nazi war criminals.

Gossipy tales in the popular press still hinted that the Fuehrer might be alive. Most of those grotesque stories dealt with his sexual and private life, his relations with Eva Braun, the children he allegedly fathered, and his health. While it had become less realistic each year to assert that he had escaped by submarine to a faraway hideout, some magazines used their imagination about his private life to raise subtle doubts in the minds of their readers about him, and therefore also about what had happened to him. Such stories added another dimension of mystery and even villainy to his career. Both had been key elements in the "Fuehrer is alive" scenario. These "tell all" tales had another function as well: to attract greater reader interest.

The press, naively in many instances, now focused on Hitler's personal qualities, including his attitudes toward sex, women, children, school, dogs, smoking, religion, art, and government. Some writers tried to reduce him from demonic to human proportions. Others attempted to belittle and deride him with their stories, which had also been one of the objectives of the earlier claims that he had lived past the war and abandoned Germany by fleeing. The marketable subject of sex had especially been used since the war to vilify him. Various sensational sources, most of them based on speculation, had proclaimed that Hitler had tendencies toward sexual perversion, that he had sired several children, and that he had gone into hiding with them (e.g., in the Antarctic or Argentine) in 1945 to train them as his successors and prepare his return to power.

Sex, for example, found plenty of attention in a series of articles on the Fuehrer published in March 1964 by the West German weekly photo magazine, *Quick*. "Without women," it commented, "Hitler's style of life would have been unimaginable." The magazine, hinting that his sexual life may have bordered on the abnormal, printed sensuous photographs of Eva Braun and Hitler's niece, Geli Raubal, who had allegedly committed suicide in 1931 because of her liaison with her uncle. A would-be American analyst investigating the matter, suggested in 1960 "that some sexual experience—possibly the contraction of a venereal disease—lay behind Hitler's antisemitism." And about the Fuehrer and Eva Braun, his former doctor, Morell, once remarked, "They slept in different beds, nevertheless I believe . . ."[3]

In the clutches of popular writers and the press, such conjecture knew few limits. It had begun shortly after the war and persisted throughout the 1950s. "Hitler liked stupid women," the *Police Gazette* had written. "He had a lot to learn when it came to being a lover." A French writer had contended, without proof, "It is notorious that Hitler did not have much of a sexual appetite (at his birth, one of his testicles had remained in the abdomen)." Declared the same writer, it had been Goebbels and his Frau, Magda, who "had gone to great lengths" to "interest the lonely man with the sexual weaknesses," Hitler, in women. They had busily introduced him to starlets, actresses, and beautiful young aristocrats. He was even accused of sexual sado-masochism, which included "coprophagous," or a "predilection for the smell and sight of excrement" of his female partners.[4]

Other sexual abnormalities of the dictator were pointed out in what was advertised as Eva Braun's "secret" diary, which she had allegedly smuggled to an Austrian friend in the winter of 1944 and 1945. "This firsthand, detailed, shockingly frank account of Adolf Hitler's love life," said the volume's editor, "will solve the sexual riddle which he represented." But historians quickly proved the "intimate notes" a fraud. One of their apparent goals had been to contribute another element of perversity to the modern anti-Christ. Hitler, they said, had suffered from a defect of the foreskin of the penis, but the operation that would have corrected the problem, circumcision, had been anathema to him. Why? "He, who hated and tortured Israel, who was the scourge of the Jews," answered the editor of the fake diary, "could not submit to the same surgical intervention which every faithful Jewish child undergoes at a tender age!"

The diary had also stated that Hitler had as many as three children. He "was not impotent," said the editor, "because Eva Braun became pregnant and bore him a child." It had been a son, born in 1942 in Dresden (a symbol of Germany's devastation at the end of the war). Hitler had married Eva Braun, so the story went, "in order to give the illegitimate child a name and to bequeath him a heritage of world politics."

This allegation had been repeated by Szabo, the postwar anti-Nazi writer in Buenos Aires, who insisted that "it is probable" such children existed. The boy, he said, had been born in Italy in January 1938. Szabo's version had rested on a British report from January 1946. Shortly after the birth, the tale said, a Japanese diplomat had announced the "blessed event" in Berlin to a group of Tokyo newsmen, but the latter had been sworn to absolute secrecy. At the time, maintained Szabo, one of Japan's leading reporters, Mino Kato, had visited Eva Braun's father in Munich. "It is important," the elder Braun had supposedly told the visitor, "that Hitler never die without a successor." Slowly the news had leaked to other journalists, including a British correspondent and several Italian newsmen; in 1946 the Englishman had published the story.

Variations of this line had appeared throughout the 1950s. For example, the *Grosse Oesterreich Illustrierte,* an Austrian magazine, suggested that Eva Braun had not really been Hitler's lover, but Bormann's. The relentless Paris Hitler hunter, *Bonjour,* had seen the love affair differently. Bormann, it said, had been heard over a secret German radio transmitter after the war talking to Hitler's children. It quoted the faithful secretary as saying that he (Bormann) would arrive soon in Germany "to give the children good reports about their father and mother."

The son, named Uschi, *Bonjour* explained, had nearly completed high school and might be taken soon to his father's postwar hideout for training in "high politics." The story bore a frightening resemblance to the "son of Frankenstein" episode and its effort to bring back the terrible monster. Hitler's successor, *Bonjour* continued, would "thereby be capable later of taking the reins of the German state in his hands," and of bringing a return of Nazism to Europe. "We only wish to warn of a possible existing danger," *Bonjour* had assured its French readers, "which is contained in these proven facts." Another such "truth," pronounced the magazine, had been a secret trip of the Fuehrer to Bavaria at the beginning of April 1945, only a month before the war's end. There he had said good-bye to his offspring, according to *Bonjour,* and taken Eva Braun back to Berlin with him.

It did not seem to matter to *Bonjour* that the boy it called Uschi and identified as Hitler's son, had been shown in November 1945 by American intelligence to be the daughter of one of Eva Braun's friends, a Frau Schneider. Nor did the magazine seem to care about falsely describing Hitler's only trip out of Berlin in the final days of the war. He had not gone to Bavaria, but had traveled east of Berlin to visit German troops bracing for the attack of the Russians. His arrival among the soldiers and hour-long conference with the commanders had been discussed by the German magazine, *Heim und Welt,* in 1952. It had based its account on the report of a young staff officer who witnessed the visit.[5]

Stories had also appeared about the other Hitler children. The oldest son, another German magazine claimed, had not been born to Eva Braun, but to a mistress of Hitler's in Munich before World War I. The alleged son, Wilhelm Bauer, had killed himself in May 1945 and left a widow and several children. Although Bauer's origins had been concealed, Hitler had rewarded him with the high paying position of director of the national Nazi publishing house in Munich. How had this bit of dubious news been uncovered? Said the magazine, it had received a letter from a Swiss merchant, who insisted he had known Hitler while the two had been in Munich on the eve of World War I.

Another story proclaimed that Hitler's eldest son had been the product of an illicit relationship between Hitler and Frau Goebbels. Their clandestine affair had gone back to 1934, when the Goebbels family resided on the island of Schwanenwerder, where Hitler had been given a small room. Magda Goebbels, an impressive and blond-ish specimen of Nordic beauty, said the story, had wished for something more than her deformed and frivolous husband. A year later she gave birth to a son, Helmut. "The resemblance of the child to Hitler,"

Bonjour had observed, "immediately became apparent." Although Hitler had remained especially close to the child and favored it over the other Goebbels children, the scandal sheet asserted, he soon broke off his intimacy with Magda and replaced her with Eva Braun.

Then in the 1960s the world suddenly started hearing from those who claimed to be the children, like Gisela Heuser of Frankfurt. Despite the protest of her parents and the unwillingness of the government to allow its publication in West Germany, a French press printed a book she had written contending that Hitler had fathered her while her mother had been in Berlin in 1936, competing in the Olympic games. Another self-proclaimed Hitler child, Franz Weber-Richter, a German flimflam artist, used the story that he was the Fuehrer's illegitimate son and had lived with his father after the war, to defraud ex-Nazis in Argentina of substantial sums of money. He told his incredibly gullible victims that he had spent eighteen months on Venus, learning from residents of the planet the secret of forming a "World Government" on the earth, which would be based in Berlin.[6]

Part of the appeal of this dizzying round of exposés rested on the fact that few people had known Hitler closely or intimately. Consequently, because his private life had been successfully concealed from the world, the most sensational of stories about him seemed to possess at least a grain of truth to them. This had even been the case with reports that he had outlived the war. *Quick* advertised its series of articles on Hitler in 1964 by asking, "Hitler—who was he really? A crazy mass murderer? A misguided genius? These questions often remain unanswered." For nearly a decade, popular American magazines like *Look, Ladies Home Journal,* and *Science Digest* had explained him by calling him "insane."

Yet this type of vague description had contributed since the war to the sense of puzzlement and mystery that had surrounded the man. Many postwar myths about him, like that of his survival, had been aided in part by the confusion about his family ancestry and personal life. Since the end of the war, rumors had abounded in the press. Had he been the son of an Austrian customs official, as most historians argued? Or born to a shoemaker or peasant named Schickelgruber? Several German newspapers, relying on the diary notes of Hans Frank, the Nazi governor of Poland executed at Nuremberg for war crimes, had reported that Hitler had been part Jewish. "Was Hitler a

Jew?" the *Hamburger Freie Presse* had asked in August 1949. His father, the paper alleged, had been an illegitimate child of a cook named Schickelgruber and a young Jew, Frankenberger, in Graz.

Some Hitler chasers in the 1950s, like *Bonjour,* had purposely tried to raise such doubts which, they thought, would enable their readers to imagine even more easily that he had not died in Berlin, but had gotten away free. "Was the man who had written *Mein Kampf,*" *Bonjour* had asked, "identical with the German corporal who was wounded by poison gas and lay in a hospital at the end of World War I?" "More important," it raised a further query, "had the one who the Nazis claimed had perished in Berlin in 1945 been Hitler?"

Adding to this aura of mystery around him, and especially to the thesis that a "double" had died in his place, had been the Fuehrer's physical appearance, which had changed during the war as he received large doses of medication and his health started to fail. Had he been sick? Did he collapse from the pressures of the war? Or had Hitler's look alike bid good-bye in the the bunker to the secretaries, Bormann, Goebbels, Kempka, Linge, and the others, thus allowing the Fuehrer to escape? His body had changed so much at the end, *Bonjour* declared, that even his closest associates hardly recognized him.

Whereas Kempka, Linge, Axmann, and the others who had been with Hitler in the bunker and used the Fuehrer's poor health as support for their contention that he had died, the popular press employed the health issue to argue the opposite. Hitler's physical weaknesses, *Bonjour* maintained, and especially his nervousness and violent trembling, had rendered it "technically" impossible for him to have held a gun and shot himself. Further, the magazine postulated, German military justice viewed suicide as totally dishonorable. It equaled desertion, and Hitler and his advisers would not have left such a shameful example for future Nazi militarists.[7] But this was curious logic. *Bonjour* offered no explanation, for example, of why Hitler had been well enough to flee a gigantic Russian attack on Berlin and Germany and continue living indefinitely when he had been too ill to murder himself. It also failed to disclose how deserting by escaping to the Antarctic had been more worthy than running away by suicide.

By the beginning of the 1960s, such stories about his health and appearance had changed noticeably. Instead of being used by Hitler hunters to create an air of uncertainty about him that had lended credence to the tale of his survival (e.g., that he had been too ill even to commit suicide), they were now employed to affirm that he had died in the bunker. That he had departed the world in his underground sanctum seemed to be the verdict of the Hitler "wave." The satirical *Mad* magazine pronounced him "good and dead" in 1960. So did several French publications. *Paris Match,* discussing the battle of Berlin, conceded bluntly that "Hitler was dead." "It has been twenty years," *Monde* admitted in 1965, "since Hitler killed himself."

Just as some people had sought to attract attention to themselves by asserting that Hitler had outlived the war, a few now tried to capitalize on his death. Even those who invented the wildest stories about his fate declared him deceased. He had been assassinated, said one popular version. Nazi enthusiasts, forever searching for new villains to sell the public, looked beyond Himmler and the SS as the accused murderers. One Nazi buff, a Frenchman Henri Ludwigg, claimed Goebbels had killed the Fuehrer. Feverishly planning the myth of Hitler's heroic death in April 1945 and not wanting him captured by the Allies so as to keep Nazism alive, said Ludwigg, the Minister had forced his leader to swallow poison and then shot him. And his proof? Following the murder, he said, a vase of flowers lay smashed on the table in Hitler's room in the Fuehrerbunker, which had shown evidence of a scuffle (presumably between Hitler and his propagandist).

The Italian paper, *Epoca,* relying on equally flimsy proof and reasoning, put forth the theory in 1964 that Hitler's brother-in-law, Hermann Fegelein, had been the killer. The Russians had then removed the body, with help from the last Nazi General Staff chief, Krebs, from the bunker to Moscow. There it had been displayed, said *Epoca,* in the Kremlin for Stalin.[8] But this was pure nonsense. *Epoca* ignored the testimony of a mountain of witnesses, including Kempka, Axmann, and the "Reich Chancellery group" of prisoners. Hitler had Fegelein shot for treason in the final days, and Krebs had committed suicide on May 1, 1945, shortly after his abortive effort to negotiate with the Russians on behalf of Bormann and Goebbels.

Michael Arnaudow, a doctor at Kiel University, also hoped to reap fame and fortune from Hitler's death. By proclaiming he had new evidence of the Fuehrer's end, Arnaudow sold an old, timeworn story in November 1964 to the German press. He had aided a group of Berlin physicians to identify beyond a doubt Hitler's charred body, said the doctor, which the Russians had found in the Fuehrerbunker a few days after his suicide. How had the identification occurred? X-ray photographs of Hitler's teeth, made in 1944, Arnaudow noted, had been recovered and matched with the teeth in the corpse. But this information had been presented eight years before to the Berchtesgaden court that had issued Hitler's death certificate. Trevor-Roper, moreover, had possessed since 1945 X-rays of Hitler's head taken late in the war and found among the medical records of his doctor, Morell.

And who was Arnaudow? Why had he waited so long to tell his story? Fear of reprisals by the Russians against his family who lived in eastern Europe, he answered. Later, the Soviets explained his precise role in the identification of the teeth. Arnaudow, they said, had been a young Bulgarian medical student in 1945 and had led them to the dental technician Heusemann, who had identified Hitler's teeth from the body found by the Russians.

At about the same time Arnaudow came forth, a California professor of dentistry, Elsworth Kelly, who had been an American soldier in Germany at the end of the war, provided a dental chart of Hitler's mouth " at the time of his alleged death." Kelly had acquired the diagram, along with a written description of Hitler's teeth, from the Fuehrer's dentist, Blaschke. While in prison after the war, the Nazi dentist had informed Kelly that his famous patient's teeth were poor and many were missing. "His few remaining teeth," Blaschke said of Hitler, "were affected with periodontal disease and were loose."

The press and films in the Hitler "wave" gave much more fanfare to the Fuehrer's health and suicide. The steady convulsing of the left side of his body and his changing appearance at the end had always been tied indirectly by his postwar pursuers to the theory that a "double" had died in his place in the bunker. A mini-propaganda war rose in the 1960s, in fact, over his health. The combatants included former Nazi and non-Nazi physicians in West Germany, the Israeli press, and military officers who had served the Fuehrer.

One popular medical explanation of his badly quivering left arm and leg, their slow paralysis, and his stooped posture had been Parkinson's disease. He had suffered progressively from the nervous disorder since 1942, according to this interpretation. Another natural ailment said to have caused the trembling was hysteria, produced by chronic stomach cramps. *Quick* added another possibility. It had been "an infectious fever of the brain," said the magazine, that had struck the dictator.

But Hans-Dietrich Roehrs, a former member of the Reich Health Leadership under Hitler, vehemently attacked each of these diagnoses. Like Trevor-Roper two decades earlier, Roehrs accused Morell of destroying the German leader's health. Morell had turned Hitler into a "pill addict," said Roehrs, giving him excessive injections of hormones, sugar, Pervitin, and strychnine. Roehrs added that the evil doctor had used his influence with the Fuehrer to become rich during the war from pharmaceutical industries he had purchased cheaply. Pills and injections produced a lucrative business for Morell, and Hitler became his best customer. And Roehr's evidence? Beyond the symptoms described by Hitler's servant Krause, Otto Dietrich, Linge, Guderian, the secretary Schroeder, and others, he relied on the testimony of Elfried Conti, wife of the Reich Health Leader. Her husband, Dr. Conti, she said, had analyzed Morell's pills prepared for Hitler and found they contained small parts of strychnine. Roehrs also cited a "mood of euphoria" which Hitler had allegedly shown during his last days. Since neither his physical condition nor the disastrous military situation seemed to warrant such behavior, Roehrs concluded, it could only have been Morell's "medications that instigated it."

Roehrs provoked immediate accusations of propaganda-mongering and slander. Morell's wife filed a law suit against him for libel. A German-language newspaper in Israel, *Freiheit,* blasted him for seeking to create a new "stab-in-the-back" legend for Germany, designed to explain away (as a similar legend after World War I) its defeat in the war. "Without a doubt an interesting, but likewise dangerous view," protested the paper. "Had this Dr. Morell not poisoned the 'Fuehrer,' Germany would have won the war."[9]

Diary notes of the Supreme Command of the German military, published in 1961, confirmed that Hitler had become at the last "a worn out, old man." These included records from an unidentified senior officer who had taken part in the military conferences in the Fuehrerbunker in March and April 1945. "Physically, he was a terrible sight," recalled the officer to interrogators after the war. "He carried himself slowly and with much difficulty, pulling his leg behind him as he came from his living quarters into the conference room of the bunker. He had lost control over his right arm, and the right hand shook continually [this was probably meant to be the left arm and hand]."

A rash of memoirs appeared from Hitler's generals and highest military advisers. Many pointed the finger at Hitler for having lost the war because of his blunderous military decisions and insistence that he, not the generals, should have the final say in such strategy. As a small part of this quarrel, the generals bickered over the meaning of Hitler's suicide. Had he really died a soldier's death, they asked, by putting a bullet in his head as the enemy came within hours of capturing him? No, decided Walter Warlimont, one of his trusted officers to the end. The Fuehrer had been a coward. As late as April 29, 1945, Warlimont said, Hitler had sent a desperate message from the bunker to his Supreme Command headquarters to the north, asking for reinforcements to rescue him. "The manner of his end," the General now criticized his former commander-in-chief, "was one last proof that to the depths of his being Hitler was no soldier."

Keitel, Supreme Commander of the German Armed Forces General Staff, also condemned his suicide. Keitel had been notorious for groveling before the Fuehrer and believing in the latter's strategical genius. Faced with the gallows at Nuremberg, however, the Field Marshal had said of Hitler:

> . . . for him—as I learned only later—to have committed suicide when he knew he was defeated, shunning thereby his own ultimate personal responsibility upon which he had always laid such great stress and which he had unreservedly taken upon himself alone, instead of giving himself up to the enemy; and for him to have left it to a subordinate to account for his autocratic and arbitrary actions, these two shortcomings will remain forever incomprehensible to me. They are my final disillusion.[10]

Jodl, chief of the military's operational staff, had defended the Fuehrer. "Hitler did not choose the easy, but the secure death," he had said in a memorandum written while waiting to be hanged at Nuremberg. "He handled himself as all heroes in history have done."[11]

But a more plausible viewpoint of why Hitler had chosen suicide seemed to others—as to Trevor-Roper two decades before—that he had no other alternative. By April 1945, reasoned most scholarly studies emerging on Nazi Germany in the 1960s, he had lost a calamitous war and instigated monstrous deeds which had left him hated around the world. He did not wish to be exhibited at a postwar trial, nor even to have his dead body put on display. Neither did it seem possible for him to escape and therefore, his game played out, he had put an end to his life. Especially studies combining research in psychology and history, like James McRandle's *The Track of the Wolf,* compared the facts surrounding Hitler's suicide with statistical data on suicide in general.

This revealed, said McRandle, "how 'typical' Hitler's death was." By European and Western standards, he had been a "suicidal personality": a male, in his fifties, born in Austria, without a formal religion, a product of the lower-middle class, a politician (and one-time artist and soldier), resided in Berlin (and once in Vienna), and had shot himself with a pistol on a Monday in April. McRandle documented wherein "at least nine times during the days preceding his death," Hitler had threatened to end it all. And on five occasions before that, "extending as far back as 1905, Hitler stated that he would kill himself, and twice he named a pistol as the weapon of destruction."[12]

The method of the suicide now overshadowed all other questions about Hitler's death. He had shot himself, most Western accounts agreed.[13] Or had he? Only the Russians probably really knew, since they had taken his bunker in the battle of Berlin and apparently discovered the remains of his mutilated body. They had hinted as much several times since the end of the war. But would the Soviet Union ever part with its secret? Many bet it would not. Nearly two decades after the war, what reason would it have had to do so?

10

Poison or a Bullet?

"Hitler poisoned himself," wrote the Russian General, B. S. Telpukhovsky, "during the second part of the day of April 30." This curt remark, buried in a history of the Soviet Army in World War II, appeared fourteen years after the fact (1959). It went virtually unnoticed in the West. At the moment there seemed to be little of significance in the statement.[1] Some viewed it as merely another Communist effort at duplicity on the subject. "The Russians," bemoaned Trevor-Roper, "are as reticent, as repressive, as ever."

Since the war's end, even including the day of Zhukov's press conference in June 1945, the Soviet Union had periodically suggested Hitler had died. The Russian film on Berlin made in 1948 had portrayed him as poisoning himself. Four years later, the *Soviet Encyclopedia* mentioned his suicide. And the Russians had released the "Reich Chancellery Group" of German prisoners who had testified to the Fuehrer's death.

Yet Telpukhovsky's pronouncement represented the first written admission by Moscow of how it believed Hitler had departed the world in 1945. It marked a beginning in another way. A steady flow of memoirs and recollections of Soviet leaders involved in World War II soon appeared in the 1960s. Most at least touched on the fate of Hitler, whom each writer keenly remembered as responsible for the wartime deaths of twenty million Russians. Then, suddenly in 1968, the Kremlin permitted the publication in the West of an autopsy report on the remains of Hitler, Eva Braun, and Goebbels, which the Russians conceded they had found only a few days after the surrender of Berlin. Hitler, said the report, had swallowed poison and had then apparently been shot by one of his servants.

In the eyes of most Western observers, the confession came two decades too late. So tardy, in fact, and still unofficial, said many, that they suspected a Russian trick. Was it because the Soviets felt they could no longer be embarrassed by the subject? Did they think it unlikely that Hitler—whom the Russians felt certain they had found and identified in 1945—would show up now, nearly a quarter of a century after his reputed end? Perhaps. Russian domestic politics seemed a more logical reason, and especially the aftermath of Stalin's death in 1953, which saw the dictator criticized and downgraded.

Even before Khrushchev's powerful denunciation of Stalin in 1956, the Red Army had returned to a position of prominence in the government. Zhukov, having been recalled from Germany in 1945 and degraded along with the rest of the Army by Stalin, became Minister of Defense. Such changes, together with the arrival of the era of nuclear weapons and long range bombers, soon brought important revisions in military strategy, doctrine, and history.

The re-evaluation downplayed Stalin's role in World War II and instead honored the Russian people and Communist party as the supreme architects of victory. Soviet historians and military writers took their cue from Khrushchev, who accused Stalin of ignorance in military affairs and of criminal negligence in permitting Russia to enter the war unprepared. Despite the Hungarian revolt in 1956 and the forcing out of Zhukov a year later, the liberal attitude toward the war continued. Moscow published a new multi-volume history of the conflict; other books and journals that dealt with the war appeared. The Kremlin even allowed the translations of foreign works (e.g., the memoirs of German and Western military leaders). Criticism of the Soviet defeats early in the war slowly expanded beyond Stalin to include the Army and government leadership.

The repeated, though still informal, Russian concession that Hitler had ended his own life on April 30, 1945, may have been a part of such rethinking. This too repudiated Stalin, who had insisted that Hitler had eluded the Russians in Berlin. Khrushchev thought that Hitler had met his end. He later recalled that Zhukov, near the close of the war, had promised him, "Soon I'll have that slimy beast Hitler locked up in a cage. And when I send him to Moscow, I'll ship him by way of

Kiev so you can have a look at him." But after Germany's surrender, the Marshal had lamented to Khrushchev, "I won't be able to keep my promise after all. That snake Hitler is dead. He shot himself, and they burned his corpse. We found his charred carcass."

The changing attitude toward the recent Soviet past continued after Khrushchev, ousted from power in 1964. While nothing like academic freedom reigned in Soviet intellectual circles, Moscow nevertheless hosted an international conference of historians the next year. Despite the Soviet emphasis on the superior Soviet contribution in World War II and the inevitability of the Communist triumph, the meeting heard other topics discussed. These included the person of Hitler, the German opposition to him, and his influence on monopoly capitalism (as the Russians called it).[2]

Another reason for the turnabout may have been the upsurge in publicity about neo-Nazi groups in West Germany and elsewhere. The extreme right wing German National Democratic party organized itself with much fanfare in 1964. Its leadership included several ex-Nazis, and the tiny party received much attention from the press for visiting the graves of Nazi war criminals buried near Landsberg. The American Nazi movement and its self-styled "storm troopers" demonstrated before the White House with anti-Semitic placards. While such groups were small, the headlines given them possibly encouraged the Russians to alter their earlier policy of silence and emphasize that Hitler had died and that he had not met a hero's end.

This effort to demythologize the Fuehrer could also have been a response to the far-reaching publicity given him at the beginning of the 1960s in the Western press, television, and cinemas. Perhaps Moscow reasoned that a deceased Fuehrer would help dampen the "Hitler wave." But in reality, the tide of publications and revelations that came from Russia after 1960 provided further speculation for a world that seemed, nearly twenty years after the fact, as curious as ever about Hitler and his destruction. As Telpukhovsky had published his comment that Hitler poisoned himself in the bunker on April 30, 1945, the Foreign Literature Publishing House in Moscow had shown an interest in Trevor-Roper's book. The Russians even proposed a translation of *The Last Days of Hitler.* But without warning, they dropped the project. When they hosted an exhibit of British books a few months later in November 1959, they demanded that some thirty volumes be withdrawn from it, including Trevor-Roper's.

Moscow seemed determined to present its own case to the world. Allowing *The Last Days of Hitler* into the country may have been too threatening to the changing Soviet views toward the past, and especially toward the World War. Marxist ideology had always placed a premium on the writing and interpreting of history. The Hitler described so vividly by Trevor-Roper did not fit the mold. Soviet writers discussed in the coming years a Fuehrer who had little courage and who had not set a holy example for his soldiers and people by shooting himself. Instead, they stressed that this Satan of fascism, cowering in his den to the last, had been swept aside by the supreme force of the future, world Communism.

Yet the Russians did not construct in the 1960s their interpretation of Hitler's end as carefully or systematically as one would have expected from a totalitarian state. Except for finally conceding that Hitler had not escaped from Berlin, the Soviets followed what they had done since 1945. They conjectured on the different methods of the dictator's death. Then they released the autopsy performed on Hitler by Russian doctors in May 1945, saying he had poisoned himself and been shot by one of his bunker associates. But why such hesitancy and diversity? Did the Kremlin hope to confuse the West further? Were the liberal tendencies under Khrushchev more genuine than imagined by outsiders? Or, without the awesome Stalin, had it been necessary to work out slowly the government's basic viewpoint, just as had happened with the Soviet account of the war?

Whatever the explanation, the gates of silence opened gradually. The Kazakhstan *Pravda* printed three photographs, never before seen, and one supposedly of the dead Hitler, in 1960. A quotation from Ilya Yakovievich Sianov, a member of the Russian detachment that had first entered the Fuehrerbunker, accompanied the photos. "This is a picture of Hitler's corpse," it said. "The hysterical maniac had shot himself at the very last moment. I saw his body. He lay there with a hole in his forehead. His servants had even no time to burn Hitler's body as he had ordered them to do." The story contrasted sharply with that of Telpukhovsky, and it provided the first Russian denial that Hitler's body had been burned. But had *Pravda* shown the world a picture of the real Fuehrer? Had not the Soviets complained repeatedly in 1945 about finding many Hitler "doubles" in the Chancellery garden?

No one could be certain. Shortly after the publication of the photograph, a new edition of the *Soviet Encyclopedia* appeared. Like its predecessor from 1952, it made clear Hitler had been a suicide. But how? The *Encyclopedia* refused to commit itself. "During the defeat of fascist Germany, the disintegration of the fascist state and the entry of the Soviet armies into Berlin," it said, "Hitler, fearing the judgment of the nations, including the German nation, ended his life by suicide in the underground Berlin imperial Chancellery."[3]

Further clues came from the memoir of the German General, Weidling, who had commanded Berlin's defense and surrendered the capital to the Russians on May 2, 1945. Condemned by a Soviet court to twenty-five years of hard labor, he had died in a Russian prison in November 1955. A Soviet military journal published in 1961 his recollections of the last days of the war and the bunker, which had apparently been written as part of his interrogation by Russian intelligence, the NKVD. Hitler, said Weidling, had both poisoned and shot himself.[4]

The General had commanded the 56th Tank Corps, stationed in Berlin at the end of the war. Through General Krebs, the last chief of the German Army General Staff, he had met personally with Hitler in the bunker on April 23, 1945. There the Fuehrer had outlined his last ditch strategy for saving the capital from the Russians, said Weidling, and appointed the General head of the city's military defenses. Since he had not met Hitler personally for many months, he had been astonished at what he saw: "Behind a table covered with maps sat the Fuehrer of the German Reich. With my entrance, he turned his head. I saw a bloated face with the eyes of one who was sick with fever. The Fuehrer tried to stand up. I noticed to my shock that his hands and one of his legs shook endlessly. With great difficulty, he finally stood up."

After exchanging pleasantries with Weidling, Hitler sat down, again with much trouble. "As he sat," the General observed, "his left leg moved continuously, his knee like a clock pendulum, only somewhat more quickly." After their discussion, Hitler had tried to rise and dismiss the officer. "Again the Fuehrer attempted to stand up, but he could not," Weidling recalled. "He had to shake my hand while sitting down. I left the room deeply disillusioned with the Fuehrer's physical condition. I was befuddled! What was to happen now? There was neither a Supreme Command of the Army nor of the military [command headquarters had been moved for safety north of Berlin]."

For the next day and a half, the Russians had pushed deeper into eastern and southern Berlin. On the evening of April 25, Weidling had again reported to the Fuehrerbunker, where he informed Hitler, Krebs, Goebbels, Bormann, and others present at a military conference that the enemy had nearly encircled the city and was driving relentlessly toward its center. Hitler's response, which came in "long, repetitive sentences," said Weidling, portrayed "the grounds which had forced him to stay in Berlin and either sink or swim." His small camarilla of still devoted military and Nazi party followers echoed his every word. They accepted without question what he said, despite the situation which worsened with each minute.

Russian shells were by now ripping up the nearby Potsdamer Platz and Leipziger Strasse. Brick and stone dust hung like a fog in the air. Streets and buildings stood gutted and ruined, many afire. Masses of frightened and wounded Berliners huddled in subways, cellars, and a few makeshift hospitals. Because of the mountain of rubble, vehicles found it impossible to move through the streets. On April 27, Weidling said, the Russians had captured the Gatow and Tempelhof airports, which left only the East-West Axis in the Tiergarten for the landing and take-off of small aircraft.

Weidling described the catastrophe to Hitler that evening, but the news became buried amidst the anger of the Fuehrer and Goebbels over word of Himmler's "treason." Later in the evening, Weidling had discussed privately with Bormann, Axmann, and several others in the bunker the insanity of fighting on and his view that the German troops, including Hitler and those in the shelter, should try a mass escape before it was too late. Bormann agreed, but one of the secretaries had whispered, "You had better keep it [the escape plan] from Dr. Goebbels."

Throughout the early hours of April 28, Weidling and Krebs had drafted an elaborate scheme to break away from the Chancellery and the city. They would use the roughly forty German tanks left in the middle of Berlin to flee westward in three large groups, along the

Heerstrasse and across the Havel River south of Spandau. Hitler, it had been decided, would be among the second group escaping, protected by two SS regiments led by Mohnke, commandant of the Chancellery. To present to Hitler the urgency of fleeing, Weidling collected records showing the drastic shortages of munitions, personnel, and hospital facilities.

That evening, the General had reported to the Fuehrer, Krebs, and the others. German forces could at best hold out only two more days, he judged. A mass sprint from the Chancellery and out of the city had been carefully planned; the sooner it began the better. But before Hitler could respond to the proposal, Goebbels ridiculed it as "laughable," and encouraged the Fuehrer to ignore it. Goebbels, Hitler's special "Reich Commissioner" for the defense of Berlin, cared little about the suffering and destruction outside the bunker. His concern, Weidling said, was that Hitler leave the appearance that he died heroically. After a lengthy pause, Hitler had refused Weidling's suggestion. "It would be best," he told the officer, "if he [Hitler] stayed in the Reich Chancellery. He saw the general situation as hopeless." The Fuehrer had repeatedly emphasized, moreover, that Germany must never surrender.

Frustrated, and especially angry at Goebbels, Weidling had still hoped Hitler would change his mind. The Russians had time on their side, and had penetrated to within a few blocks of the Chancellery on April 29. At another military conference that evening, Weidling and Goebbels had quarreled bitterly. But in a surprising move, Hitler agreed to permit "small groups" to escape the Chancellery area, and left it to Weidling to organize the breakaway with his section commanders. Weidling asked himself, "What did the Fuehrer mean by 'breakthrough in small groups'? How did he think this directive could be carried out? Was this not a veiled capitulation?" He set the exodus for April 30 at 10 P.M.

Only a few hours before it began, however, the Chancellery countermanded Hitler's order. Weidling, after taking nearly an hour to move a few blocks from his headquarters to the Chancellery to see what had caused the dramatic reversal, learned of Hitler's suicide, which had occurred around 3:15 P.M. that afternoon. Much to his disappointment, Goebbels now tried to negotiate an armistice with the Russians, rather than surrendering. Weidling had protested Goebbels' decision, but the Minister stubbornly clung to Hitler's directive never to give up.

What had happened to the Fuehrer? On the evening of May 1, more than a day after Hitler's death, Weidling had heard the details from Krebs and his adjutant, General Burgdorf. Two days before Hitler's suicide, they told Weidling, the Nazi leader had married Eva Braun. Then had come the grisly self-murders. "The Fuehrer poisoned himself and his wife on April 30," said Weidling, "but in addition he had shot himself." After having learned of Hitler's fate, the next day, May 2, the General had surrendered his garrison to the Russians.

His memoir illustrated several things about Hitler's last days. The fact that the Russians allowed its publication indicated the strength of their conviction that the Fuehrer had perished in the bunker. Weidling offered substantial testimony to support that conclusion. He described a Hitler, for example, even more ill than what other witnesses had said. Weidling pictured him as a sick weakling, hardly able to stand up or walk, and manipulated by Goebbels. The world learned also of the plan and argument of Weidling for the desperate escape, which Hitler spurned for himself on several occasions. Goebbels, and not the Fuehrer, had been the arch-villain for the General. The fanatical Minister had insisted on a hero's death by his remaining in Berlin. And, although he added a new dimension to Hitler's suicide (i.e., that he had both poisoned and shot himself), Weidling reaffirmed what had been told many times previously.

But on the method of the infamous death, the Soviets could not agree. The official multi-volume *History of the Great Patriotic War of the Soviet Union* added no details. Foreigners found especially confusing the version of an East German writer, German Rosanow. Moscow carefully censored his work. In a book advertised by its publisher as "truths about the German imperialism," Rosanow used the testimony of Axmann and the decision of the Berchtesgaden court in 1956 to show that "Hitler had shot himself in the mouth, Eva Braun had taken poison." He also provided a photograph showing a corpse with a mustache and dressed in a uniform, lying amidst the Berlin ruins, which Rosanow erroneously identified as the dead Hitler. The body had been too well preserved to have been that of the authentic Fuehrer. Truth, however, was not his objective in printing the photo.

Rather, it served a propaganda function, with its caption reading, "Once Hitler had married his longtime friend, Eva Braun, he removed himself in a cowardly way from responsibility for his criminality."[5]

Such widely diverging stories coming out of Russia, and the willingness of the government to allow discussion, encouraged this question: what, really, did the Soviets know about Hitler's end? In search of an answer, Cornelius Ryan, author of the best-selling *The Longest Day,* visited Moscow for two weeks in April 1963. Preparing a book on the battle of Berlin, the popular writer received permission from Khrushchev to interview Soviet army officers involved in the investigation in May 1945 of what had happened to Hitler. Those field marshals queried by Ryan included Vasily D. Sokolovsky, Zhukov's chief of operations in the battle and his successor as Soviet commander in Germany after the war; Ivan Konev, head of one of the Red Armies that had stormed Berlin; and Vasily Chuikov, leader of the Eighth Guards Army that participated in the main thrust into Berlin and accepted the surrender of the German Berlin garrison.

Sokolovsky, having acquired Khrushchev's blessing for the interview, told Ryan, "You should be informed that the Soviet Union officially regards Hitler as dead." He and the other marshals said that the Russians had found at the beginning of May 1945 a body, partially consumed by fire and wrapped in a blanket, near the Fuehrerbunker. A bullet had ripped through its right temple and blown out some of its teeth. Hitler's dentists, whom the Russians had flushed out of hiding in Berlin, then identified the remains as those of the Nazi leader.

Earlier, said the marshals, General Krebs had given the Soviets a letter from Bormann and a document alleging to be Hitler's third will and testament (i.e., beyond his political and personal testament) that proved that the Fuehrer had died. What had happened to the remnants of his body? The Russians had cremated them just outside Berlin, they told Ryan, but they would not say where. Some doubt existed among the marshals, moreover, that Eva Braun's body had been found.

Former German prisoners, like Echtmann, Heusemann, Guensche, Kempka, Helmut Kunz, Reitsch, and Theodor von Dufving, Weidling's former staff chief, also answered questions for Ryan. Guensche, Hitler's SS adjutant who had stayed with the Fuehrer to the end and helped burn the body, recalled the dictator's last moments. Hitler and

Eva Braun had disappeared into his room on the afternoon of April 30, 1945, after bidding their friends in the bunker good-bye. "It was about three-thirty or three-forty," said Guensche. "I tried to do away with my feelings. I knew that he had to commit suicide. There was no other way out."

As Guensche waited, he told Ryan, there had been a brief anti-climax. A distraught Magda Goebbels had rushed up to Hitler's door, demanding to see the Fuehrer and to beg him not to go through with what he had set himself to do. Guensche knocked on the door and opened it:

> The Fuehrer was standing in the study. Eva was not in the room, but there was a tap running in the bathroom so I assume she was there. He was very annoyed at me for intruding. I asked him if he wanted to see Frau Goebbels. 'I don't want to speak to her any more,' he said. I left.
>
> Five minutes later I heard a shot.
>
> Bormann went in first. Then I followed the valet Linge. Hitler was sitting in a chair. Eva was lying on the couch. She had taken off her shoes and placed them neatly together at one end of the couch. Hitler's face was covered with blood. There were two guns. One was a Walther PPk. It was Hitler's. The other was a smaller pistol he always carried in his pocket. Eva wore a blue dress with white collar and cuffs. Her eyes were wide open. There was a strong stench of cyanide. The smell was so strong that I thought my clothes would smell for days—but this may have been my imagination.
>
> Bormann didn't say anything, but I immediately went into the conference room where Goebbels, Burgdorf, and others that I cannot now remember were sitting. I said, 'The Fuehrer is dead.'"[6]

A short while later, Guensche continued, those present wrapped both bodies in blankets and "placed them in a shallow depression outside the bunker entrance."

Heusemann, the dental assistant, had also talked to Ryan. Caught up in the atmosphere and glamor of her privileged position in the Nazi hierarchy, she had thought little of the war or its consequences. Blond, vivacious, and young, she had worked as an assistant to Blaschke, Hitler's dentist. Totally trusted by the Nazi elite, she had attended nearly all of the Fuehrer's entourage, and once Hitler himself. That occasion had been the highlight of her career. She and Blaschke had been called to the Fuehrer's headquarters in East Prussia in November 1944. "Hitler's face," she later recalled for Ryan, "particularly the right cheek was terribly swollen. His teeth were extremely bad. In all he had three bridges. He had only eight upper teeth of his own and even these were backed by gold fillings." While at his so-called "wolf's lair" in the east, the dentists had pulled one of his teeth, a wisdom tooth on the right side.

After the Fuehrer had moved into the Berlin bunker at the beginning of 1945, Heusemann traveled back and forth daily between Blaschke's dental office and the Reich Chancellery. Wherever Hitler went, she had sent a set of dental tools and supplies there. Following his suicide and the surrender of Berlin, the Russians had ferreted her out on May 7, 1945, and taken her to Finow, near Eberswalde, about twenty-five miles northeast of the capital. There she identified Hitler's jaw and dental work. Two days later, she testified to Ryan, the Soviets had picked her up again and transported her to the town of Erkner, where she identified the bodies of Goebbels and his children. Apparently, because of her recognition of Hitler's teeth, she spent the next eleven years in a Soviet prison, mostly in solitary confinement.

Ryan concluded that Hitler had shot himself. None of those he questioned, mostly army officers, had mentioned poisoning. Even the General, Telpukhovsky, who had earlier claimed Hitler died from poison, apparently reversed himself. "The body was badly charred," he told Ryan of the remains in the Chancellery garden which the Russians identified as Hitler's, "but the head was intact, though the back was shattered by a bullet. The teeth had been dislodged and were lying alongside the head."[7]

The Soviet officers questioned by Ryan did not disagree over how Hitler had killed himself, but on the date of the suicide. Chuikov had been the first Russian to hear of the death from General Krebs on the morning of May 1, 1945, while the Nazi officer made a futile effort to negotiate with the Soviets. According to the Marshal, Hitler had probably ended everything on May 1 or 2, not on April 30, as accepted by most sources. Why? Because, said Chuikov, Russian soldiers had found Hitler's scorched body in a smoldering rug in the Chancellery garden on May 2. Moreover, he said, General Krebs had confused the time of the suicide while discussing it with the Russians. When Krebs had first informed Chuikov of it, he had said Hitler died "at 15.00 hours today [May 1]." But immediately, the Nazi had corrected himself and said "yesterday [April 30]."

Later in their talks, Chuikov thought he had again detected confusion on Krebs' part. It came during the German General's description of Hitler's arrest of Goering in the final days for treason. "Goering? He is a traitor," said Krebs. "The Fuehrer cannot stand him. Goering proposed that the Fuehrer should hand over control of the state to him, and the Fuehrer had expelled him from the Party." Instantly, Krebs had caught himself, saying, "Before his death Hitler expelled him from the Party." Right from the beginning, said Chuikov, suspicion rose on his part about the Fuehrer's fate. "Here was a muddle for a start," he commented, "first the Fuehrer cannot stand Goering—in the present tense; then he expelled him from the Party—in the past tense."

Some, like Trevor-Roper, challenged the Marshal. "Not correct," said the British historian when he later read Chuikov's report, adding "I think it's a perfectly genuine misrecollection of a detail." Hitler's corpse had not been buried in a rug on May 1 or 2. "The man who buried Hitler is still alive," he asserted. "His name is Mengershausen. I have interrogated him. He buried the body in a bomb crater—probably not very scientifically—on the evening of April 30."[8]

Ryan's experience in Moscow with Chuikov and the others seemed to indicate one thing. Differences still remained that had surfaced in the summer of 1945 between the military and political branches of the Soviet regime over what had happened to Hitler. Ryan had been permitted to talk only with the army leaders. Unavailable to him were intelligence and medical sources, which would soon put forth the theory that Hitler had poisoned himself. Those most anxious to denounce the Fuehrer's suicide as cowardly and resulting from poison instead of a bullet, did not include the Red Army.

What may have been an effort by certain political elements in the Kremlin, partly for propaganda reasons, to downgrade both Hitler's suicide and what the Soviet marshals had said about it, started in July 1964. Igor Yegorov, who had been among the Russian units searching for Hitler's body in the ruins of the Chancellery in May 1945, published his recollections in a Soviet weekly magazine, *Nedelya*. Claiming to have interrogated persons who witnessed Hitler's death,

Yegorov concluded that the dictator had been too ill and shaky to have shot himself, as so many others had described. "His hands trembled and his head jerked, his morale had crumbled completely," said the Russian investigator. "Hitler was virtually unable to shoot himself."

Yegorov also found it difficult to believe that the fascist leader, as alleged by Weidling, had the nerve both to poison and shoot himself. Instead, he declared, Hitler had killed himself with poison, and his corpse had then been shot in the mouth by one of his henchmen. Nor did Yegorov think that the Nazis, who had put a bullet into their dead master, had the purest of motives. They had shot him, Yegorov concluded, to help build the myth that the Fuehrer had died a more "honorable death."

This pronouncement again thrust the issue of Hitler's demise squarely into the arena of propaganda and politics. Not only did Yegorov contribute a new side to the accusation that the Nazis had purposely encouraged the story of Hitler's gallant end, but he injected the idea that the Fuehrer had in fact died a skulking death. Was it not a tradition of the German Army, he asked, for a disgraced officer to shoot himself? Were not poison and drugs considered a woman's way of suicide? Yegorov, since he presented no proof (e.g., documents or testimony), seemed intent on discrediting further the hated fascists and their leader.

Hitler had ordered poison tried on his favorite dog, Blondi, and her pup, to test its efficiency, said Yegorov, and later he and Eva Braun had retired to his private room. Bormann, Axmann, and one of Hitler's servants waited anxiously outside. Linge, the Fuehrer's valet, had readied and loaded two pistols which had been left in the room. After some delay, "Hitler had asked for another fifteen or twenty minutes to muster up courage" to kill himself, Yegorov said. When the time had elapsed, Hitler's aides opened the door to the room; there "two corpses lay on the sofa, Eva and Adolf, both having taken poison."

And the evidence? "Hitler's remains were checked later" by the Russians, Yegorov added. "In the jaw there were discovered small bits of a poison pellet." Bormann had then sent one of the Fuehrer's bodyguards into the room, Yegorov declared, and he had "raised the head of the still warm corpse and shot Hitler in the mouth. Then he dropped the pistol on the floor near Hitler's lifeless hand. In this way there was created the myth that the Commander-in-Chief of the Third Reich shot himself, and thus the honor of the Officer Corps of the Nazi Army was saved."[9]

The Soviets carried Yegorov's story a step further during the following year. On the twentieth anniversary of the end of the war, they published what amounted to an "unofficial" version of Hitler's death. The vehicle was Yelena Rzhevskaya, a Soviet writer who had been an interpreter late in the war for the headquarters of the Russian Third Assault Army. She had been assigned on April 29, 1945, to an elite team of Red Army officers given the job of capturing or finding Hitler in Berlin. She provided the most detailed account yet from the Soviet Union.

That day, according to Rzhevskaya, Russian troops slowly overcame stiff Nazi resistance in the heart of the city, fighting their way through the Tiergarten and along Unter den Linden. They reached to within five hundred yards of the German Parliament, the Reichstag, and not much further from the Chancellery, under which the Red Army believed Hitler had hidden himself. But only three days later, on May 2, could Rzhevskaya and her group, headed by a Lieutenant Colonel Ivan Klimenko, break into the Chancellery bunker. Except for the report of General Krebs to the Russians the previous day, saying Hitler had ended it all by his own hand, the investigators knew little of the whereabouts of their coveted target.

On entering the bunker, they had started sifting through scattered documents and interrogating those few of Hitler's staff that still remained there. They found papers of Bormann, showing his efforts after April 20 to shift the Fuehrer's headquarters to Berchtesgaden. Rzhevskaya also said she had come across a dozen thick volumes of diaries from Goebbels' hand and an announcement of Mussolini's death, containing a scribbled notation allegedly by Hitler, "hung by the feet." Already that evening, with the help of a Nazi garage mechanic, Karl Schneider; a cook, Wilhelm Lange; and a Vice Admiral seized while trying to flee, Voss; the Russians discovered "the half charred bodies of Goebbels and his wife" in the Chancellery garden. About the same time, they found the corpses of the six Goebbels children in the bunker, each poisoned.

The team soon began gathering information about Hitler. Most of the Nazis captured in the Chancellery told the Russians on May 3 that in the last days, they had heard rumors of Hitler's death. Schneider, for example, said he had not seen the Fuehrer, but had been told of his suicide by Kempka, the chauffeur. "This news had gone from mouth to mouth, everyone talked about it," related the mechanic, "still no one knew exact details." Schneider had suspected something unusual, however, since he had been ordered to round up gasoline on April 29 for sending to the bunker.

"The Fuehrer is dead, and nothing remains of his body," the cook, Lange, had been told on April 30 by the caretaker of Hitler's dogs. "Among the employees of the Reich Chancellery, rumors spread that Hitler had poisoned or shot himself and his body had been burned." A technician at the Chancellery, Wilhelm Zinn, had also heard on April 30, around six P.M., that the Fuehrer had killed himself. Voss told the Russians, "Goebbels reported Hitler's death to me." And Rzhevskaya's group heard other stories. Said one, the Fuehrer had flown out of Berlin with the lady pilot, Reitsch. Another had him fleeing through a secret underground passage to safety in the Tyrol. The Russians frequently heard that a "double" had died in the Fuehrer's place, and on May 3, they uncovered a body resembling Hitler's. Voss and other Nazis, however, could not identify it as the dictator.

Puzzled, the Russians concluded that Hitler's remains had been destroyed along with those of Eva Braun, his new bride. The search had now shifted on May 4 to the garden, especially on a tip from one of the Chancellery's last dentists, Helmut Kunz. Kunz told his interrogators that he had heard from Rattenhuber, the commander of Hitler's detective guard, that the Fuehrer's body had been set afire in the garden. Meanwhile, one of Klimenko's soldiers uncovered two severely blackened corpses outside the bunker, one a male and the other a female, believed to be those of Hitler and Eva Braun. He also unearthed the remains of two dogs, which had been poisoned and which Klimenko's team later learned were Hitler's. A report of the investigators, written the next day and quoted by Rzhevskaya, described the scene. "The bodies were badly burned and could not be identified without additional statements," it said. "The bodies lay in a bomb crater, three meters in front of the entrance to Hitler's bunker, and were covered with a layer of earth."

Through the testimony of other witnesses and the recognition of the teeth in the corpses, the Russian search team had soon determined their identity. Guensche, Hitler's adjutant, had been seized while hiding in a Berlin brewery, and he claimed to the Russians Hitler had poisoned himself, after having seen the poison kill his dog, Blondi, and her puppy. Later, Guensche would reverse his story when interviewed by Ryan. But Rzhevskaya, who accepted the version Guensche told the Russians, apparently based her choice on the adjutant's vague statement that on returning to the Fuehrer's room shortly after his body had been burned, he had noticed "a strong smell of almonds coming from there (cyanide)." Could that not have been from the suicide of Eva Braun?

Rzhevskaya quoted another prisoner of the Russians, the guard Mengershausen, as testifying that while patrolling the Chancellery and surrounding area on April 30, he had seen Guensche and the valet, Linge, carry the bodies of Hitler and Eva Braun into the garden, near the bunker exit, and set them afire. Rattenhuber, also captured by the Russians, informed them that Mengershausen and another SS man, on orders from Guensche, had buried the molten and smelling corpses in the grave "with Hitler's poisoned dogs."

The "decisive argument," said Rzhevskaya, had been her own locating on May 9 and 10 of two dental technicians in Berlin who had worked on Hitler's teeth, Heusemann and Echtmann. Using X-ray photographs and other dental records of Hitler's found in the Reich Chancellery, they recognized the teeth from the man's remains that had been unearthed as those of the Fuehrer. In pursuit of the technicians, Rzhevskaya had carried Hitler's teeth around Berlin in a cigar box, stuffed into a satchel.

Based on these and other records, Klimenko's investigation unit completed a report on May 13, 1945, which identified the nearly consumed remains unearthed in the garden on May 4 as those of Hitler and his wife. In the nearby suburb of Berlin-Buch, a commission of Soviet military doctors, who had performed an autopsy on the bodies, decided that Hitler had ended everything with cyanide poison. "From the burning of the considerably mutilated bodies," Rzhevskaya quoted the commission, "no visible traces of deadly wounds or illness could be established. In the mouth slivers of glass were found, a thin phial, part of the lining and the bottom."

But the poison did not explain everything, added Rzhevskaya.

What about the shot allegedly heard by some of Hitler's associates, like Linge and the pilot Baur, on that afternoon of April 30? They had told others that the Fuehrer had shot himself. Linge, Rzhevskaya proclaimed, had sneaked into Hitler's room after his chief had taken poison and put a bullet into him. And how had the Russians arrived at this startling explanation? Mainly through the testimony of Rattenhuber, who they said had entered Hitler's room shortly after the suicide and had admitted to them that he had "perceived a powerfully bitter smell of almonds." Momentarily, he said, Linge had approached him:

> Therewith he [Linge] explained to me that he had to carry out the hardest command of his life from the Fuehrer. I looked at Linge with astonishment. He told me that Hitler had ordered him before his [Hitler's] death to leave the room for ten minutes, then re-enter, to wait ten minutes more and execute the directive. Linge went quickly into Hitler's room and returned with a Walther pistol, laying it on the table before me. In this exhibition I recognized the personal revolver of the Fuehrer. Now it was clear to me what the command of Hitler's contained.[10]

Hitler, Rattenhuber told the Russians, had doubted the effectiveness of the poison he swallowed, and a fear had obsessed him of being seized, alive or dead, by the Soviets. He had therefore directed his valet to fire a bullet into his head, making certain he would not survive. Rzhevskaya reasoned from all this that Hitler had been made wary of the poison because of its poor effect on one of his dogs, which he had allegedly seen writhe in pain while dying. According to Soviet doctors who had done an autopsy on the dogs, she said, each had been poisoned and shot.

The wound which the Soviets had supposedly found in the scorched carcass of Eva Braun, declared Rzhevskaya, provided further evidence that Linge had shot his Fuehrer. Russian doctors had performed a post-mortem on what was left of her on May 8, 1945, finding the bullet fired by Linge at Hitler had also accidentally hit her in the chest. Eva Braun too had already died from a cyanide capsule. Rzhevskaya, in a blast leveled at Trevor-Roper and those in the West who maintained that Hitler had perished by a bullet, said the "one is badly informed, the others again wish to glorify the circumstances of his death." But the final judgment, she said, could not be mistaken: "Hitler was dead. Everything was certain, all was clear."

In what may have been an example of the fading belief that Hitler had survived, Rzhevskaya's account found little immediate interest in the West. Perhaps the unofficial status of her story elicited the dwarfish reaction. Or, possibly, it resulted from her words first appearing in an obscure Moscow journal and not being very widely read. No one, for instance, questioned her dubious inferences from the testimonies of Rattenhuber and Guensche. *Look* magazine summarized her remarks under the melodramatic headline, "Hitler's Jaw was in Her Handbag," referring to her journey around Berlin with Hitler's teeth to find someone to identify them.

Rzevskaya impressed a British reviewer. "I do not think," he responded, "that there is any doubt that the Russians found and identified Hitler's and Eva Braun's bodies." "Personally," he continued, "I am more inclined to accept the findings of the Red Army doctors regarding the cause of Hitler's death than Professor Trevor-Roper's version based on the hearsay accounts of Hitler's and Bormann's secretaries, and those of Kempka and the despicable Axmann." Still, only the complete publication by Moscow of the available evidence and documents suppressed by Stalin and mentioned by Rzhevskaya could dispel all remaining doubts.

In quest of such records, another Western writer, following Ryan's model, trekked to Moscow in the spring of 1965. Erich Kuby, an editor for the West German magazine, *Der Spiegel,* questioned several army officers in the Soviet capital as well as Rzhevskaya and Klimenko, chief of the special Russian search team ordered in Berlin on April 29, 1945, to locate Hitler. The editor's mission ended in frustration, however, as he failed to clarify how the Fuehrer had died or what the Russians had done with the corpse.[11]

Klimenko's story for Kuby closely paralleled Rzhevskaya's. His unit found what proved to be Hitler's carcass, he said, in the Chancellery garden on May 4, after an exploration of the Chancellery, its cellars, and bunker, and the interrogation of Nazi prisoners such as Voss, Schneider, and Lange. The latter yielded that Hitler had killed himself, after marrying his long-time mistress, Eva Braun. During their search, the Russians discovered several bodies that had mustaches and uniforms similar to Hitler's. One "double," found near an emergency exit of the bunker, even fooled Voss, who had been with the Fuehrer to the end and erroneously identified the look-alike as the dictator.

A Soviet soldier, said Klimenko, unearthed "two half burned bodies, wrapped in a gray blanket" about three meters from the entrance to the bunker. They were what was left of a man and a woman, and had been buried with two dogs in a bomb crater. Mengershausen, a key witness for the Russians, had admitted to Klimenko's group that while patrolling the Chancellery on April 30, he had seen Hitler and Eva Braun carried out of the bunker and set afire by Guensche and Linge. He led Klimenko to the spot where his hunters had found the bodies, and after further interrogation conceded that he had helped keep the corpses ablaze. "That night [May 4]," Klimenko recalled, "my people wrapped the bodies in a blanket and carried them from the Reich Chancellery, laid them in two boxes, put them in an auto and took them to our staff." Several days later, the Russians identified the remains as those of the German tyrant and his wife.

Kuby also uncovered in Moscow a former Russian officer, Viktor Bojew, who had belonged to a Soviet tank division that had crashed into Berlin and who said he had talked to Goebbels by telephone on April 26, 1945. Despite the raging battle in the city, phone connections remained good with the German Propaganda Ministry and the Fuehrerbunker. Bojew spoke fluent German, and he decided with two Russian reporters to call Goebbels and have "a bit of fun." Much to their suprise, after speaking with several persons, Bojew had finally reached the Minister. "When and in what direction will you escape Berlin?" he had asked the Nazi leader. "This question is much too insolent to be answered," came the abrupt reply. Seconds later, when queried whether he knew that the Soviets "already hold a gallows for you," Goebbels hung up the phone.

The Russians emphasized to Kuby that Hitler had not left Berlin at the end of the war, but had poisoned himself in the bunker. "We knew with certainty," Klimenko told him, "that Hitler was dead." General Antonov, a Soviet officer who had greeted a small delegation of Nazi officials that had crossed the battleline in Berlin on May 1, 1945 (after Krebs' mission), to negotiate with the Russians, confirmed this. Discussing the episode with Kuby, Antonov said that the Nazis had talked about Hitler's marriage, his death, and the poisoning of his dog, Blondi, and then his taking poison himself. Rzhevskaya gave Kuby a similar story, quoting from a Russian autopsy report.

But it had not been testimony from the Russians that persuaded the *Spiegel* editor of the possibility Hitler had swallowed poison. Linge, Hitler's valet, he said, who had stated in 1955 that the Fuehrer had shot himself in the right temple, had contradicted his previous story in an interview with Kuby. According to the journalist, Linge said he had also seen a bullet wound on Hitler's left temple and that he suspected the dictator had shot himself with the left hand. Why? Because when the servant had entered the suicide room on April 30, moments after the deed, the Fuehrer's head lay slumped to the right, with blood oozing from the right temple only. Moreover, he told Kuby, Hitler sat upright on the sofa in the room, with "his hands placed in good order on his knees." The servant even appeared confused about where Hitler's revolvers lay when he had entered the apartment. A decade before, he had testified that both pistols had been on the floor. But now, Linge maintained that one had been on the table in front of the dead Hitler.

Linge later denied Kuby's story. The editor thought the valet's uncertainty important enough to question whether Hitler had shot himself. Why had the right-handed Fuehrer chosen such an insecure way to die, pulling the trigger with his badly trembling left hand? Why, furthermore, had he sat so undisturbed on the couch, if he had just been struck by a bullet from point-blank range in the side of the head? Had the fanatical Linge, Goebbels, and Bormann, the only persons really to see Hitler dead (i.e., his face and skull), asked Kuby, agreed secretly after the suicide to foster the myth that "our great Fuehrer had shot himself like a man"?

Kuby's inquiry raised more questions than it answered. Even the Russians needed scrutinizing, he said. Had they perhaps altered their autopsy report on Hitler, mentioned by Rzhevskaya, for "an ideological reason"? "A Hitler who poisoned himself unmanly," he suggested, "fits into the Communist picture much better than a Hitler who had grabbed for a pistol. He also fits better into the psychological category in which I have classified Hitler." Kuby's conclusion? "Probably the most photographed, most documented person of our time, vanished through well-known means into the unknown."

11

The Autopsy

"Birthdays we are happy not to celebrate: Hitler would have been 80 on Sunday," *The Times* of London called to its readers' attention in April 1968. If he had been alive to blow out his candles, Hitler would probably have laughed at learning that over two decades after the battle of Berlin, the final word on his fate had not yet been issued by the Soviet Union. He would also have delighted in witnessing the strongest revival of Nazism in West Germany since the World War.

Organized into the tiny National Democratic party in Germany, the neo-Nazis experienced their greatest electoral successes in the spring of 1968, capturing nearly 10 percent of the vote in Baden-Wuerttemberg. Anti-Soviet and anti-American, the neo-Nazis saw themselves as upholding the rights of Germans to lands they had lost when Hitler's Reich had collapsed, especially territories now under Polish, Czechoslovakian, and Soviet rule. The National Democrats vowed to reunify the two Germanies, rehabilitate Hitler and Nazism, and show that the Fuehrer had been a noble crusader against World Communism, but that the Jews, Roosevelt, and Churchill had subverted his policies. Other Germans showed an interest in re-examining the recent past. In a public opinion poll, 43 percent of the nation agreed that "it is high time to get rid of the claim that Germany was to blame for the outbreak of World War II." Such activity elicited a stampede of publicity in the German and foreign press, and it particularly disturbed Moscow.

The Soviets found equally disconcerting the new *Ostpolitik,* or "Eastern policy," of the Bonn government, designed to establish normal diplomatic relations with the countries of eastern Europe for the first time since the war. The Kremlin angrily denounced the policy as a trick to lure the east European states out of the Soviet orbit and into economic ties with the Federal Republic. The Russians easily singled out the neo-Nazis as proof of the rebirth of revanchism and reckless nationalism among the Germans. Whenever possible, they used the National Democrats to justify the Soviet accusation that the Federal Republic (à la Hitler) still held territorial ambitions in eastern Europe, and that no Communist regime should fall prey to this menacing power.

The Russians felt themselves genuinely threatened. Their press pictured the National Democrats not as a small minority party, but as a leading political force in the Federal Republic. The Soviet invasion of Czechoslovakia in 1968, to suppress liberal, pro-Western sympathies there, represented in part a further illustration of how seriously they regarded the German situation. Moscow became determined to prevent close ties, without its permission, between the eastern European states and the Federal Republic.

This eagerness to remind the world of Germany's aggressive expansion eastward in World War II and to undercut the neo-Nazis, may also have been responsible for the unofficial publication by the Soviets in August 1968 of their autopsy report on Hitler. The report, mentioned by various Soviet sources in the 1960s, appeared amid a journalist's lengthy dissertation on how his body had been discovered and by the strongest propaganda claim yet that the suicide had a shameful meaning for Nazi followers. Hitler, the Russians said again, had not died bravely by putting a revolver to his head, as the Nazis and the West had proclaimed since 1945. He had swallowed poison, and then one of his aides had shot him.

The method through which the Soviets published their autopsy results indicated that they wished to score a point for their side of the propaganda battle. Moscow did not release them without comment, as the British had done in November 1945 with their announcement of Hitler's suicide. Instead, it buried the report in a book by a Soviet journalist and former intelligence officer, Lev Bezymensky, titled *The Death of Adolf Hitler*. It tried to justify the mysterious Russian handling of the death since the war, the argument that it had been caused by poison, and the assertion that the Nazis had tried to create a last, desperate legend out of their leader's demise. This, coupled with a quarter century of preconceived ideas in the West about what had happened to Hitler, assured mixed foreign reactions for the Russian findings.

Except for a few minor details, *The Death of Adolf Hitler* echoed what the Soviets had stated earlier. Before the capture of Berlin, said Bezymensky, the Red Army had no "precise information as to Hitler's whereabouts." Nor did it "trust the news releases in the official Nazi press," declaring the Fuehrer to be in the capital guiding its defense. Only on May 1, 1945, had the Russians learned of Hitler's suicide from the Nazi general, Krebs, who had crossed the battleline in the ruined city to negotiate fruitlessly with the enemy. The Red Army immediately forwarded the information to Moscow and Stalin.

When the city had surrendered the next day, a small unit of the Soviet Counter Intelligence Service (abbreviated SMERSH, for the Russian words meaning "death to spies"), headed by Klimenko, started searching the Chancellery, its bunker and garden, and interrogating German prisoners. Bezymensky quoted heavily from an official report by Klimenko. On the outskirts of the capital, the Russians had seized Hitler's adjutant Guensche, and later recognized and questioned him. Nearer the Chancellery, they captured the guard, Mengershausen, who had witnessed the burning of Hitler's body. SMERSH quickly discovered the bodies of Goebbels and his wife, Klimenko had said, "at the emergency exit of the Fuehrer's bunker." The unit found the Minister's children and Krebs inside the shelter a day later, all having yielded their lives to poison. Over twenty Nazi prisoners, including Wilhelm Echolt, chief of Goebbels' bodyguard, identified them. "Goebbels' death," affirmed Bezymensky, "was proved beyond any doubt."

The hunt for Hitler, said Klimenko, had taken a strange turn. The Fuehrer's remains were uncovered by the Russians, not immediately identified, reburied, and disinterred again. After a corpse "in mended socks" that resembled Hitler had been found two days before, but not recognized positively, SMERSH had begun looking in the rubble-strewn Chancellery garden. Around noon on May 4, in a crater near the bunker door, it dug up two bodies, one a male and the other a female, which had been buried with loose papers, the remains of two dogs, and a bazooka. "Of course at first I didn't even think that these might be the corpses of Hitler and Eva Braun," said Klimenko, "since I believed that Hitler's corpse was already in the Chancellery and only needed to be identified." Consequently, SMERSH wrapped the bodies in blankets and placed them back in the ground. Inside the Chancellery, witnesses busily identified the other dead.

The body produced on May 2 and thought by SMERSH to be Hitler's proved to be a fraud. So on the morning of May 5, Klimenko had returned to the garden crater and unearthed the corpses. Who were they? Was the male Hitler? Steps began to obtain the answers. First, Soviet patrols had arrested Mengershausen and taken him to the crater, where he testified that shortly after noon on April 30, while on guard duty at the Chancellery, he had seen Guensche and Linge carrying the deceased Hitler and Eva Braun into the garden. He had also watched carefully, Mengershausen stated, as Guensche had poured gasoline on the dead and set them ablaze. A bit later, the corpses, nearly destroyed by the fire, had been placed in a crater close to the bunker door and covered with dirt.

SMERSH transported the bodies and those of the dogs in wooden boxes to its headquarters at Buch, north of Berlin, on the morning of May 5. There a team of forensic doctors had performed autopsies on Goebbels, his family, and Krebs. Death for each had come by poison, concluded the physicians. They even examined Blondi, Hitler's dog. It too had succumbed to cyanide, a finding later supported by the story of the prisoner, Guensche, who described how the animal had been poisoned at its master's order to test the effectiveness of the deadly potion.

According to the autopsy report, completed by the doctors on May 8, 1945, the male corpse from the crater suspected of being Hitler's had been "greatly damaged" and "severely charred" by fire. A piece of the cranium as well as all of the skin were missing. The left testicle could also not be located, either in the scrotum or on the spermatic cord inside the inguinal canal, nor in the small pelvis. The doctors worked with what remained, including parts of the occipital bone, left temporal bone, lower cheekbones, nasal bones, and the upper and lower jawbones.

The report contained an extensive summary of the dead man's teeth, the keys that unlocked his identity. In the upper jaw were nine teeth, connected and protected by a gold bridge; the lower jaw had fifteen. It also held something else—poison. "Splinters of glass, parts of the wall and bottom of a thin-walled ampule," said the doctors, "were found in the mouth." "Death in this instance," they determined, "was caused by poisoning with cyanide compounds." In addition to the crushed glass capsule in the mouth, the doctors found other indications of poison: a "marked smell of bitter almonds" coming from the body and the "presence of cyanide" in the internal organs.[1]

Despite the bones and dental work they had to deal with, the forensic specialists could not show that this was Hitler's body. They nevertheless provided a vital clue. They removed from the corpse the lower jaw and the gold bridge from the upper jaw. On May 9, SMERSH officials had taken the jaw and bridge into Berlin, hunting for Hitler's dentist. Their search yielded the dental assistant, Heusemann, who had directed the investigators to the office of Blaschke, the Fuehrer's dentist. They recovered X-ray photographs of Hitler's teeth as well as his complete dental file.

Heusemann, and later the dental technician Echtmann, said Klimenko, had "described Hitler's teeth from memory in minute detail," and this "corresponded precisely with the entries in the medical history and with the X-ray pictures that we had found." They had also recognized the jawbone and bridge "unequivocally as those of Adolf Hitler," plus identifying the teeth and bridgework of the female corpse from the crater as those of Eva Braun.[2] Based on Heusemann's interrogation alone, Klimenko had judged in his report, "it may be presumed that the teeth as well as the bridge described in the document [i.e., the autopsy] are those of Chancellor Hitler." What had the Russians done with the corpses? They "were now completely burned and their ashes strewn to the wind."

Where the reports of the autopsy and Klimenko left off in *The Death of Adolf Hitler,* Bezymensky seized the remaining pages in the book to interpret what the "facts" suggested. Hitler's missing testicle, mentioned in the autopsy, provided an example. In a question reminiscent of those raised earlier by the popular press in the West, Bezymensky asked: did this prevent Hitler from having a "normal sexual life"? Apparently wishing to give his own answer and deride the dictator simultaneously, he recalled a statement allegedly of Himmler that Hitler had contracted syphilis "in his early years."

The Soviet writer described as illogical the Western theory that

Hitler had shot himself. But instead of addressing himself to the version of Trevor-Roper and the British, he criticized the most vulnerable Western viewpoint, that of Linge. He berated Linge's remark made to *Der Spiegel* that Hitler had shot himself in the left temple with the left hand, and noted that the Nazi leader had been neither left handed nor in possession of a steady left and right hand. What had such stories of Linge and the other Nazi prisoners (e.g., Kempka, Axmann, and Baur) meant? "The confusion and lack of conformity in the statements indicate that the collaborators of Hitler who managed to escape from the bunker purposely tried to hide the truth in order to foster the legend that the Fuehrer had shot himself like a man."

Sketching a cringing and scheming Hitler in his final moments, regardless of historical accuracy, seemed to give Bezymensky much satisfaction. As Berlin fell and the situation had become hopeless, he said in *The Death of Adolf Hitler,* the Fuehrer had "broken down completely." Then he had refused to accept his defeat, and instead fully supported frantic efforts among Himmler and other Nazis to maneuver the Western powers into a separate peace with Germany and a split with the Soviet Union. Even when Soviet soldiers had penetrated Berlin, he had dreamed of dividing his enemies. "Hitler, Goebbels and Ribbentrop lived in a world of illusions," observed the journalist. "This was not yet the year 1954."

Bezymensky went to some length, and with no evidence to support his argument, to state that Hitler, after dying of poison, had been shot by one of his bunker subordinates. Part of the tyrant's skull was missing, the autopsy report had stated. To make certain he had died and that he would not fall into the arms of the Red Army, the Russian writer deduced, someone had shot the Fuehrer in the head. And the proof? Two questionable remarks of German prisoners, captured and interrogated by the Russians in May 1945.

One, SS commandant of the Chancellery Mohnke, had allegedly told his captors on May 20 that Linge had informed him Hitler "had committed suicide and that he [Linge] had executed the most difficult order in his life." The other, commander of Hitler's detective body-guard, Rattenhuber, had told the Soviets in 1951, "I came to the conclusion that Hitler did not entirely trust the effect of the poison on his organism and there ordered his valet Linge to go into his room after a certain lapse of time and shoot him." "Such a request," Bezymensky said, "cannot be considered entirely senseless." But while he stressed that Linge had been the culprit, he asserted without any explanation, that "Soviet researchers are of the opinion that it was Guensche who pulled the trigger." Then, leaving his readers gasping for something more, Bezymensky added that only one thing could be certain—"Hitler poisoned himself."

Speculation also stood at the crux of his analysis of why the Soviet Union had kept silent on Hitler's fate for so long. To begin with, he said, it had been a "senseless exaggeration" of the West to assume "that the Soviet Army battled for Berlin merely because Adolf Hitler was there. It had other, more important goals." Why had the results of the Soviet investigation and autopsy, even though the Kremlin had considered them conclusive, remained unpublished for twenty three years? "Not because of doubts as to the credibility of the experts," Bezymensky assured his readers. Rather, it had been Stalin who had "showed considerable interest in the fate of Hitler."

The Russian Premier, hinted Bezymensky, had been responsible for Marshal Zhukov's curious behavior in June 1945. By stating at his famous press conference on June 9 that Hitler "could have flown away from Berlin at the very last moment," the Russian commander in Germany had shocked the world. Of Hitler, Zhukov had allegedly told Bezymensky, Stalin had "frequently inquired about him and indicated that investigations should be continued" during 1945. But in his memoir published a year after *The Death of Adolf Hitler,* Zhukov gave little indication of pressure placed on him by his boss to say that Hitler had escaped.

When Zhukov had first informed Stalin from Berlin on May 1, 1945, of Krebs' report that Hitler had killed himself, the Premier reportedly answered, "So that's the end of the bastard. Too bad it was impossible to take him alive. Where is Hitler's body?" It had been "burned" came the reply. Had Zhukov believed the stories of Krebs and the Nazi Propaganda Ministry official, Fritsche, the first Germans to testify to the Russians that Hitler had ended his own life?

Circumstances made me doubt at first the truthfulness of the account of

Hitler's suicide, all the more so because we could not find Bormann either. I thought then that perhaps Hitler had escaped at the last moment when there was no hope of any outside help for Berlin.

I stated that conjecture in Berlin at a press conference for Soviet and foreign correspondents.

Some time later, after careful investigation and questioning of Hitler's medical staff, etc., we began to receive additional and more concrete evidence confirming Hitler's suicide.

Personally I am inclined to believe there are no grounds for doubting that Hitler committed suicide.[3]

The Field Marshal also discussed his meetings with the Western commanders, Eisenhower and Montgomery, at the beginning of June 1945, dealing with the Allied administration of Germany. Had differences with his counterparts over this issue prompted both himself and Stalin to declare Hitler possibly alive, with the aim of enhancing Russia's political and military claims in Germany? Zhukov never suggested this had been his or Stalin's objective at his press conference on June 9. But he remembered from this crucial period the suspicions he and Stalin had about Anglo-American intentions in Europe. "I feel," Stalin once told him, "the British want to retain the German troops [in the British zone of Germany] so that they can be used later." On another occasion, he had warned the Marshal, "You will probably have to act alone against the others [i.e., the Allied commanders] in settling a number of questions. But it won't be the first time we've had to fight alone."

Zhukov pictured his meeting with the other commanders in Berlin on June 5, 1945, as much less cordial than either Montgomery or Eisenhower had described it.[4] First, he said, he had argued with General Tooey Spaatz, chief of the American Strategic Air Command, who had accompanied Eisenhower to the former German capital, about Anglo-American flights over the Soviet zone into the city. Then, Montgomery and the Marshal had disagreed over which battle, El Alamein or Stalingrad, had been of the greatest significance for the Allied victory. By the time Eisenhower could intervene and soothe both men, they had differed over a more substantial question: the insistence by Montgomery that Anglo-American troops be allowed immediately to occupy their respective zones in Berlin, which lay at the time under the control of the Red Army. After the meeting, Zhukov said, "I called up Stalin and told him of Montgomery's claims." Within four days, the Marshal held his controversial press conference, saying he thought Hitler had survived. Three months later, the Russians accused the British of hiding Hitler in their zone.

Bezymensky, in opposition to Zhukov, stressed in *The Death of Adolf Hitler* that Stalin had been "skeptical" of the announcement of Hitler's demise, principally "because he did not wish to accept the fact that Hitler had 'escaped' his just punishment" by the Allies. Moreover, the Russians had other reasons, he said, for having withheld the autopsy report. One had been "to hold it in reserve" in the event someone might slip into the role of "the Fuehrer saved by a miracle," and resurrect the Nazi threat. The Russians had also continued their investigation after 1945, "in order to exclude any possibility of error or deliberate deception" on the part of the Nazis. Had it been clear how Hitler had died, "the Soviet side would long ago have made an official declaration. We have no interest whatsoever in hiding the truth."

Despite the previous Russian accounts that had said much the same, *The Death of Adolf Hitler* provoked an instant controversy around the world. His critics eagerly urged him to appear personally in the West to defend what he had said. For a few weeks, it seemed their dream might come true. He scheduled a visit to the international book fair in Frankfurt, in September 1968, to promote the sale of his work. But only hours before he was to hold a press conference there, the Kremlin canceled his trip. It feared possible protests by neo-Nazis or radical leftist students, it said, showing their unhappiness about the Soviet invasion of Czechoslovakia.

Linge, one of those accused by Bezymensky of shooting Hitler and thereby administering the *coup de grace* to his former master, denied the story in a television interview with the BBC and in meetings with the West German press. Why had the Russians invented such a theory, the media asked? "Because they thought Hitler was a coward," Linge responded. Newsmen questioned the other one-time Russian prisoner and Nazi accused of shooting Hitler, Guensche, at his home in Cologne. "Cyanide played no part in the death of Hitler," he said firmly. "I stand by my earlier statements that Hitler shot himself."

The Death of Adolf Hitler evoked an outburst of disbelief from

Trevor-Roper, whose version of Hitler's last days in the Fuehrer-bunker and conclusion that he had shot himself in the mouth had become the standard account in the West. "Nonsense," he said of Bezymensky's work, "only a Soviet editor could expect to get away with it." The Regius Professor of History at Oxford charged Bezymensky with failing to explain why Stalin had decided to "suppress the documents and falsify the evidence in 1945." Instead of fearing that someone might later pretend Hitler was alive (as Bezymensky had maintained in Stalin's defense), Stalin had purposely hidden the facts to create the pretense that Hitler had survived. "There were only two rational explanations of Stalin's action," argued Trevor-Roper. "Either he was genuinely unconvinced by the Russian inquiry, or he deliberately falsified its results for political purposes."

The British professor suspected the autopsy report, too. He noted erroneously that the Russian doctors writing the report had only hinted at Hitler's poisoning. The doctors' statement had been unequivocal—"death in this instance was caused by poisoning with cyanide compounds." Trevor-Roper also pointed out that the doctors had cautioned that the body had been "severely charred." Furthermore, he asked, how could they have observed that part of the cranium was missing and then pass over that fact without discussing it? By ignoring the broken skull, had the Russians tried to explain away a gunshot wound? How unfortunate, Trevor-Roper rightly complained, that "we are not allowed to read the original text or know the history of this important document."

Some reviewers of Bezymensky's book contributed more confusion than enlightenment to the controversy. Harrison Salisbury, analyzing it in a lengthy article in *The New York Times,* remarked that Trevor-Roper and another Western writer, Shirer, had "concluded that Hitler shot himself after having shot his mistress Eva Braun." In an angry letter to the *Times,* Trevor-Roper corrected the statement, saying he "nowhere stated that Hitler shot his mistress. She was stated to have swallowed poison." Neither did he appreciate Salisbury's contention that knowledge about the Soviet team (SMERSH) finding the bodies of the Fuehrer and Eva Braun represented something new. "These facts have been known, and in print since 1956," he countered, "when I published, in the third edition of my book a full and circumstantial account of the Russian investigation and its sequel."[5]

The list of those who doubted the veracity of the autopsy grew. In its official history of World War II, the United States Army asserted flatly, "Hitler shot himself with a pistol. The evidence that he shot himself appears to be conclusive, despite a report by a former Soviet intelligence officer that Hitler bit on a cyanide capsule." A West German television program in November 1971 questioned whether the Soviets had ever found Hitler's partially cremated body. German viewers saw an X-ray picture of Hitler's teeth taken by one of his doctors, Giesing, in September 1944.

The photo, proclaimed Giesing, who appeared on the program with the former American prosecutor at the Nuremberg trials, Robert Kempner, differed radically from the jaws described by the Soviets. Giesing and Kempner also contended that Hitler had two testicles, rather than one as asserted by the Russians. The West German historian, Werner Maser, who published Giesing's X-ray photo of Hitler's head and described it, explained such doubts about the teeth and corpse allegedly found by the Russians:

> In the original (though less so in the above reproduction) the steel pin in the lower right incisor is plainly evident. The false teeth in the lower jaw of the corpse, believed by the Russians to be Hitler's were not attached to the lower right incisor. Similarly the dentition of their corpse differed materially from that of Hitler, both in the number of the teeth and in the way the bridge was held in place of the upper jaw.[6]

And maintaining that Hitler had undergone numerous checks of his testicles and genitalia, Maser insisted that the Fuehrer "had possessed both testicles." Showing that a professional historian could also deal in rumor, he quoted Guensche as alleging that the missing genital gland had been removed by Hitler's loyal followers before the Russians had arrived at the bunker. But for what purpose? To disguise the dictator's remains? To keep it as a relic for future Nazis to venerate? As if to imply that conventional sexuality required two testicles, Maser declared: "There is no doubt about the fact that Hitler's sexual life was normal." But more important, Maser, like Bezymensky and some other writers about Hitler, seemed to have a political message. Had the Fuehrer's policies of aggressive nationalism and expansion also been "normal"? Maser apparently thought as much, by closing his analysis with an appeal for German unification and a condemnation of East Germany.

Others saw the autopsy report not only as a weapon of propaganda, but as a final chapter in the bizarre mystery surrounding Hitler's fate. "Now suspicion has become certainty," said *Der Spiegel*, convinced Hitler had died of poison. "Old and new Nazis in the Federal Republic wanted to compose from Hitler's death an anti-Communist hero epic," commented the left-wing Berlin journal, *Die Weltbuehne.* "The publication of the autopsy report destroyed the myth. It has clarified how cowardly and wretchedly Hitler slunk away from life, totally in accord with his character and the fascist system."

What became the most powerful argument for the autopsy appeared in the fall of 1972 at the international meeting of forensic sciences, held in Scotland. Reidar Sognnaes, a professor of anatomy and oral biology at the University of California at Los Angeles, produced evidence that Hitler had perished and that the Soviets had autopsied the right body. Sognnaes drew on German, American, and Soviet sources. He had studied at length the autopsy findings and the photographs of Hitler's dental bridgework and of some of his natural teeth still in the lower jawbone, published by Bezymensky. An analysis of the photos, he said, revealed that "in the lower jaw, several of the natural teeth were remarkably well-preserved, being attached to the charred remnants of the mandible." He also found significant from Bezymensky's book a Soviet pathologist's sketch of the teeth and tooth replacements of Hitler's upper and lower jaws, accompanied with annotations made by Heusemann.

Sognnaes relied as well on the interrogation report from 1945 of Blaschke, Hitler's dentist. This included the dentist's careful description of Hitler's teeth (complete with diagrams), a history of the Fuehrer's dental treatment, and a discussion of Hitler's final dental examination in mid-February 1945 in the Chancellery. Also crucial for Sognnaes' study had been copies of the X-ray plates of Hitler's head, found by the Allies in 1945 among the records of the Fuehrer's doctor, Morell, and misfiled in the National Archives in Washington, D.C., until Sognnaes discovered them in 1972. Disagreeing with Giesing's viewpoint that the X-rays proved the Russians had not found Hitler's remains, Sognnaes stated that they presented "excellent odontological forensic evidence for identifying Hitler."

He pointed out that the X-rays showed two of the most characteristic features of Hitler's dentistry. One, a "window crown on the maxillary left incisor," had been mentioned by Blaschke to American interrogators in 1945. The other, "a telephone bridge in the lower right jaw," Sognnaes said, "is very clearly seen in several of the X-rays and is in harmony with the snapshots of the jaw fragment reproduced in the Russian autopsy report." Sognnaes was certain of his proof:

> The accumulated evidence now provides definite odontological proof that Hitler did in fact die, and that the Russians did indeed recover and autopsy the right body . . . The individual identified by means of the 1945 Hitler files located in the U.S. National Archives in 1972, is the same person as that whose 1945 autopsy report was published in 1968 on the basis of the previously unknown documents from Soviet Archives of 1945.[7]

Unlike the mixed reaction that had greeted the British report in 1945 declaring Hitler dead and the publication of the Russian autopsy, Sognnaes' work received sweeping acclaim, except for irreconcilables like Giesing and Maser. It authenticated what the world had strongly suspected, but refused to admit, since the end of the war: Adolf Hitler had died in his bunker on April 30, 1945, and the Russians found and identified his remains a few days later. "It is irrefutable," the Paris paper, *L'Express,* said of the study. Sognnaes also persuaded the American psychohistorian, Peter Loewenberg, who commented, "The accuracy of the Soviet identification of Hitler's body was conclusively established from three independent sources—German, American, and Soviet—by leading forensic dentists." Even Ladislas Farago, the professional Nazi hunter who claimed in 1974 to have found Bormann living amidst a "Fourth Reich" of former Nazis in Latin America, admitted that Sognnaes had "resolved once and for all the lingering mystery of Hitler's death."[8]

Further testimony suggesting that Hitler had been physically unable to escape Berlin in April 1945 strengthened this already formidable scientific evidence. Albert Speer, Hitler's capable Munitions and Armaments Minister who had visited the Fuehrer a last time in the Fuehrerbunker on the night of April 23-24, 1945, described him as "empty, burned out, lifeless." Speer, after having been released in 1966 from a Berlin prison where he had lived since the Nuremberg trials, discussed his last meeting with Hitler at length. "Believe me, Speer," Hitler had told him, as heavy Soviet artillery fire could be heard outside the besieged bunker, "it is easy for me to end my life. A brief moment and I'm freed of everything, liberated from the painful existence."

Goebbels' final diary notes from February and March 1945, which had been seized by the Red Army in Berlin, confirmed this. Three decades later, the Soviets released them for publication in the West. On no less than five separate occasions during March, the Minister had lamented about Hitler's declining health, noting on the 30th, "I have never seen his hand so shaky as during this conversation. It is truly saddening to me to see the Fuehrer in such a bad physical state." Three days before, he had recorded his leader's decision to stay in the heart of the Goetterdaemmerung he had created, and perish. Regarding the role of Nazi officials next to the Fuehrer in the destruction of the Jews, Goebbels left the most open confession yet. "Anyone in a position to do so should kill these Jews off like rats," he wrote on March 13. "In Germany, thank God, we have already done a fairly complete job. I trust that the world will take its cue from this."[9]

Several new witnesses from the bunker scene appeared, adding their versions to the long string of testimony since 1945. Johannes Hentschel had been the chief electrician for the Chancellery and its bunker, and the last German to leave the underground fortress alive on May 2, 1945. Captured by the Russians, he spent the next ten years in a prison. "The garden looked like a cemetery during a gravediggers' strike," the aging Hentschel said in recalling what he had seen as he left the shelter that morning. "Bodies lay around in unnatural, dislocated positions, with heads cut off and bowels ripped out, and here and there an arm and a leg." He had recognized only the corpses of Goebbels and his Frau, who "were not burnt, only singed." Of Hitler, Eva Braun, and others from the last days, he saw nothing. Not even a Hitler look-alike, which the Russians claimed to have uncovered later in the garden? "No," Hentschel replied firmly. "I have never seen a Hitler double, neither dead nor living. And I strongly doubt that Adolf Hitler ever saw one."

Ernst-Guenther Schenck, another who had ended the war in the ill-fated Chancellery ruins, had also spent a decade in Russian jails. A former SS doctor, Schenck had been called in mid-April 1945 to work in a makeshift hospital in the cellar under the Chancellery, about a hundred and fifty meters from Hitler's bunker. He vividly remembered being called to the Fuehrer's sanctum late in the evening of April 29, where he had met Hitler for the first time. "My initial reaction on meeting Adolf Hitler face to face," he said, "was to snap to attention and salute. I was a mere colonel in a not very presentable uniform; he was still Fuehrer, Chancellor and Supreme Commander-in-Chief of the Armed Forces. My whole body seemed to freeze. A chill went up and down my upper spine."

Soon, however, Schenck had looked at Hitler with a doctor's eye. The pathetic man he saw bore little resemblance to the former, mesmerizing idol of the masses so familiar to millions. "I knew, of course, that this was Adolf Hitler and no double," he observed.

> Today I can see him there still, although the whole scene lasted only about four, maybe five minutes. . . .
>
> I was profoundly shocked, and reacted, I suppose, as any doctor would have, not without sympathy. And yet it was far too late, in more ways than one, for any mortal doctor. At fifty-six, the Fuehrer was a palsied, physical wreck, his face wrinkled like a mask, all yellow and gray. The man, I am sure, was senile, without the dignity of silver hairs.[10]

After his audience with Hitler, Schenck had stayed in the bunker into the early morning of April 30, talking and drinking with Guensche, Krebs, Baur, Rattenhuber, Kempka, and others. While on his way to one of the shelter's toilets, he had walked past Hitler's quarters and seen the Fuehrer, sitting at a small round table, talking intently with his most trusted former surgeon and now a doctor in the Chancellery hospital, Werner Haase. They did not notice Schenck, who watched Hitler closely for the second time within two hours:

> It was pitiful. His flabby left hand, in which he was clasping his steel-rimmed spectacles, was also clutching the table. His whole left arm, up to the shoulder, was trembling and, now and then, shuddering. This arm kept tapping the table rhythmically. To brace himself, he had wrapped both his left calf and foot around one leg of the table. This leg was throbbing, shaking. He could not control it.

Now, most doctors would agree with me, I think, that these are the classic symptoms of paralysis agitans, what in English I believe you call Parkinson's disease. If my quick diagnosis was correct, this meant that Hitler, even had he lived, would in a very few years have been a hopeless cripple, able to gaze only at the ground.[11]

Later, Schenck learned from Haase, who himself suffered from tuberculosis, what his long conversation with the Fuehrer had been about. Less than an hour after Hitler's death on the afternoon of April 30, Haase told his fellow physician that he and the Fuehrer had discussed the most foolproof method of suicide. Haase, apparently the last doctor to counsel and serve the dictator, despite the many other physicians Hitler had kept around, recommended to him that he shoot and poison himself simultaneously. To that end, Haase had supposedly been the one to poison Hitler's dog, Blondi, in order to assure the Fuehrer of the poison's effectiveness. He had also given Hitler careful instructions on the pistol-and-poison procedure of self-destruction. "Place the muzzle of the revolver directly at your right temple, right-angled at eyebrow level," Haase said. "Then squeeze the trigger and bite into the cyanide capsule at the same time." Despite the probability that such an immediate, point-blank blast from a 7.35 caliber Walther pistol would have blown away an entire side of Hitler's cranium (something none of his aides like Linge or Axmann had reported seeing), Schenck appeared persuaded by Haase that Hitler had ended it all in this way. What had happened to Haase? Already weak and ailing, he apparently died in a Soviet prison.

Such revelations indicated that it would have been physically impossible for Hitler to have fled Berlin in the last hours of the fighting. They substantiated, at least in the sense of suggesting he had not lived beyond the war, the autopsy findings and work of the dental forensic experts. Despite such evidence, only a couple of Western writers could bring themselves to admit the validity of the autopsy. James O'Donnell, the first bureau chief for *Newsweek* in Germany after the war, concluded from the testimony of Schenck and others that Hitler had both poisoned and shot himself.[12]

Robert Waite, an historian in America who published a psychobiography of Hitler in 1977, thought that the autopsy had proven Hitler a monorchid (i.e., having one testicle), which explained to Waite's satisfaction the Fuehrer's sexual perversions. He offered more psychological grounds than anyone that suggested Hitler had a masochistic, coprophilic urge and other abnormal inclinations. Given Hitler's continual concern about his scrotum and his lifelong habit in moments of tension of covering it protectively with folded hands, Waite stated, he believed the testimony of Linge that he had discovered Hitler in the death room with his hands folded carefully in his lap. The Fuehrer, said Waite, took poison and then someone, but not Linge or Guensche, as the Russians assumed, had shot him.

Who, then, had pulled the trigger? Eva Braun, replied Waite. And why? The answer, surmised the historian from Williams College, lay in Hitler's psyche. He did not trust the poison he swallowed. Indeed, Waite continued, Hitler had never been able to trust people. And in his hour of defeat and destruction, with his nation, army, and beloved SS having failed him, "there was only one person he could rely upon" to perform the *coup de grace*. Not Guensche, Linge, or Bormann, all members of the SS, but Eva Braun. "She was a woman of courage who had flown into a doomed city to be with him; she had demonstrated her obedience by fulfilling his every wish and his most unusual sexual demands; she was a sportswoman who knew how to handle pistols," said Waite.

Linge thought Hitler himself had fired the shot which entered his left temple and exited from his right. But the Fuehrer was not left-handed, his hand shook so badly that he could not control it, and Linge and others had recalled that blood had trickled out of his right temple, not the left. This indicated the bullet had only entered from the left, Waite judged, "if the shot were made an inch or two away from Hitler's skull—as would probably have been the case if Eva Braun-Hitler had shot him." A shot fired with the muzzle pushed tightly against the skull, he added, "would have produced a gaseous recoil, leaving a large hole at the point of entry and probably pulling portions of the brain out with it."

Thus, if Hitler had been found sitting upright on the sofa and with his hands resting neatly on his knees, or folded over his crotch, it appeared unlikely he had shot himself. Waite discounted the possibility that Hitler had been shot in the mouth, mainly because of the Russian autopsy, which had found no sign of a wound in the oral cavity, but mentioned discovering there glass shards from a cyanide ampule. The historian described the Fuehrer's death:

> Thus, we conjecture, that at about 3:30 on the afternoon of 30 April 1945, Adolf Hitler swallowed a lethal dose of cyanide, clasped his hands over his crotch, and waited for his dutiful bride who, following his orders, shot him through the left temple either with her own 6.35 Walther pistol or with his 7.65. She then tucked her feet beneath her as she liked to do when listening to phonograph records, took poison herself, and died seated beside the man she loved.
>
> Hitler's body was badly burned but not completely consumed. Apart from the evidence of the Russian autopsy, there is another reason for believing that the bodies were not totally destroyed. Linge stresses the lack of effective planning and the confusion surrounding the whole incident.[13]

Except for Waite and O'Donnell, almost all Western writers and scholars refused to accept, and some even to mention, the Soviet autopsy. John Toland, author of a best-selling biography of Hitler, also criticized the conclusions of Sognnaes, the dental professor. But instead of addressing himself to Sognnaes' thesis, which stated that Hitler had died and the Russians had autopsied the correct corpse, Toland attacked him on a point Sognnaes never stressed: that the dictator had poisoned himself. Other Fuehrer biographers, like Robert Payne, dismissed entirely the autopsy and its verification by arguing that the Russians "have produced no satisfactory evidence."

Nor has any West German account of Hitler acknowledged the significance of the autopsy and the tide of memoirs and histories published in the Soviet Union after 1959. Juergen Thorwald's standard work on the end of the war, revised and updated in 1975, completely ignored the Russian material. Joachim Fest, in his monumental study of Hitler, attacked the "contradictions in the Soviet story," and contended that politics motivated the Russians:

> These contradictions tend to indicate that the Soviet version of Hitler's suicide has a political coloration. It sounds like a last echo of the attempts constantly made during Hitler's lifetime to refute him by belittling him, as though a certain mentality could not bear to concede

abilities and strength to the morally reprehensible. It was the story of the Iron Cross or his gifts as political tactician or statesman all over again: he was now begrudged the courage required for the obviously sterner death by a bullet.[14]

Whereas the doubts about what had happened to the Fuehrer had centered for two decades on the mysterious circumstances surrounding his fate in Berlin in 1945, the division of opinion in academic circles today is more inspired by international politics and rivalries. The question of how he committed suicide has become a reflection of the principal attitude that arose from the war, which divides the world conveniently into "democracy and communism," "God and heathen," and "good and evil."

To dispute the sacred view of Trevor-Roper and the British in favor of the "Communist version," is traitorous in the West. Only three decades after the deadliest war in history, scholars like Maser, and to a lesser extent Fest, defend Hitler in the question of how he died. Their Hitler was "normal" and capable of bravery. In Maser's view, the dictator also stood for admirable political goals like a powerful, unified Germany and the battle against Communism. Fest, too, seems sympathetic to the idea that Hitler had acted as a protector of Germany and Europe from mighty alien forces—a "'soulless' American capitalism, on the one hand, and 'inhuman' Russian Bolshevism on the other hand."

The same applies to the Russians. They blindly insist Hitler poisoned himself and departed the world a coward, yet ignore the remark in their own autopsy saying that part of the dead Fuehrer's skull could not be found. They intended the release of the autopsy to discredit neo-Nazism and to recall for the world Germany's historic aggressiveness toward the east. What ensures that this controversy will persist is that the "friend-enemy" ideology governing our contemporary world rests as much on myth as on truth. But one of the myths is no longer whether or not Hitler survived—it is the belief that the Western and Russian interpretations of his fate not only cannot be reconciled, but cannot be harmonized.

12

Epilogue

Till a decade ago, whenever a Sunday paper ran short of a sensational headline or someone in Rio de Janeiro wished to make the front page, up popped the allegation that Hitler still lived. Even droopy parties could receive new life if their hosts suddenly announced that "the Fuehrer" had been seen that morning in Caracas, Buenos Aires, or Tokyo. People spotted him without a mustache, his hair dyed red, a patch over one eye. The man-on-the-street, oblivious to Trevor-Roper and Bezymensky, but familiar with his favorite magazine or newspaper, imagined such stories might be true.

As late as 1969, German authorities still arrested Hitler "look alikes." Incredibly, one Albert Pankla had been detained 300 times by mistake since 1945. Pankla, a retired German miner and the unfortunate Hitler "double," proclaimed on his eightieth birthday that he was "not a retired Fuehrer." Wearing his mustache and hair much like the onetime dictator, Pankla told the police and press, "I'm fed up with being taken for the other fellow." The press loved the story. "No, it's not Adolf," laughed a headline in the London *Daily Mail,* "it's Albert."

By the 1970s, Hitler too would have been in his eighties. It seems impossible that anyone could think him alive or that he had survived the war. Not only was he in wretched health by the time of his last (fifty-sixth) birthday in 1945, but he had been missing and presumed dead by most Allied authorities for nearly thirty years. And despite the multitude of theories about his alleged escape in 1945 to Latin America, the Antarctic, and other corners of the world, he had not reappeared. Except for the gruesome description of his scorched remains in the Russian autopsy report, no serious trace of him had been found.

Some who had believed in his survival, like the American Gospel preachers, Herbert and Garner Ted Armstrong, revised their thinking.[1] Since the war, they had warned their followers in the Worldwide Church of God that Hitler had not died, but had wriggled out of the Allied grasp in 1945 and gone to Argentina. He would return by 1972 to unite Europe, they had prophesied, create a new Empire with the help of the modern anti-Christ, the Pope, and seek world domination. Either for tactical reasons or because they ceased to believe Hitler could still be living, they abandoned this idea in favor of the view that the European Common Market was the Roman Papal Empire resurrected, with, of course, Germany at its head.

Yet the myth of Hitler's survival, in spite of the towering evidence amassed since 1945 that he died in his underground hideout in Berlin, continues to fascinate us. We remain in the throes of the "Hitler wave" that began nearly two decades ago. The volume of publications, films, and television documentaries on the Fuehrer and the war is rapidly reaching unmanageable proportions. About his fate, we know both too much and too little: too much about his last days and moments in the Fuehrerbunker, too little about how precisely he ended it all. Although we have a mountain of testimony from near witnesses, plus an autopsy, no one can say for certain *how* he committed suicide. While this may be irrelevant alongside our knowledge that he in fact died, in this day of technology and science, there is an obsession with knowing exactly what he did to remove himself from humanity.

Perhaps it is this piece of the puzzle, still missing, that allows the myth to live on, whether it be in magazines, books, films, or television. Indeed, its entertainment appeal is equally important. As one historian has recently noted, there is a Hitler industry: "Adolf Hitler sells." This is as true of his death or alleged survival as of most other aspects of his life and career. How he is pictured, whether as dying or having outlasted the war, is significant for its influence on the public's view of who he was and what he did. Did he die like a coward, full of fear and self-pity? Did he face death like a hero? Or was he clever and superhuman enough to have sneaked through the huge Russian net that had surrounded him at the last?

That he had masterminded a plot to throw the world off his tracks, revealing again his unique evil genius, is a dangerous theme that remains with us. It is now the preserve mainly of the entertainment industry, and thereby seemingly harmless enough on the surface. But by ignoring the "fact" of Hitler's death, such depictions, wittingly or not, leave the impression for present and future generations that Hitler, although the worst mass murderer in history, had been a sort of superman who fooled the world one final time. It is possible in these scenarios that he could become a hero of the darker side of the human soul, that of the animal and the beast. As with much of the "Hitler wave," the popular and marketable accounts of the Fuehrer's fate romanticize him, disregarding completely historical truth.

Most disturbing is the erroneous view the stories seem to leave of Hitler. His alleged survival against impossible odds, they imply, is proof of something nearly inhuman and godlike. This is the kind of myth-making that could potentially spark an unconscious desire among some for a "new Hitler"—a charismatic and legendary figure who could lead a mass protest against oppressive evils like Communism or decadent Western culture. In this regard, a recent survey of what children in West Germany know about Hitler raised many eyebrows, because of the ignorance and confusion the youth displayed.

Dieter Bossmann, a Flensburg high school teacher, made the study, and found that Hitler had become a dim silhouette of the past for the average German youngster. Of 2,070 essays on "What I Have Heard About Adolf Hitler," written by students aged fourteen to sixteen, Bossmann considered only four to be adequate responses. He found most of the compositions "appalling," he said. One student wrote that Hitler was born between 1920 and 1925 and "played a leading role in getting Germany back on its feet after World War II." "Hitler was our old Fuehrer," said another. "He did not allow young people to wear their hair long." Yet another wrote that "aside of his many bad deeds, Adolf Hitler also did some good things, such as building the first autobahn."

And what did they think had happened to Hitler? "In the war he hid himself and just gave orders," one student wrote. "When another meeting took place, and the bad situation was made known, he said, 'I'll be back in a moment.' In the room next door, they heard a shot.

When they came in, it was too late. They pulled him out and packed him in his bunker. But it could be that he fled and is running around in Russia somewhere—out of his mind." Another youngster declared, "He shot himself. Hitler was married."

A survey in 1975 of all ages of West Germans, taken by the weekly magazine *Stern,* revealing that nearly 40 percent thought Hitler had been "one of the greatest German statesmen," is equally disconcerting. As previous polls indicated, the percentage has risen steadily since 1964.[2] As a small part of this "second coming of Adolf Hitler," in the words of the American magazine *Argosy,* there appeared stories of what television, Hollywood, and the press believed had happened to him at the end of the war. The American film, *Hitler: The Last Ten Days,* which did not show, but implied, that Hitler shot himself, achieved the most accuracy. It starred Alec Guinness and told the story of Gerhard Boldt, a military officer in the Fuehrerbunker till a few hours before the suicide.

While Guiness earned ample plaudits for his capturing of Hitler's mannerisms, the film disappointed serious students of Nazi history. It failed to deepen our understanding of Hitler, how he seized power in Germany, and why. "The true Hitler does not allow itself to be squeezed into this scheme," commented the *Neue Zuercher Zeitung.* "What the audience is presented with is an ever wilder, narrow-minded fellow, housed in a macabre underworld, persecuted by fantastic delusions, an unreal caricature—and was this the man before whom millions had trembled?" Perhaps. *Hitler: The Last Ten Days* illustrated what had been known in varying degrees since 1945. The Nazi dictator had faced death like both a demon and a human, at times insane with self-pity, fear, and despair, yet rational enough to plan and execute coldly his self-murder and that of his new bride.

If some in the entertainment world have sought the truth, others continue to exploit the myth, menacing as it is. In a "special collector's edition" published in 1977, the *Police Gazette* printed once more its series of sensational "Hitler is alive" stories, which its barber shop and drugstore readers had carefully followed two decades earlier. Hitler's escape, the magazine proclaimed, "is an episode of World War II that excites the imagination of today's generation." Not bothering to mention either Trevor-Roper or the Russian autopsy of Hitler's remains, the *Gazette* insisted, "The *important fact* is that Adolf Hitler's body *was never found—only corpses dressed in Hitler's clothes.*"[3]

The past decade has witnessed several other contributions to the myth of his survival. A recent novel (and now a movie) of death and the science of heredity, *The Boys From Brazil,* weaves a story about Josef Mengele, the notorious doctor and "angel of death" at Auschwitz, who escaped to Latin America after the war and tried to create genetic reproductions of Hitler. To save the Aryan race, Mengele had experimented with Hitler's skin cells while in hiding to reproduce ninety-four young boys who were not the Fuehrer's sons, as the evil doctor explained, "but another himself [Hitler], not even a carbon copy but another original." In the final, dramatic scene, as both Mengele and Yakov Liebermann, the aging Nazi hunter who had been pursuing the war criminal, die in a violent confrontation, Mengele described his diabolical scheme:

> He's [Hitler's] alive. This album is full of pictures of him, ages one through thirteen. The boys are exact genetic duplicates of him. . . . Exact genetic duplicates. They were conceived in my laboratory, and carried to term by women of the Auiti tribe; healthy, docile creatures with a businesslike chieftain. The boys bear no taint of them; they're pure Hitler, bred entirely from his cells. He allowed me to take half a liter of his blood and a cutting of skin from his ribs—we were in a biblical frame of mind—on the sixth of January 1943, at Wolf's Lair.[4]

An Austrian writer, Werner Brockdorff, has alleged that he spent "twenty years studying the sources and traveling in many lands on different continents" to show how Hitler and other prominent Nazis had outsmarted the Allies and escaped. Much of Brockdorff's story had a common ring. Hitler had not really died in the bunker, he said, but a double, created by Stumpfegger and Bormann, had perished in his place. Meanwhile, the Fuehrer and Eva Braun had fled through West Berlin to a plane, which carried them to Flensburg. From there, a submarine had taken them to Ireland and across the Atlantic by December 1945 to the coast of Argentina.

Bormann had looked after the Fuehrer's every wish, said Brockdorff, having stockpiled money and purchased some of the best land in Argentina during the war. The deposed Hitler lived sumptuously in a "miniature Berghof" that "resembled Berchtesgaden," surrounded by "peasant houses in which the guards lived." Brockdorff's imagination seemed unlimited, as he described Hitler's comfortable retirement: "The course of his day included sleeping until 11:00, looking at political reports after lunch, taking a walk, and in the evening in enthusiastic monologues for his friends until late in the night, much of which was written down." Except for losing his empire, Brockdorff seemed to imagine the Fuehrer still in Germany. And what of Eva Braun and Hitler? "It is asserted," fantasized the writer, "that they were never so happy as after 1945. At the Argentine Berghof she was the woman of the house and respected as such by everyone. She was always near to her husband; in Germany she often never saw him for months at a time."

An innocent piece of historical fiction? Hardly. Brockdorff denied every fact of Hitler's death that had been established since 1945. Instead of telling the truth about the destructive and nihilistic nature of Nazism, which led so many German leaders, including Hitler himself, to commit suicide in their hour of reckoning, he depicted Hitler and his henchmen as shrewd and skillful geniuses at outwitting the enemy. The Allies never defeated Brockdorff's Fuehrer; he broke away from Berlin and lived happily ever after. One realizes the author is not the self-styled Nazi hunter he would have his readers believe.

Aside from glorifying Hitler and Bormann, he gives us another example of how the Fuehrer's fate has become entwined in postwar politics and propaganda. Why had Hitler been able to live unmolested and at ease in Argentina? Brockdorff's political sympathies give us a cue. He is a Pan German nationalist, both anti-Russian and anti-American. Hitler, he proclaimed, had lived under the protection since 1952 of the American intelligence agency, the CIA, which feared that the Fuehrer's "mere existence could call forth an upsurge of national feelings and fascist alternatives to the democracies." In fact, Brockdorff argued, without evidence, "Hitler and his company received regular financial support from the CIA, as long as the secret remained a secret." Of the Russians, he said, they were liars, as their autopsy had clearly revealed.[5]

Other recent accounts alleging the Fuehrer's survival had included a diary and a transcript of tape recordings. Supposedly written by

Hitler, the former detailed his being flown by a mysterious pilot named "Walter" out of Berlin on April 30, 1945, to the mountains of Tibet. Once there, he and Eva Braun had lived until 1947, when the diary stops, in a monastery at the foot of the Himalaya mountains. A copy of tape recordings of the Fuehrer, purportedly made during the final days of his life in the bunker, bore the provocative title, *I am Adolf Hitler.* More authentic from his final moments, however, was a letter, believed to be one of his last signed papers, which went on auction in New York in June 1979. Bids were first expected to start at $50,000, which would have made the letter one of the most expensive documents ever sold. "I shall stay in Berlin," Hitler had written on April 24, 1945, to a German field marshal who had urged him to leave the capital and join Nazi forces in the mountains of Bohemia. But the bid for the letter never materialized. Prospective buyers realized that it only said Hitler would remain in the capital and that it had been typewritten.

The survival legend has also persisted through the stories of more "Hitler children." The newest of these sagas is a novel, *The Fuehrer Seed.* It is the account of the rise to power in West Germany of Kurt Hauser, who eventually learns he is really Kurt Hitler, son of the Nazi tyrant and Eva Braun. The young Hauser, first as candidate for mayor of West Berlin and then as Germany's apparent man of destiny, decides (after the astonishing revelation of his identity by Bormann, hiding in South America) to follow in his father's footsteps.

Even a professional historian, whom one might assume would be above indulging in such fantasies, has fallen prey to the idea of Hitler's return through one of his children. Werner Maser, the West German historian and Hitler biographer, set Europe buzzing in November 1977 by claiming to have discovered an illegitimate son of the Fuehrer living in France. Although never providing proof, Maser identified the "son" as Jean Marie Loret, an unemployed railroad worker, supposedly born in 1918 to Hitler, then a corporal in a German regiment stationed in World War I France, and a French peasant girl named Charlotte. The boy had been placed in an orphanage, stated Maser, and became during World War II a ranking French police official who worked closely with the Gestapo. Only in 1948 had Loret learned the shocking identity of his father which, according to the German historian, had ruined the son's family and marriage.

Maser, having become obsessed with proving the normality of Hitler's sexual life and disputing the Russian autopsy report that had discussed Hitler's monorchism, had no full documentation for his outrageous assertion. He could only relate that he had first come across Loret's path in 1965, when his research had taken him to the small French village of Wavrin. There, he said, elderly residents still recalled Charlotte, her German soldier, and later her infant son. After locating Loret, a long search into the Frenchman's past had convinced the historian that Hitler had been Loret's father. "The resemblance between Loret and Hitler is striking," Maser declared. "Particularly when Loret takes his glasses off, though of course he has no mustache. Still, he is his father's son."

There are others, similar to Maser, who continue to receive a twisted enjoyment from speculating on the sex life of the Fuehrer and Eva Braun. Totally unfounded have been claims by a former SS member that he had bedroom movies of the couple, filmed secretly by the Elite Guard at Eva Braun's orders for her protection, should her lover's enchantment with her wane. The German-born movie queen, Marlene Dietrich, successfully blocked in March 1977 the premiering of a film, *Adolf and Marlene,* which pretended to show explicit scenes of her meeting with the dictator at his Bavarian retreat during the war. Rumors had once abounded that Hitler had a crush on the actress, but she hated both him and Nazism and fled Germany during his regime.

Television, too, has discovered the myth. One program showed the British detective group, the "New Avengers," seeking to stop a gang of Nazis on a Scottish island from bringing the Fuehrer back to life. According to the plot, the nearly dead Hitler had been airlifted out of Berlin at the end of the war and kept in a coma or inanimate till a doctor had decided to bring him to life. In an old fashioned gunbattle, the Avengers shot the Nazis. And in the center of the fireworks, bullets riddled Hitler's coffin, killing him once and for all.[6]

What is encouraging about the future use of the Hitler escape stories (or his return in some form) is their potential for teaching us about ourselves and contemporary issues that affect us. An example is *The Trial of Adolf Hitler,* a novel published in 1978 by Philippe van Rjndt.[7] After having slipped away from his bunker and the flames of Berlin in April 1945, and reaching a tiny Bavarian village where he is able to hide for the next quarter of a century, Hitler is imagined by

Rjndt walking into the Bavarian Prosecutor's Office on April 30, 1970, and surrendering himself. What ensues in this thought-provoking story is an enormous international trial, held at the United Nations with judges from the United States, the Soviet Union, West Germany, Israel, and England.

The charges against Hitler in the trial are almost routine. A few incidents and scenes are presented to document what everyone knows—that he had been responsible for more crime and violence, more human suffering, than anyone else in history. At the end, when Hitler is executed by a lone Israeli paratrooper on a small, abandoned Pacific island, the reader feels that the punishment is fully justified but that it hardly solves the basic problems raised in the book. The evil Hitler did, says Rjndt, lives after him. It exists in the neo-Nazis, planning and organizing for a Fourth Reich; in the African, Arab, and Latin American nations where some of the authoritarian and military values of Hitler receive strong support; in Russia, which has preserved much of Hitler's totalitarian spirit and style; and in the United States, which ended the World War in an atomic holocaust and borrowed a large part of the Nazi espionage system for their own use in the Cold War.

The mystery surrounding Hitler's fate will doubtless never be completely solved. Few surprises, if any, remain. That he died, is certain. But exactly how? The controversy that has raged over this subject since 1945 is another illustration among many, including the much broader upsurge of interest in Hitler since the 1960s (i.e., the "Hitler wave"), that the Fuehrer's presence never vanishes. His life is the basic trauma of our century, the wound through which our humanity bleeds. The idea that he outlasted the war and cheated his enemies of their just revenge, a belief that has persisted through three decades, reminds us again that myths do not die easily and that truth is rarely given birth without a struggle. Neither myth nor truth can be laughed away by irresponsibility. Only if Hitler is moored in human reality will he stay dead. If not, he shall remain as he has been since 1945: a nightmare of the past that will forever haunt us.

Yet, ironically, there is much evidence that like most legends, the world not only enjoys the myth of Hitler's survival, it needs it. The Russians especially treasure it. Ever vigilant toward a potential revival of Nazism, they analyze the Western curiosity about Hitler as an effort to "humanize" the tyrant and make him solely responsible for fascism, instead of seeing the latter as a result of capitalist society. Noting the Fuehrer had been dead twenty-nine years, the Communist youth paper, *Komsomalskaya Pravda,* declared in 1974: "Nothing essential can be added to his vile biography. It is not without purpose that Hitler is taken out of the mud. Literary and biographical notes are being used to make the public ready again for accepting the idea of a military coup. It explains the desire to revive the idea of a dictator."

In the West, the stories of Hitler possibly being alive, or returning to terrorize humanity, resemble the many returns of the Frankenstein monster. Just as numerous sequels were made to the original 1931 Frankenstein movie (even though the monster, played by Boris Karloff, died horribly in the flames of the old mill), so since 1945 have sequels to the Hitler survival myth appeared in the form of fanciful tales about Eva Braun, the "bride of Hitler," and the different "children of the Fuehrer." As with Frankenstein's monster, a terrifying creature formed from dead people, Hitler is to us *of* humanity, but not humanity—the arch killer with a criminal's brain. In 1933, in fact, as the Nazi leader had risen to power in Germany, a British writer compared him to the movie monster.[8]

Why this infatuation with the murderous Nazi beast? We seem to need him for the perverse entertainment that thinking about and seeing him can give us. Evil intrigues us equally as much as goodness, perhaps even more. The myth that Hitler survived reflects the latent animal in us, that failure of spirit and love which is the source of all evil. On the other hand, keeping Hitler "alive," either for political reasons or entertainment, may even symbolize our need to love one another, despite our sins and crimes, in order to live through this world of uncertainty and maintain the humanity which Hitler could not find in himself and which he extinguished in those around him.

It may be true as well that the survival myth has mirrored an unwillingness on the part of the world to allow Hitler to have the peace of death, in light of the mass crimes he perpetrated. The thought that he possibly outlived the war could also signify an unconscious feeling of the public that world order has not yet been totally restored and that harmony among men and nature has not been achieved. But how could the earth be returned to peace and tranquility when the drug-ridden demagogue and murderer of millions who plunged it into six years of hell had apparently died so easily and escaped so completely the vengeance of his enemies?

Had he been Satan in a human body? The modern anti-Christ? A recent German rock opera titled *Der Fuehrer,* opened with the haunting, unholy sounds of an occult seance in which Hitler, Faust-like, enters into a pact with the Devil. Slowly Germany's bloody history under Hitler, from the burning of the books to the slaughtering of the Jews and misery and destruction of war, unfolds. At the end, in the Fuehrerbunker, the Devil returns to take his prize. Doomed, Hitler suffers the agony each of his enemies has wished for him both during and since the war. As Satan crept closer, Hitler uttered a final, piercing scream, "There, there, over in the corner—it's he, it's he, he's come for me."[9] Our imaginations insist on bringing him back to life so that we may condemn and kill him again and again, the pleasure he so fiendishly deprived the world in 1945.

Notes

Preface

1. H. R. Trevor-Roper, *The Last Days of Hitler* (3rd ed.; New York: Macmillan, 1965). His study was originally published in 1947, and this third edition appeared first in 1956.

2. The autopsy report was published by the Soviet journalist Lev Bezymensky, *The Death of Adolf Hitler: Unknown Documents from Soviet Archives* (New York: Harcourt, Brace and World, 1968), pp. 44–49. Also, note Werner Maser, *Hitler,* trans. Peter and Betty Ross (London: Allen Lane, 1973), p. 314; and Michael A. Musmanno, *Ten Days to Die* (2nd ed.; New York: MacFadden Books, 1962), p. 216.

3. James P. O'Donnell and Uwe Bahnsen, *Die Katakombe: Das Ende in der Reichskanzlei* (Stuttgart: Deutsche Verlags-Anstalt, 1975), pp. 377-78; and pp. 196-97 above, in this study.

4. See Trevor-Roper's analysis of the Soviet behavior to 1956 in *Last Days of Hitler* (3rd ed.), pp. 36–53.

1.   Myth in the Making

1. A transcript of the famous announcement is in International Military Tribunal, *Trial of the Major War Criminals* (hereafter *TMWC;* Nuremberg, 1947–49), Document No. 444–D, XXXV:116–18; and the mysterious voice episode is recounted in *The New York Times* (hereafter *NYT*), May 2, 1945.

2. Leonardo Blake, *Hitler's Last Year of Power* (London: Andrew Dakers Ltd., 1939), pp. 72–76.

3. *The Gallup Poll: Public Opinion, 1935-1971* (New York: Random House, 1972), I:339.

4. For example, see the photos in *Deutsche Allgemeine Zeitung* (Berlin), September 20, 1944; *Hamburger Fremdenblatt,* July 31, 1944; *NYT,* July 23, 1944; and *Daily Telegraph* (London), December 9, 1944.

5. Transcripts of German radio broadcasts may be found in the *Voelkischer Beobachter* (Munich), published through April 28, 1945; *NYT;* and British Ministry of Information, *News Digest,* Nos. 1744–1747 (EH Series), April 26–30, 1945. The first public admission that Hitler was in Berlin came on April 22, in a radio statement by Hans Fritsche, an official of the German Propaganda Ministry.

6. *Pravda* (Moscow), April 24–25, 1945, quoted in *Moscow News* (London), April 25, 1945. The Allies captured Axmann after the war and showed that he had visited Hitler's underground bunker in Berlin on several occasions during the last days of April. He had been there on April 30 and examined the dead bodies of Hitler and his new wife, Eva Braun. No evidence surfaced that he tried to form a "children's army" in Bavaria (see above, p. 83).

7. An accusation of the Soviet government paper, *Izvestia,* during the second week of April. Such "benevolence," it argued, formed an essential part of Nazi plans to go underground in preparation for another war. "As may be seen from the history of the Reichsbank's gold reserves, the Germans are trying to use the Allied occupational zone for saving foreign-exchange values and army cadres."

8. On the Nazi report of Greim's visit, see *News Digest,* No. 1747 (EH Series), April 30, 1945; and on Goering's resignation, *Voelkischer Beobachter,* April 25-26 and April 28, 1945. Hitler had in fact relieved Goering of his offices, the world learned after the war (see below, pp. 212-13, n.6). Greim received the order from the Fuehrer on April 23 to report to the bunker; he arrived three days later (see above, pp. 77-78, 84). Goering had last seen Hitler in Berlin on April 20.

9. Information about Hitler's poor health had reached the Americans at the beginning of March 1945. The origin of that report had been the SS, commanded by Himmler. SS officials had told the Swiss of Himmler's willingness to meet with Charles Burckhardt, president of the International Red Cross. See United States Department of State, *Foreign Relations of the United States,* 1945 (hereafter *FRUS;* Washington, D.C.: U.S. Government Printing Office, 1967), II:1138.

10. The Soviet reports of their progress later proved to be quite accurate. If anything, their bulletins were a bit conservative. The Red Army's struggle for the inner "citadel" of the city and the continual shelling of the Chancellery had begun on April 27. Bitter house-to-house fighting occurred in the center of Berlin on April 28, and difficult battles were waged the next day in the nearby Grunewald, Reich Sport Field, Anhalter Railroad Station, Potsdamer Platz, and Tiergarten. On April 30 the fighting intensified in the Tiergarten, Friedrichstrasse, Weidendamm Bridge, and Potsdamer Platz, and the Russians took the Reichstag building.

2. Hero's Death or Suicide?

1. British Broadcasting Company (hereafter cited as BBC), *Daily Digest of World Broadcasts and Radio Telegraph Services* (hereafter cited as *Daily Digest*), No. 2, 115–16 (May 1–2, 2–3, 1945); and *Soviet War News* (London), May 3, 1945.

2. Leonard O. Mosley, *Report from Germany* (London: Victor Gollancz Ltd., 1945), p. 99.

3. As, for example, *The Palestine Post* (Jerusalem), May 2, 1945.

4. BBC, *Daily Digest,* No. 2, 116 (May 2–3, 1945).

5. This represented only a sample of the mass American reaction. See the *NYT,* May 2, 4, 1945; *San Francisco Chronicle,* May 5, 1945; and *Los Angeles Times,* May 2, 1945.

6. *News Digest,* No. 1751–53 (EH Series), May 4–7, 1945.

7. According to Bernadotte, who published his memoirs after the war, Eisenhower had the correct version of the talks (see above, p. 70). The Allies revealed after the war how unreliable a witness Schellenberg, captured in Sweden, had been (see above, p. 99).

8. Fritsche, later acquitted at Nuremberg and released by the Russians, verified this account. He was the first major Nazi prisoner who had been near Hitler's bunker headquarters in Berlin in the last days to be freed by the Russians (see above, pp. 89–91). The communiques are in BBC, *Daily Digest,* No. 2, 116 (May 2–3, 1945); *Soviet War News,* May 4, 1945; and *NYT,* May 3–5, 1945.

9. *Yank: The Army Weekly,* III, No. 50 (June 1, 1945), 14–19, published "a sample of public opinion on the subject of Hitler's death."

10. Hitler did leave a testament, but copies of it would not be discovered for another six months (see above, pp. 86–88).

11. An ear, nose, and throat specialist, Giesing had in fact attended Hitler after July 20, 1944. But the Allies disproved his testimony that he had last attended Hitler on February 15. He and Brandt had become involved in September 1944 in a conflict with Morell over Hitler's declining health. Morell won and Hitler dismissed Brandt and Giesing from his service (see below, p. 213 n.8). Giesing had X-rays, which he produced long after the war, of Hitler's skull and jawbones. He used the pictures to assert that the Russians had not found Hitler's body, as they claimed in the 1960s (see above, p. 189). Both Morell and Brandt survived the war and became prisoners of the Allies (see note p. 38).

12. This untrue story should not be confused with another account, testified to by numerous witnesses after the war, that Hitler had a complete collapse of confidence during one of his military conferences in the Berlin bunker on April 22.

3. Missing: The Corpse

1. *Pravda,* May 3, 1945, as quoted from Moscow radio; BBC, *Daily Digest,* No. 2, 116 (May 2–3, 1945).

2. *Le Monde* (Paris), May 6–7, 1945; and *Evening Standard* (London), May 4, 1945.

3. BBC, *Daily Digest,* No. 2, 120–21 (May 6–7, 7–8, 1945). Several Western sources after the war proved true the discovery of the large number of suicides in the area of the Reich Chancellery.

4. The Russians later confirmed this report at a news conference on June 6, 1945 (see above, pp. 46–7). Since the bodies were uncovered on May 3–4, it is possible they were the same ones identified by the Russians in 1968 in the autopsy they published on the remains of Hitler and Eva Braun. According to that report, they disinterred Hitler's body from a shallow bomb crater in the garden of the Chancellery and tentatively identified it with witnesses on May 4.

5. The Fuehrerbunker lay fifty feet below the so-called old Chancellery building (Hitler had constructed a new Reich Chancellery during the war) and its garden, and amid other underground bunkers in the government district. Contrary to the lavish portrait of the bunker painted in these days by the Soviets, it could hardly be described as an "underground city." It consisted of eighteen rooms, all small, cramped, and uncomfortable, and a central passage. These included conference rooms, map-room, quarters for Hitler's doctors, a first aid area, and the private apartments of Hitler and Eva Braun. Hitler's comprised a bedroom and a study. The best pictoral and written descriptions of "these miserable underground hutches" (in the words of Hugh Trevor-Roper, the British historian who wrote in 1947 the standard Western account of Hitler's death) are O'Donnell and Bahnsen, *Die Katakombe,* pp. 20–25; and Trevor-Roper's article in *Life,* XXII (March 17, 1947), 106–22.

6. Goering, like most Nazis, had a wild and perverted imagination. He filled his account, the world eventually learned, with self-glorification and inaccuracy. He had fled from Berlin to Berchtesgaden on April 21, after Hitler had singled out him and the Luftwaffe for incompetency. Hitler had not sentenced him to die, but had removed him on April 23 from the multiple offices Goering held. Not long afterward, Goering was arrested. It was Bormann who had ordered the traitorous Reich Marshal "exterminated," whether Hitler authorized the directive has never been shown. Finally, Goering had not mustered the courage to "phone" the Fuehrer from

Berchtesgaden, offering to take power, but had sent Hitler a telegram. The best firsthand account is Karl Koller, *Der letzte Monat* (Mannerheim: Norbert Wohlgemuth Verlag, 1949), pp. 36–70. Koller, a former Luftwaffe chief of staff, had urged Goering to send the telegram to Hitler (pp. 36–37) and had been with the demoted Reich Marshal at the end.

7. See part of Herrgesell's story in Felix Gilbert, ed., *Hitler Directs His War: The Secret Records of His Daily Military Conferences* (New York: Oxford University Press, 1951), pp. ix–xiii; and his statement in *Time,* XXI (May 21, 1945), 40 f.

8. Later research would show that Morell last saw Hitler on April 22, 1945, that he had contributed to the ruin of the Fuehrer's health with his many drugs and injections, and that Brandt and another doctor, Erwin Giesing, had warned Hitler personally of Morell's treatment. Some of Morell's pills, they told the dictator in the fall of 1944, contained poison. But Hitler relied too much on Morell's drugs and no longer listened to reason and arguments. He ousted Brandt and Giesing from his inner circle, and even had Brandt arrested.

9. Quoted in *Le Monde,* May 14–15, 1945.

10. There is a vast literature regarding this aspect of the Cold War. As examples, see Tony Sharp, *The Wartime Alliance and the Zonal Division of Germany* (Oxford: Clarendon Press, 1975), pp. 125-58; John Gimbel, *The American Occupation of Germany: Politics and the Military, 1945–1949* (Stanford: Stanford University Press, 1968), the introductory chapters; John Backer, *The Decision to Divide Germany: American Foreign Policy in Transition* (Durham, N.C.: Duke University Press, 1978); Winston S. Churchill, *Triumph and Tragedy* (Boston: Houghton-Mifflin, 1953), p. 569; and *FRUS,* 1945 (Washington, D.C.: U.S. Government Printing Office, 1968), III:304–5.

11. BBC, *Daily Digest,* No. 2, 122–30 (May 8–17, 1945); *Pravda,* May 6, 1945, and *Izvestia,* May 16, 1945, are quoted in various American newspapers.

12. Robert E. Sherwood, *The White House Papers of Harry L. Hopkins* (London: Eyre and Spottiswoode, 1949), II:880; Charles E. Bohlen, *Witness to History 1929–1969* (New York: Norton, 1973), p. 220; *FRUS,* 1945 (Washington, D.C.: U.S. Government Printing Office, 1960), I:29–30.

13. Accounts of this unofficial press conference are in *NYT,* June 7, 1945; *Evening Standard,* June 6, 1945; *Baltimore Sun,* June 7, 1945; and Trevor-Roper, *Last Days of Hitler* (3rd ed.), p. 54. The Goebbels telegram of May 1 actually said Hitler had died "yesterday"—i.e., on April 30—"at 15.30 hours" (note above, pp. 79, 99–100). The Russian autopsy report published in 1968 concluded that Hitler had died of poison and his body had been found by the Soviets on May 4.

4. "He could have flown away"

1. The best accounts of the press conference are *Evening Standard,* June 9, 1945; *NYT,* June 10, 1945; *Soviet News* (London), June 11, 1945; *Newsweek,* XXV (June 18, 1945), 57–58; Herbert Moore and James W. Barrett, *Who Killed Hitler? The Complete Story of How Death Came to Der Fuehrer and Eva Braun* (New York: Booktab Press, 1947), pp. 137–38; and on the interest of the Allies in the diaries of Hitler's adjutants, mentioned by Zhukov, see Trevor-Roper, *Last Days of Hitler* (3rd ed.), p. 21. Regarding the earlier Soviet admission that the bodies of Goebbels and his family had been "virtually identified," note the *Red Star* announcement quoted on p. 34 above.

2. Suggested by Hugh Trevor-Roper, "The 'Mystery' of Hitler's Death," *Commentary,* XXII (July 1956), 7–8. On Vishinsky's role, see John R. Deane, *The Strange Alliance: The Story of Our Efforts at Wartime Cooperation With Russia* (Blooming-ton, Ind.: Indiana University Press, 1973), pp. 173–76; and Bohlen, *Witness to History,* p. 220.

3. Matthew P. Gallagher, *The Soviet History of World War II: Myths, Memories, and Realities* (New York: Praeger, 1963), pp. 18–19; and Seweryn Bialer, ed., *Stalin and His Generals: Soviet Military Memoirs of World War II* (New York: Pegasus, 1969), pp. 493–94. The American press frequently noted Zhukov's honoring of Eisenhower, e.g., see *San Francisco Chronicle,* May 10, 26, and June 6, 1945.

4. Bernard Law Montgomery, *The Memoirs of Field Marshal The Viscount Montgomery of Alamein K.G.* (Cleveland: World Publishing Co., 1958), pp. 319–21; and the repeated Soviet propaganda charges that week over Moscow radio and in the press, BBC, *Daily Digest,* No. 2, 152–54 (June 7–10, 1945); and *Soviet War News,* June 8, 1945.

5. Copies of the *Red Star* articles and Zhukov's statement, as broadcast by Moscow radio on June 9–10, 1945, are in BBC, *Daily Digest,* No. 2, 154–56 (June 9–12, 1945).

6. *Evening Standard,* June 9, 1945. Apparently even the incredibly thorough Trevor-Roper overlooked the *Red Star* account. See the *Evening Standard*'s criticism of him (June 16, 1950) for failing to cite the Red Army paper in the first two editions of his book, *Last Days of Hitler.*

7. History, as well as the Soviet Union, have vindicated the *Red Star* story; they have not been so kind to Zhukov's press conference. Zhukov and Chuikov later published their memoirs and confirmed the Krebs visit to Chuikov's headquarters on May 1, 1945. See pp. 169–70, 185–86 above.

8. Ladislas Szabo, *Je sais que Hitler est vivant* (Paris: Sfelt, 1947), p. 69. I agree

with Geoffrey Barraclough, "The Nazi Boom," *The New York Review of Books,* XXVI (May 17, 1979), 18, that these and similar stories became "grist to the mill of the Western gutter-press" in the 1950s and 1960s. "Once historians began prying into Hitler's sex life and alleged sexual aberrations," he adds, "anything was permissible, provided it was sordid, scurrilous, and scandalous enough." Chapters eight and nine above cite numerous examples of what he is talking about. But in the summer of 1945, even the "respectable" press published speculation on the sex life of Hitler and Eva Braun, e.g., *Newsweek,* XXV (June 4, 1945), 56–61, and XXV (June 18, 1945), 57–58; and *NYT,* June 12, 1945.

9. See his remarks in *Neue Zuercher Zeitung,* June 12, 1945; and *NYT,* June 12, 1945.

10. Such sensationalism pure and simple, is found in Michael Beauquey and V. Ziegelmeyer, *Le disparu du 30 avril* (Paris: Les Productions de Paris, 1964), pp. 268–69; Johannes von Muellern-Schoenhausen, *Die Loesung des Raetsels Adolf Hitler: Der Versuch einer Deutung der geheimnisvollsten Erscheinung der Weltgeschichte* (Vienna: Verlag fuer Foerderung wissenschaftliche Forschung, 1959), pp. 236–37; and Szabo, *Je sais que Hitler est vivant,* p. 123. Also, see *Soviet News,* June 16, 1945; *NYT,* June 21, 1945; and *The Stars and Stripes* (Paris), June 12, 1945.

11. Moscow's suggestions are in BBC, *Daily Digest,* No. 2, 158–59 (June 13–15, 1945). Also, see *New York Herald Tribune,* June 11, 1945.

12. *Chicago Times,* July 16, 1945; and the other papers.

13. *Le Monde,* July 18, 1945; and *NYT,* July 18, 1945.

5. Death in the Bunker

1. Statement of Karnau, *NYT,* June 21, 1945. Karnau was imprisoned at Nienburg and examined by Canadian and British authorities, which eventually included the English intelligence officer-historian, Trevor-Roper. The latter thought him a key witness who tried to recollect the truth, not tell a preconceived story. Sometimes his memory failed him, however, as when he said he had seen Hitler on the morning of May 1 (the Fuehrer, it would be shown later, died on April 30). The guard persistently affirmed to Trevor-Roper that he saw on the ground outside the bunker the corpses of Hitler and Eva Braun burst suddenly, as if by spontaneous combustion, into flame. This seemed compatible with the version of Erich Kempka, Hitler's chauffeur (see above, pp. 68–9), who also witnessed the crude cremation and testified that Hitler's adjutant, Guensche, had lit the bodies by throwing a burning rag on them from a point invisible to Karnau. The stories of Kempka and Karnau, told independently to Trevor-Roper, were simply two aspects of the same fact.

2. Statement of Kempka, ibid. After his arrest, the former chauffeur underwent

interrogation by both American officers and, later, Trevor-Roper, at Moosburg. Kempka had escaped the bunker with Bormann and others on the night of May 1. They had moved northward along the Friedrichstrasse, and Kempka became one of the few who crossed the river Spree successfully and moved east along the Invalidenstrasse toward Charlottenburg. He hid for a day among Yugoslav women in a railway arch, while the Russians celebrated the fall of Berlin. Captured for a time, he escaped, swam the Elbe river, and achieved American captivity. See Trevor-Roper, *Last Days of Hitler* (3rd ed.), p. 276.

3. *NYT,* June 21, 1945. Kempka had also visited Goebbels and his family to bid them goodbye on the afternoon of May 1, only a few hours before their suicides.

4. Count Folke Bernadotte, *The Curtain Falls: Last Days of the Third Reich,* trans. by Count Eric Lewenhaupt (New York: Knopf, 1945), pp. 105–10, 132; and Brandt's statement, *NYT,* June 22, 1945. Also on Brandt's collision with Morell in the fall of 1944, leading to the former's dismissal from Hitler's court, see above, p. 213 n. 8. Regarding Himmler's negotiations, see above, p. 13.

5. *NYT,* July 31, 1945 (Gorbatov's statement); and *The Times* (London), July 9, 1945 (Bruck's statement). In his memoirs, A. V. Gorbatov, *Years Off My Life: The Memoirs of General of the Soviet Army A. V. Gorbatov,* trans. Gordon Clough and Anthony Cash (New York: Norton, 1965), p. 221, he reaffirmed "Hitler committed suicide."

6. *Soviet News,* July 5, 1945.

7. Isaac Deutscher, *Stalin: A Political Biography* (2nd ed.; New York: Oxford University Press, 1967), pp. 531-32. Stalin's remarks are recorded variously in FRUS, 1945 (Washington, D.C.: United States Government Printing Office, 1960), II:123–24, 126, 526, 538; James F. Byrnes, *Speaking Frankly* (New York: Harper and Brothers, 1947), p. 68; William D. Leahy, *I Was There* (New York: McGraw-Hill, 1950), p. 396; C. R. Attlee, *As It Happened* (New York: Viking Press, 1954), p. 206; and Churchill, *Triumph and Tragedy,* pp. 654–57.

8. John Wheeler-Bennett and Anthony Nicholls, *The Semblance of Peace: The Political Settlement After the Second World War* (New York: Norton, 1974), p. 399; Gallagher, *The Soviet History of World War II,* pp. 3, 23–31; *FRUS, 1945,* III:830, 832, 852–56, 859; Lucius D. Clay, *Decision in Germany* (Garden City: Doubleday, 1950), pp. 104–5; and Earl F. Ziemke, *Battle for Berlin: End of the Third Reich* (New York: Ballantine Books, 1968), pp. 153–57.

9. Discussed at length in *NYT,* September 9, 1945.

10. *Evening Standard,* June 24, 1945; Muellern-Schoenhausen, *Die Loesung des Raetsels Adolf Hitler,* p. 237; *Soviet News,* August 31, 1945; and Eisenhower's

remarks in *NYT,* October 7, 13, 1945. Such stories about Hitler's escape, which remained unproven, often had a tiny element of plausibility. Stumpfegger, it is true, had been a pupil of Gebhardt, and the latter (called by other Nazis a "detestable," corrupt, and selfish intriguer) had served as Himmler's personal doctor. Gebhardt had also carried out experimental operations on Polish girls at the Auschwitz concentration camp. When Hitler fired Brandt in the fall of 1944, Stumpfegger, a competent orthopedic surgeon specializing in the regeneration of bones, replaced him at the Fuehrer's headquarters. He gave total and unconditional loyalty to Hitler and became one of those blind, true believers who remained in the Fuehrerbunker to the end. Careful not to alienate the powerful Morell (who had gained Brandt's removal from Hitler's circle), Stumpfegger had established a surgical station under the Chancellery, adjacent to the bunker.

As shown after the war, Stumpfegger had not gone to Ravensbrueck for his surgical instruments, but to Gebhardt's clinic at Hohenlychen. All of this is detailed in Trevor-Roper, *Last Days of Hitler* (3rd ed.), pp. 131–32, 153, 172, 188, 215. Stumpfegger escaped with Bormann and others from the bunker on the evening of May 1, and died from cyanide poisoning near the Invalidenstrasse Railroad Bridge, north and east of the Chancellery. Remnants of his skeleton, along with those of Bormann, were unearthed in December 1972 by construction workers in West Berlin, and identified by pathologists. See *Frankfurter Allgemeine-Zeitung,* April 12, 1973. Thus, by hardly even the barest thread of implication, storytellers in 1945 claimed Stumpfegger had manufactured a "double" to die in Hitler's stead.

11. Trevor-Roper, *Last Days of Hitler* (3rd ed.), p. 45; and Moore and Barrett, *Who Killed Hitler?, p. 138.*

12. *The Gallup Poll,* I:527.

13. The text of the British statement is in *NYT,* November 2, 1945. By April 28, 1945, as Russian communiques thereafter had revealed, the Twelfth Army, commanded by General Wenck and fighting previously along the Elbe River southwest of Berlin, had been smashed by the Red Army. Hitler had planned since April 21 for Wenck to move toward Potsdam and from there fight his way into the southern part of the capital. But for many days now, the Fuehrer's orders had bore little relation to reality, as he moved imaginary battalions and non-existent formations which naturally never attacked.

14. Ibid.

15. *Time,* XXII (November 12, 1945), 36.

16. Look for these and other such stories in Ray Petitfrère, *Sous le signe du fusil* (Tamines: Duculot-Roulin, 1945); Beauquey and Ziegelmeyer, *Le disparu du 30 avril,* pp. 269–73; Reuben Ainszstein, "How Hitler Died: The Soviet Version," *International Affairs,* XLIII (April 1967), 307; H. R. Trevor-Roper, "Is Hitler Really

Dead?" *Commentary,* XI (February 1951), pp. 124–25; *The New Yorker,* XXI (November 24, 1945), 56–60; and Musmanno, *Ten Days to Die,* pp. 218-19.

17. *Le Monde,* October 19, 1946; and Dwight D. Eisenhower, *Eisenhower's Own Story of the War* (New York: Arco Publishing Co., 1946), pp. 118-19. And on Uschi, see *Sunday Express* (London), November 18, 1945; *Newsweek,* XXVI (November 26, 1945), 48; and Szabo, *Je sais que Hitler est vivant,* p. 72.

6. The Last Days

1. Statement of Axmann in Trevor-Roper, "The 'Mystery' of Hitler's Death," pp. 10–11. Axmann also told interrogators in 1946 that he assumed, though it had not been apparent from Hitler's corpse, that in shooting himself in the mouth, the Fuehrer must have shattered his dental fittings, since otherwise the Russians could not have identified his body. These fittings had in fact been preserved and identified (see above, pp. 70–72). Axmann had escaped from the Fuehrerbunker with Bormann and the others on the night of May 1, and testified that he had seen Hitler's secretary dead near a railroad bridge on the Invalidenstrasse, north of the Chancellery. He had probably been the last survivor of Hitler's court to see Bormann. Axmann then continued on his way alone, finally joining a few Hitler Youth who hid out for six months in the Bavarian Alps.

2. Hitler's breakdown had occurred on April 22 (see above, p. 37). Reitsch's testimony is in Robert E. Work, "Last Days in Hitler's Air Raid Shelter," *The Public Opinion Quarterly,* X (Winter 1946–47), 565–81. Excerpts also appeared in the *News Chronicle* (London), December 28–31, 1945; and *NYT,* December 6, 1945. She has recently revised her story, coloring it with even more pro-Hitler sentiment, in *Hoehen und Tiefen, 1945-77* (Munich: DSZ-Verlag, 1978); and "Mein Erleben im Hitler-bunker," *National-Zeitung* (Munich), July 28, 1978.

3. Probably another accidental error of time on Reitsch's part. Hitler received the report of Himmler's treachery on April 28 (see above, page 77).

4. Trevor-Roper, *Last Days of Hitler* (3rd ed.), pp. 240–41; *The Times* (London), January 1, 1946; and Trevor-Roper, "Is Hitler Really Dead?" pp. 125–27. At the time of their discovery and first publication, some doubted the authenticity of the testaments because of un-German characteristics in the typescript. These were not in the original documents, however, and it became apparent they had been introduced into the photographic reproductions printed in the newspapers by editors who wished to restore the blurred lettering.

5. Trevor-Roper, "Is Hitler Really Dead?" pp. 127–28. Below had been Hitler's Luftwaffe adjutant and served in the Fuehrer's entourage for eight years. One of the many in the Fuehrerbunker who did not relish suicide as a way out of the disaster, Below had asked Hitler on April 29 if he might be permitted to escape the shelter.

Since the Fuehrer had just allowed three other adjutants to leave the bunker to reach Wenck, he sent Below with a postscript of his testament to the Supreme Command of the German Military, by then in Schleswig-Holstein. Below had left at midnight on April 29–30, fleeing along the East-West Axis westward to the Kant Strasse, under Russian fire, and to the Reich Sport Field. There he found the other adjutants (including Gerhard Boldt, see above, pp. 93–95) and journeyed south with them to a bridgehead at Pichelsdorf, sailed down the river Havel, and landed safely on the western bank between Gatow and Kladow. This had become a classic escape route in the final days of Berlin.

6. See the Nuremberg interrogations of Fritsche and Kempka, *TMWC,* XVII:186, 447–54. Also, note Hildegard Springer, ed., *Es sprach Hans Fritsche: Nach Gespraechen, Briefen und Dokumenten* (Stuttgart: Thiele-Verlag KG, 1949), pp. 24–30, 37–39, 50–62; and *The Times* (London), July 4, 1946. Regarding Echtmann's experience with the Russians, see above, p. 72. On Bormann's death, see below, p. 224 n. 19.

7. Semmler had disappeared after April 17, 1945. His wife later published his diary notes; see Rudolf Semmler, *Goebbels—The Man Next to Hitler* (London: Westhouse, 1947), pp. 187–88.

8. Schroeder's statement and Kelley's diagnosis, the latter not always based on historical fact, are in Douglas M. Kelley, *22 Cells in Nuremberg: A Psychiatrist Examines the Nazi Criminals* (New York: Greenberg, 1947), pp. 201–5, 215–18, 224–25, 234–35.

9. Gerhard Boldt, *In the Shelter with Hitler,* trans. by Edgar Stern-Rubarth (London: Citadel Press, 1948), pp. 5–7, 12–31, 41–72. On Boldt's escape route, see above p. 219 n. 5. Also, Boldt erred in his statement that Hitler had made it known on April 21 he would stay in Berlin. This occurred at the stormy military conferences the next day.

10. H. R. Trevor-Roper, *The Last Days of Hitler* (New York: Macmillan, 1947), especially pp. 5–6, 15–26, 28–38, 50–51, 57, 184–85.

11. Ibid., pp. 51–52, 145, 200–201; and on Wenck, pp. 122–23, 152, 162–63, 191, 194. *Life,* XXII (March 17, 1947), 106–22, published a shorter version of the death.

12. Trevor-Roper, *Last Days of Hitler* (1st ed.), pp. 201–203.

13. Ibid., pp. 57–70.

14. Trevor-Roper, "Is Hitler Really Dead?" pp. 120–25; ibid., pp. 52–53; and his article in *The New York Times Magazine,* April 24, 1955.

15. See his introduction to the third edition of *Last Days of Hitler,* pp. 19–20; and

his article, "Is Hitler Really Dead?" pp. 121–22. For the reviews, note *Le Monde,* December 20, 1947; *Evening Standard,* June 16, 1950; *Time* (August 18, 1947), 98–100; *Nation,* CLXV (September 20, 1947), 287; and *New Republic,* CXVII (September 22, 1947), pp. 29–30. Note Heimlich's foreward in Moore and Barrett, *Who Killed Hitler?,* and especially pp. 113–24.

7. Officially Dead

1. Clay's statement is in *NYT,* May 28, 1948. A picture of Noll, showing his remarkable likeness to Hitler, is in *NYT,* January 10, 1950.

2. Muellern-Schoenhausen, *Die Loesung des Raetsels Adolf Hitler,* p. 249; The *Times* (London), November 27, 1947, October 16, 1948; and *New York Herald Tribune,* December 2, 1947, September 14, 1948.

3. *Frankfurter Allgemeine-Zeitung,* December 4, 1953; and *Der Spiegel,* No. 49 (December 3, 1952), 32–33.

4. Described in the *Muenchener-Merkur,* July 19, 1952; and *The Times* (London), April 10, 1953.

5. *Der Spiegel,* No. 38 (September 15, 1949), 14–15; Walter Schellenberg, *The Schellenberg Memoirs,* ed. and trans. by Louis Hagen (London: Andre Deutsch, 1956), p. 112; and Karl Wilhelm Krause, *Zehn Jahre Kammerdiener bei Hitler* (Hamburg: Hermann Laatzen Verlag, 1949), pp. 43–45.

6. Otto Dietrich, *The Hitler I Knew,* trans. by Richard and Clara Winston (London: Meuthen, 1957), pp. 101, 213, 225.

7. Joachim Schultz, *Die letzten 30 Tage: Aus dem Kriegstagebuch des OKW,* ed. by Juergen Thorwald (Stuttgart: Steingrueben-Verlag, 1951), pp. 21–22, 60; Walter Luedde-Neurath, *Regierung Doenitz: Die letzten Tage des Dritten Reiches* (3rd ed.; Goettingen: Musterschmidt Verlag, 1964), pp. 25, 29; and Koller, *Der letzte Monat,* pp. 61, 93–94, whose notes had been available to Trevor-Roper.

8. Probably either Fraulein Elisabeth Schroeder or Fraulein Johanna Wolf; see Albert Zoller, *Hitler privat: Erlebnisbericht seiner Geheimsekretaerin* (Duesseldorf: Droste Verlag, 1949). Also, note Karl Wahl, *". . . es ist das deutsche Herz:" Erlebnisse und Erkenntnisse eines ehemaliges Gauleiters* (Augsburg: Self-Published, 1954), pp. 390–91; and Heinz Guderian, *Panzer Leader,* trans. by Constantine Fitzgibbon (New York: E. P. Dutton, 1952), pp. 342, 442–44.

9. Zoller, *Hitler privat,* pp. 26, 33, 61–69, 121–22, 194–96, 204, 233. Recently, it has been argued, and by a rape of the evidence, that Hitler knew nothing of the mass

murders; see David Irving, *Hitler's War* (New York: Viking Press, 1977). For a detailed demolition of Irving, see the article by Charles W. Sydnor, Jr., "The Selling of Adolf Hitler: David Irving's *Hitler's War*," *Central European History*, XII (June 1979), 169–99.

10. Erich Kempka, *Ich habe Adolf Hitler verbrannt* (Munich: Kryburg Verlag, 1950), pp. 106–10. On his initial statement in June 1945, see above, pp. 68–70.

11. Ibid., pp. 111–20.

12. Louis P. Lochner, ed., *The Goebbels Diaries* (Garden City: Doubleday & Co., 1948), pp. 130–32, 192. Also on Goebbels' observations about the Fuehrer's failing health, note the memoir of his aide, Wilfred von Oven, *Mit Goebbels bis zum Ende* (Buenos Aires: Duerer-Verlag, 1950), II:231, 296–98.

13. Compare *Bol'shaya sovetskaya entsiklopediya* (2nd ed.; Moscow: Gosudarst-vennoe Nauchnoe Izdatel'stvo, 1952), XI: 454, with Georges Blond, *The Death of Hitler's Germany*, trans. by Frances Frenaye (New York: Macmillan, 1954), p. 289.

14. The statement of Spalcke in *Sueddeutsche Zeitung* (Munich), December 30, 1953. The word on Heusemann confirmed what the Russians and Dr. Bruck told the Allies about her in June 1945; see above, pp. 70–72.

15. Echtmann's statement in *The Times* (London), October 15, 1954; his story also confirmed that of the Russians and Dr. Bruck in June 1945, see above, p. 72. Trevor-Roper, *Last Days of Hitler* (3rd ed.), pp. 32–53, first discussed the Soviet investigation into Hitler's death.

16. This German prisoner, whose story appeared in *Der Fortschritt* (Duesseldorf), May 5, 1955, has remained anonymous.

17. Linge's statement in the *Chicago Daily News*, October 22–29, 1955. In 1965, after an interview with Erich Kuby, an editor of *Der Spiegel*, Linge became the center of controversy because he had apparently contradicted himself by telling Kuby he had also seen a bullet wound in Hitler's left temple and that he thought the Fuehrer had shot himself with the left hand. See above, pp. 178, 184.

18. Statement of Linge in *Frankfurter Allgemeine-Zeitung*, October 11, 1955.

19. Hans Baur, *Hitler's Pilot*, trans. by Edward Fitzgerald (London: Frederick Muller, 1958), pp. 171–72, 182, 184, 187–210.

20. Ibid., pp. 210–41.

21. *Das Bild,* January 26, 1956. And the statement of Mengershausen in *The Times* (London), January 13, 1956; and Trevor-Roper, *Last Days of Hitler* (3rd ed.), pp. 34, 41–42.

22. See the court's report, Bavarian Ministry of Justice, "Betreff: Verfahren zur Feststellung des Todes Hitlers," October 25, 1956, a copy of which is in the Wiener Library, London. The statements of Rattenhuber and Guensche are in Trevor-Roper, *Last Days of Hitler* (3rd ed.), pp. 33–34; Schneider in *Jerusalem Post,* October 21, 1955; and Kunz in *New York Herald Tribune,* October 21, 1955.

23. Bavarian Ministry of Justice, "Betreff . . . ," October 25, 1956.

24. The court's decision received wide publicity in West Germany; see, for instance, *Westdeutsche-Allgemeine* (Essen), October 26, 1956; *Koelnische Rundschau,* October 26, 1956; *Die Welt* (Hamburg), October 26, 1956; and *Der Tagesspiegel* (Berlin), October 26, 1956.

25. *Der Spiegel,* No. 7 (February 9, 1955), 34–35; and Musmanno, *Ten Days to Die,* pp. 31–32, 200–205.

26. For example, Walter Goerlitz and Herbert A. Quint, *Adolf Hitler: Eine Biographie* (Stuttgart: Steingruben Verlag, 1952), pp. 622–23.

27. Alan Bullock, *Hitler: A Study in Tyranny* (New York: Bantam Books, 1961), pp. 720-21. The book first appeared in 1952.

8. Scenario of Survival

1. *The Gallup Poll,* I:647.

2. For example, Edouard Saby, *Le tyran nazi et les forces occultes* (Paris: Editions de l'Ecole Addeiste, 1945), pp. 51–66, 89–108; and Erich Mueller-Gnagloff, *Vorlaeufer des Antichrist* (Berlin: Wedding-Verlag, 1948), pp. 282–83, 328. Today, over thirty years after World War II, Hitler remains the world's most despised historical figure. At London's Madame Tussaud's Wax Museum, where many of the past's great personages are on display in life-size models, a poll taken of visitors chose him "the most hated man in history," ahead of Richard Nixon and Idi Amin; see *Parade,* April 10, 1977. Also, note Andrew Ewart, *The World's Wickedest Men: Authentic Accounts of Lives Terrible in Their Power for Evil* (New York: Taplinger, 1963), pp. 9, 163, 169–70; and David Wallechinsky, Irving Wallace, and Amy Wallace, *The Book of Lists* (New York: Morrow, 1977), pp. 1, 9.

3. Muellern-Schoenhausen, *Die Loesung des Raetsels Adolf Hitler,* p. 237.

4. The quotations from *Bonjour* in this chapter come from *Heim und Welt,* which

reprinted much of the French magazine's argument in a run of its own series of articles to debunk the Hitler survival myth, "Ist Hitler wirklich tot?" Nos. 26–34 (June 29–August 24, 1952). For Koller's viewpoint of Hitler's death, see above, p. 107.

5. Details of this supposed episode are in Beauquey and Ziegelmeyer, *Le Disparu du 30 Avril,* pp. 251–86.

6. *NYT,* November 23, 1951 and January 8, 1954. Quotations from the *Gazette*'s series in the 1950s and 1960 in this chapter are taken from the "special collector's edition" published in *The National Police Gazette,* CLXXXII (January 1977), which reprinted the earlier articles.

7. Muellern-Schoenhausen, *Die Loesung des Raetsels Adolf Hitler,* pp. 235–37.

8. I have been unable to locate Slawin's pamphlet, but extensive quotes from it and *Bonjour* appear in *Heim und Welt,* No. 26 (June 29, 1952), 4. On Weidling's memoir released by the Russians in 1961, see above, pp. 163–66. Slawin's report also tallied with one in *Soviet News,* July 5, 1945; see above, p. 72.

9. Szabo, *Je sais que Hitler est vivant,* pp. 100–124; and above, pp. 75–76, 216–17 n. 10.

10. Josef Greiner, *Das Ende des Hitler-Mythos* (Vienna: Almathea-Verlag, 1947), pp. 339–43. Greiner, a notorious liar, probably never knew Hitler in Vienna.

11. Muellern-Schoenhausen, *Die Loesung des Raetsels Adolf Hitler,* pp. 235–36.

12. See above, p. 60.

13. See above, pp. 62–64, for an account of the original reports from 1945.

14. Heinz Schaeffer, *U-977—66 Tage unter Wasser* (Wiesbaden: Limesverlag, n.d.).

15. James Morris, *The Preachers* (New York: St. Martin's Press, 1973), pp. 319–41; and Werner Smoydzin, *Hitler Lebt! Vom internationalen Faschismus zur internationale Hakenkreuzes* (2nd ed.; Pfaffenhofen/Ilm: Ilmgau Verlag, 1967), p. 50.

16. *Newsweek,* LV (February 22, 1960), 57; and *Der Courier* (Toronto), December 20, 1956.

17. *Evening Standard,* May 12, 1950; *The Times* (London), September 15, 1949; *Daily Telegraph* (London), August 15, 1956; Muellern-Schoenhausen, *Die Loesung des Raetsels Adolf Hitler,* p. 237; and *New York Herald Tribune,* January 22, 1953.

18. Curt Riess, *Joseph Goebbels* (London: Hollis and Carter, 1949), pp. 440–41.

19. Construction workers in West Berlin unearthed a skull, identified by pathologists as Bormann's, in December 1972; *Frankfurter Allgemeine-Zeitung,* April 12, 1973.

20. *Frankfurter Allgemeine-Zeitung,* April 13, 1957; *Jerusalem Post,* June 16, 1950 and August 27, 1954; and James Larratt Battersby, ed., *The Holy Book and Testament of Adolf Hitler* (Manchester, U.K.: The Kingdom Press, 1951), pp. 12, 19–21, 34–45, 52–56, 75.

21. *Heim und Welt,* 30–34 (July 27–August 24, 1952), containing numerous "letters to the editor." A woman in Berlin whose husband had worked at the end of the war near the Lehrter Railroad Station, wrote that her spouse had received a small notebook on May 6, 1945, which contained writing in German. The husband had received the tiny book from a Belgian laborer who had in turn received it from a Russian claiming he read no German and had discovered it in a leather jacket. The Berlin couple were astonished to find on page one Bormann's name, address, and phone number. The book allegedly included daily entries from January–May 1, 1945, the last day showing only the remark, "attempt to break out." Other entries had mentioned Goering's expulsion from the Nazi party; Hitler's marriage, testament, and death; and a notation by Bormann, "The world now stands at the end of the sword. We stand and fall with the Fuehrer!" The Russians, said the woman writer, later confiscated the notebook. This may have been Bormann's diary, especially since the Soviet Union admitted in 1965 it had found the volume and described it precisely as had the *Heim und Welt* letter writer. See Yelena Rzhevskaya, *Hitlers Ende ohne Mythos,* trans. by Werner Hanke ([East] Berlin: Deutscher Militaerverlag, 1967), p. 49. Bormann's skeletal remains were also found in the vicinity of the Lehrter Station in 1972 and identified.

9. A Hitler Wave

1. *The Testament of Adolf Hitler: The Hitler-Bormann Documents, February–April 1945,* ed. by Francois Genoud, trans. by R. H. Stevens (London: Cassell, 1961), p. 57.

2. *Sueddeutsche Zeitung,* June 4, 1959; and on the films, *Der Spiegel,* No. 32 (August 3, 1960), 56–57; No. 36 (August 30, 1961); No. 34 (August 14, 1967), 104-5.

3. Noah D. Fabricant, *13 Famous Patients* (Philadelphia and New York: Chilton Co., 1960), pp. 45–46; *Quick,* March 23, 1964; *Frankfurter Allgemeine-Zeitung,* February 20, 1965; and *Collier's Encyclopedia* (New York: Crowell-Collier and Macmillan, Inc., 1966), XXXIII:630.

4. George Mac, *La vie et la mort d'Hitler* (Paris: Editions Medicis, 1946), pp.

144–50, whose sources allegedly included Jenny Jugo, a cinema star Mac claimed had been introduced to Hitler in 1937, and Hitler's niece, Geli Raubal. How he received the information from the women, Mac fails to say. Such rumors had circulated before the end of the war, as noted by an American intelligence report from 1943, Walter Langer, *The Mind of Adolf Hitler: The Secret Wartime Report* (New York: New American Library, 1972), pp. 138, 230–32. A former Nazi party member and Hitler enemy, Otto Strasser, who claimed he had in turn learned such things from Geli Raubal, discussed Hitler's masochistic and coprophilic tendencies with American intelligence. H. D. Vernon in *The Journal of Abnormal Psychology,* 37 (1942), 301, 304–6, and R. Collin in *The Spectator,* No. 5 (19 Jan. 1934), 77, came to the same conclusions. The Russian autopsy of Hitler's remains, published in 1968, noted the Fuehrer's monorchism (see above, p. 182). The most recent generation of psychohistorians has accepted Hitler's sexual perversion; see especially, Robert G. L. Waite, *The Psychopathic God Adolf Hitler* (New York: Basic Books, 1977), pp. 237–43.

5. On the Uschi affair as it had risen in 1945, see above, pp. 81–82. The quotes from *Bonjour* are from the German magazine, *Heim und Welt,* 29–30 (July 20–July 27, 1952), which reprinted much of the French magazine's series of articles alleging Hitler's survival. See also, Paul Tabori, ed., *The Private Life of Adolf Hitler: The Intimate Notes and Diary of Eva Braun* (London: Aldus Publications, 1949), pp. 49–53.

6. The "Hitler children" are discussed in *Le Monde,* June 30, 1966; *Frankfurter Rundschau,* December 13/14, 1962; and *New York Herald Tribune,* September 14, 1949.

7. Bonjour's arguments are in *Heim und Welt,* especially 31–34 (August 3–August 24, 1952).

8. *Zeit,* July 26, 1968; and Henri Ludwigg, *L'assassinat de Hitler,* trans. from the Spanish by R. Jouvan (Paris: Editions France-Empire, 1963), p. 73.

9. Hans-Dietrich Roehrs, *Hitlers Krankheit: Tatsachen und Legenden* (Neckargemuend: Kurt Vowinckel Verlag, 1966), pp. 12–14, 17, 20, 53–58, 63–67, 73, 79, 84, 106–22, 129–42, 146, 153–56, 186–87; and Johann Recktenwald, *Woran hat Adolf Hitler gelitten?* (Mitten/Basel: Ernst Reinhardt Verlag, 1963), pp. 8–20, 114. Regarding Arnaudow, note *Zeit,* July 26, 1968.

10. Walter Goerlitz, ed., *The Memoirs of Field Marshal Keitel,* trans. by David Irving (New York: Stein and Day, 1966), republished in 1979 as *In the Service of the Reich,* p. 235. See further, Percy Ernst Schramm et al, *Kriegstagebuch des Oberkommandos der Wehrmacht, 1940–1945* (Frankfurt/Main: Bernard & Graefe Verlag fuer Wehrwesen, 1961), IV:1701–2; and Walter Warlimont, *Inside Hitler's Headquarters, 1939–45,* trans. by R. H. Barry (New York: Praeger, 1964), p. 516. Admiral Doenitz, *Memoirs: Ten Years and Twenty Days,* trans. by R. H. Stevens (London:

Weidenfeld and Nicolson, 1958), pp. 439–45, is significant only insofar as explaining his version of why he had told the world Hitler had died a hero's death on the evening of May 1, 1945. His reasons were dubious at best. Given the chaos in Berlin, he said, the telegram he had received from Goebbels that afternoon had been unclear to him regarding Hitler's death. Doenitz simply assumed the Fuehrer had died heroically. Also, by delaying the announcement of the death till that evening and by implying Hitler had died fighting the Russians, the Admiral said he hoped to avoid the total collapse of the German forces.

11. Schramm et al, *Kriegstagebuch,* IV:1721.

12. James H. McRandle, *The Track of the Wolf: Essays on National Socialism and its Leader, Adolf Hitler* (Evanston, Ill.: Northwestern University Press, 1965), pp. 146-51.

13. These included William L. Shirer, *The Rise and Fall of the Third Reich* (New York: Fawcett Publications, 1965), pp. 1468–75; Werner Haupt, *Berlin 1945: Hitlers letzte Schlacht* (Rastatt: Erich Pobel, 1963), pp. 178–79; Juergen Thorwald, *Das Ende an der Elbe* (rev. ed.; Munich/Zurich: Droermersche Verlagsanstalt, 1975), pp. 176–79; and Hans Hegner, pseud., *Die Reichskanzlei, 1933–1945: Anfang und Ende des Dritten Reiches* (3rd ed.; Frankfurt/Main: Verlag Frankfurter Buecher, 1960), pp. 400–401.

10. Poison or a Bullet?

1. B. S. Telpukhovsky, *Velikaia otechestvennaia voina Sovetskogo Soviza, 1941-1945* (Moscow: Gosudarstvennoe izdatel'stvo politicheskoi lituratury, 1959), p. 478.

2. *Zeit,* May 7, 1965; Nikita Khrushchev, *Khrushchev Remembers,* ed. and trans. by Strobe Talbot (Boston: Little, Brown and Co., 1970), pp. 218–19.

3. *Sovetskaia istoricheskaia entsiklopediia* (Moscow: Gosudarstvennoe nauchnoe, 1961–1963), IV:459; and on the *Pravda* photo, *L'Express,* September 25–October 1, 1972. Regarding the 1952 *Encyclopedia,* see above, p. 112.

4. See the translation of the memoir of Helmut Weidling in the East German journal, *Wehrwissenschaftliche Rundschau,* 12 (January–March 1962).

5. German L. Rosanow, *Hitlers letzte Tage* ([East] Berlin: Dietz Verlag, 1963), pp. 106-7, 129; and *Die Ergebnisse des Grossen Vaterlaendischen Krieges, Geschichte des Grossen Vaterlaendischen Krieges der Sowjetunion* ([East] Berlin: Deutscher Militaerverlag, 1968), V:331-32.

6. Cornelius Ryan, *The Last Battle* (New York: Simon and Schuster, 1966), pp. 497–98; and *Jerusalem Post,* May 6, 1963. To my knowledge, except for an excerpt in

Trevor-Roper, *Last Days of Hitler* (3rd ed.), Guensche's statement had never been published before.

7. Ryan, *The Last Battle,* pp. 54–56, 504–6. Heusemann's account (also to my knowledge published for the first time) matched perfectly what the Russians and a Berlin dentist had told the Allies in June 1945 about her identification of Hitler's dentistry, and what she had said to a fellow prisoner while in a Soviet jail. See above, pp. 70–72, 113.

8. *NYT,* February 23, 1964; and Vasily I. Chuikov, *The Fall of Berlin,* trans. by Ruth Kisch (New York: Ballantine, 1969), p. 236.

9. *Nedelya,* July 11, 1964, quoted in *Jerusalem Post,* July 13, 1964.

10. Rzhevskaya, *Hitlers Ende ohne Mythos,* p. 82 and passim.

11. See his series of articles in *Der Spiegel,* 19–24 (May 6–June 9, 1965); and Erich Kuby, *Die Russen in Berlin, 1945* (Munich: Scherz Verlag, 1965), pp. 186–236.

11. The Autopsy

1. See the autopsy report, Bezymensky, *The Death of Adolf Hitler,* pp. 44–49.

2. The Heusemann episode had been known in the West since 1945; see above, pp. 70–72, 113, 174.

3. G. K. Zhukov, *The Memoirs of Marshal Zhukov,* trans. by Novosti (New York: Delacorte Press, 1971), pp. 622, 626. The other Field Marshal involved in the taking of the city, I. Konev, *Year of Victory,* trans. by David Mishne (Moscow: Progress Publishers, 1969), pp. 119, 158, 169–70, 178, 183, 188, 190, also said that Hitler had remained and died in Berlin.

4. Zhukov, *Memoirs,* pp. 660–62. Compare, for example, Montgomery, *Memoirs,* p. 324; and Dwight D. Eisenhower, *Crusade in Europe* (Garden City: Doubleday, 1948), pp. 435–37. Regarding that first Berlin meeting, see above, pp. 45–46.

5. *NYT,* August 2, 3, 8, 1968 and September 21, 1968; and H. R. Trevor-Roper in *The Sunday Times* (London), September 29, 1968.

6. See Maser, *Hitler,* pp. 304–5; *Jerusalem Post,* November 26, 1971; and Office of the Chief of Military History, *United States in World War II: The European Theater of Operations, The Last Offensive* (Washington, D.C.: Office of the Chief of Military History, United States Army, 1973), p. 459.

7. Reidar F. Sognnaes and Ferdinand Stroem, "The Odontological Identification of Adolf Hitler: Definitive Documentation by X-rays, Interrogations and Autopsy Findings," *Acta Odontologica Scandinavica,* XXXI (1973), 43, 68; Reidar F. Sognnaes, "Some Old and New Adventures in Dental Research," *Harvard Dental Alumni Bulletin,* 32 (1972), 56–59; *Der Spiegel,* No. 32 (August 5, 1968), 32; and *Die Weltbuehne,* No. 40 (October 1, 1968), 1256. *Zeit,* August 6–20, 1968, published lengthy excerpts from Bezymensky's book, but without editorial comment.

8. Ladislas Farago, *Aftermath: Martin Bormann and the Fourth Reich* (New York: Simon and Schuster, 1974), p. 28; *L'Express,* September 25–October 1, 1972; and Peter Loewenberg, "Psychological Perspectives on Modern German History," *Journal of Modern History,* 47 (June 1975), 245 n. 68.

9. Hugh Trevor-Roper, ed., *Final Entries 1945: The Diaries of Joseph Goebbels,* trans. by Richard Barry (New York: G. P. Putnam's Sons, 1978), pp. 40, 121, 128, 245–48, 277, 281; and Albert Speer, *Inside the Third Reich,* trans. by Richard and Clara Winston (New York: Macmillan, 1970), pp. 479–80.

10. See his statement in O'Donnell and Bahnsen, *Die Katakombe,* pp. 187–88. Also, note Ernst Guenter Schenck, *Ich sah Berlin sterben: Als Arzt in der Reichskanzlei* (Herford: Nicolaische Verlagshandlung, 1970), pp. 116–18.

11. O'Donnell and Bahnsen, *Die Katakombe,* pp. 191–92. Other testimony of Hitler's very poor physical health came from Blaschke and one of the Fuehrer's former secretaries, Johanna Wolf. Kempner interrogated both of them in 1947; Robert Kempner, *Das Dritte Reich im Kreuzverhoer: Aus den unveroeffentlichen Vernehmungsprotokollen des Anklagers* (Munich: Bechtle Verlag, 1969), pp. 44, 65.

12. O'Donnell and Bahnsen, *Die Katakombe,* pp. 211-21. Glenn B. Infield, *Eva and Adolf* (New York: Grosset & Dunlap, 1974), p. 251, also accepted the poison-bullet theory. Infield's account is hardly scholarly, however.

13. Waite, *The Psychopathic God,* pp. 415–22. With much less evidence and sophistication, David Lewis, *The Secret Life of Adolf Hitler* (London: Heinrich Hanau, 1977), pp. 207, 214–17, came to a similar conclusion.

14. Joachim C. Fest, *Hitler,* trans. by Richard and Clara Winston (New York: Vintage Books, 1975), pp. 748–50; Thorwald, *Das Ende an der Elbe,* pp. 176–79; Robert Payne, *The Life and Death of Adolf Hitler* (New York: Praeger, 1973), pp. 567–68; and John Toland, *Adolf Hitler* (Garden City: Doubleday, 1976), pp. 892–93. Toland, in his previous book on the end of the war, *The Last 100 Days* (New York: Random House, 1966), p. 530, said Hitler had shot himself in the mouth. Without explaining his change, he states in his biography (p. 888) that the Fuehrer had put the bullet in his right temple. A. J. Ryder, *Twentieth Century Germany: From Bismarck to Brandt* (New York: Columbia University Press, 1973), p. 450, declares: "Although

the Russians, who arrived on the scene two days later, have never publicly revealed the facts, they are known to have disinterred the bodies and, after identification to have secretly removed them to an unknown destination, probably in Russia." Moreover, the British popularizer and would-be scholar, David Irving, in *Hitler's War,* without citing his source, follows Trevor-Roper nearly exactly in his version of Hitler's death. See especially, Sydnor, "The Selling of Adolf Hitler," pp. 196–97. Finally, note the statement of Marlis G. Steinert, *23 Days: The Final Collapse of Nazi Germany,* trans. by Richard Barry (New York: Walker, 1969), p. 294 n. 68: "The supposition that Hitler poisoned himself or that Eva Braun shot him is probably based on a tendentious Soviet account. It is, however, possible that he both took poison and shot himself."

12. Epilogue

1. See Scott Edwards, "The Wonderful World of Garner Ted Armstrong," *The Humanist,* 38 (January/February 1978), 11; and above, p 140.

2. Those Germans polled in 1975 responded to this question: "Would you say that without the war [i.e., without the years 1939–1945], Hitler would have been one of the greatest German statesmen?" See the article by Heinrich Jaenecke in *Stern,* No. 21 (May 15, 1975), 66. Note also, Sydnor, "The Selling of Adolf Hitler," p. 170; and Dieter Bossmann, ed., *Was ich ueber Adolf Hitler gehoert habe . . .* (Frankfurt/Main: Fischer Taschenbuch Verlag, 1977), pp. 335–55. Other students in Bossmann's sample claimed, variously, that Hitler had "killed himself in the gas chamber," that he "committed suicide in 1948, after he had killed his wife and children," and that "Adolf Hitler lives in Brazil, as I have learned from the newspaper." A ten year old said, "I do not know how he [Hitler] died. But my mother has said that he is in hell with Konrad Adenauer."

3. The italics are those of *The National Police Gazette,* 182 (January 1977), 3, 6. The *Gazette*'s articles from the 1950s and 1960 are discussed extensively in chapters eight and nine above.

4. Ira Levin, *The Boys From Brazil* (New York: Random House, 1976), pp. 240–41.

5. Werner Brockdorff, *Flucht vor Nuernberg: Plaene und Organisation der Fluchtwege der NS-Prominenz im "Romischen Weg"* (Wels, Austria: Verlag Welsermuehl, 1969), pp. 194–202. Compare his tale, for example, to those discussed above in chapter eight that appeared in the 1940s and 1950s. Other lunatic fringe writers, similar to Brockdorff, have persisted with the absurdity that Hitler had been part Jewish. One, Kardel, *Adolf Hitler—Begruender Israels* (Geneva: Marva, 1974), pp. 164–68, proclaimed that the "half Jewish" Hitler had been the modern founder of the state of Israel and that the "part Jewish" doctor, Morell, by worsening the Fuehrer's health with drugs and pills, had encouraged the destruction of the Jews. For

the relation of this theme to the Hitler survival myth, see above, pp. 152–53. The most recent suggestion "that Hitler did not die in the bunker," Glenn Infield, *Hitler's Secret Life: The Mysteries of the Eagle's Nest* (New York: Stein and Day, 1979), pp. 272–88, resurrects (like Brockdorff) the familiar stories from the earlier survival theorists: a double had perished in Hitler's place, Nazi pilots had whisked the Fuehrer out of Berlin, Bormann had masterminded the flight, Hitler had fathered a child, and someone suspected as the dictator had been allegedly seen in Brazil in 1978.

6. "The New Avengers," CBS Friday Night Movie, September 15, 1978; *NYT,* March 18, 1977; *Time,* CX (November 14, 1977), 45; *Newsweek,* VIIC (May 28, 1979), 23; Werner and Lottie Pelz, *I am Adolf Hitler* (Richmond, Va.: John Knox Press, 1971); and Albert Wallner, *Moench-Story: Hitlers Flucht aus Berlin am 30.4.1945* (Horn, Austria: Verlag Ferdinand Berger, 1968). Maser's story about Hitler's alleged son resembled a silly fantasy from 1949 about another "son of the Fuehrer," Wilhelm Bauer; see above, p. 151. Moreover, an X-ray showing Hitler's head, taken from the files of the doctor Morell, sold at a New York auction in July 1977 for $375. On the controversy over such X-rays, see above, pp. 189–91. Finally, note Gus Weill, *The Fuhrer Seed* (New York: William Morrow, 1979).

7. Philippe van Rjndt, *The Trial of Adolf Hitler* (New York: Summit Books, 1978).

8. Johannes Steel, *Hitler as Frankenstein* (Adelphi, U.K.: Wishart and Co., 1933), p. 176; and *NYT,* January 28, 1974.

9. *NYT,* October 13, 1977. The script for a similar British play is in G. Hulme, *The Life and Death of Adolf Hitler* (Buckinghamshire, U.K.: Colin Smythe Ltd., 1975), especially pp. 235–46. It portrayed Hitler as shooting himself, as Trevor-Roper had said nearly thirty years before, in the mouth. But not before the one who had concocted the greatest planned crime in history had undergone a small bit of torment. The audience saw Hitler in his last moments beset with a final obsession beyond his poor health, his fear of capture by the Russians, his false hopes of victory, and his ranting against the incompetency of those around him. Nightmares of Jews being knifed haunted him, the play added to the story of his finale in the fateful bunker, when in fact on waking he realized he had dreamed of stabbing himself.

Bibliography

Adler, Hans. *Berlin in jenen Tagen: Berichte aus der Zeit von 1945–1948.* Berlin: Kongress-Verlag, 1959.

Ainszstein, Reuben. "How Hitler Died: The Soviet Version," *International Affairs,* XLIII (April 1967), 307–18.

American Magazine. "Loneliest Man in Hollywood," CXXXVII (May 1944), 133.

Arbeiter-Zeitung (Vienna). "Wenn er seinen Prozess noch erlebt hatte : . . ," Summer 1961.

Atlanta Constitution. "Adolf Killed by Bomb," May 3, 1945.

———. "British Foreign Office Believes Death Report," May 2, 1945.

———. "Burned Hitler, Eva After Suicide, Valet Liberated by Soviet Relates," October 10, 1955.

———. "Doom Closing Swiftly on 'Rats of Europe,'" May 12, 1945.

———. "Fuehrer Looms as German Hero, as Hitler Myth Begins to Form," May 4, 1945.

———. "His Doctor Suspects Adolf Hiding," May 7, 1945.

———. "Hitler and Great Love Hinted in Death Pact," May 4, 1945.

———. "Hitler, Did, Too, Have Some Mourners," May 7, 1945.

———. "Hitler is Dead, Say Nazis," May 2, 1945.

———. "Hitler Not in Berlin, Pravda Says; Russians Push Search for Body," May 4, 1945.

———. "Hitler's Body Found, Russian Source Says," June 7, 1945.

———. "Hitler's Death Confirmed By Court as Suicide in 1945," October 26, 1956.

————. "Hitler's Death Marks End of an Era," May 4, 1945.

————. "If Hitler is Dead, Good Riddance," May 2, 1945.

————. "Lest We Forget," May 10, 1945.

————. "Moscow Asks for Immediate Death for Doenitz, Other Nazi Leaders," May 14, 1945.

————. "Mystery Still Wraps About Adolf Hitler," May 2, 1945.

Attlee, C. R. *As It Happened.* New York: Viking Press, 1954.

Backer, John H. *The Decision to Divide Germany: American Foreign Policy in Transition.* Durham, N.C.: Duke University Press, 1978.

Baltimore Sun. "Congressmen Report on Horror Camps," May 16, 1945.

————. "Hitler and Eva Reported Safe," July 17, 1945.

————. "Hitler's Body Thought Found," June 7, 1945.

————. "Von Rundstedt Explains Why Reich Lost War," May 5, 1945.

Barraclough, Geoffrey. "The Nazi Boom," *The New York Review of Books,* XXVI (May 17, 1979), 18–21.

Battersby, James Larratt, ed. *The Holy Book and Testament of Adolf Hitler.* Manchester, U.K.: The Kingdom Press, 1951.

Baur, Hans. *Hitler's Pilot.* Trans. Edward Fitzgerald. London: Frederick Muller Ltd., 1958.

Bayerische Staatsministerium der Justiz. "Betreff: Verfahren zur Feststellug des Todes Hitlers." October 25, 1956.

Beauquey, Michael and Ziegelmeyer, V. *Le disparu du 30 avril.* Paris: Les Productions de Paris, 1964.

Bernadotte, Count Folke. *The Curtain Falls: Last Days of the Third Reich.* Trans. Count Eric Lewenhaupt. New York: Knopf, 1945.

Bezymensky, Lev. *The Death of Adolf Hitler: Unknown Documents from Soviet Archives.* New York: Harcourt, Brace and World, 1968.

Bialer, Seweryn, ed. *Stalin and His Generals: Soviet Military Memoirs of World War II.* New York: Pegasus, 1969.

Bild, Das. January 26, 1956.

Blake, Leonardo. *Hitler's Last Year of Power.* London: Andrew Dakers Ltd., 1939.

Blond, Georges. *The Death of Hitler's Germany.* Trans. Frances Frenaye. New York: Macmillan, 1954.

Bohlen, Charles E. *Witness to History: 1929–1969.* New York: Norton, 1973.

Boldt, Gerhard. *In the Shelter with Hitler.* Trans. Edgar Stern-Rubarth. London: Citadel Press, 1948.

Bol'shaya sovetskaya entsiklopediya. 2nd ed. Vol. XI. Moscow: Gosudarstvennoe Nauchnoe Izdatel'stvo, 1952.

Bondy, Louis W. "Hitler and the Stars," *Enquiry* (December 1949), 39–41.

Bonker, Frances. *The Mad Dictator: A Novel of Adolph Hitler.* Boston: Chapman and Grimes, 1950.

Bossmann, Dieter, ed. *Was ich ueber Adolf Hitler gehoert habe . . .* Frankfurt/Main: Fischer Taschenbuch Verlag, 1977.

Boynton, G. R. and Loewenberg, Gerhard. "The Decay of Support for Monarchy and the Hitler Regime in the Federal Republic of Germany," *British Journal of Political Science,* IV (October 1974), 453–88.

British Broadcasting Corporation. *Daily Digest of World Broadcasts and Radio Telegraph Services,* No. 2, 115–34 (May 1–21, 1945); 152–58 (June 7–14, 1945).

Brockdorff, Werner. *Flucht vor Nuernberg: Plaene und Organisation der Fluchtwege der NS-Prominenz im "Romischen Weg."* Wels, Austria: Verlag Welsermuehl, 1969.

Bromberg, Norbert. "Psychoanalyst Says Hitler had 'Psychotic Character.'" *Science Digest* (September 1961), 15–16.

Bross, Werner, ed. *Gespraeche mit Hermann Goering waehrend des Nuernberger Prozess.* Flensburg/Hamburg: Verlagshaus Christian Wolff, 1950.

Bullock, Alan. *Hitler: A Study in Tyranny.* Rev. ed. New York: Bantam Books, 1961.

Bund, Der (Berne). "Ist Martin Bormann noch am Leben?" February 17, 1953.

Butcher, Harry C. *My Three Years with Eisenhower.* New York: Simon and Schuster, 1946.

Byrnes, James F. *Speaking Frankly.* New York: Harper and Brothers, 1947.

Cartier, Raymond. "Le Jour Ou Hitler Mourut," *Paris Match* (June 23, 1962), 67–83.

Chicago Daily News. "The Yanks Were Coming For Adolf," October 22, 1955.

Chicago Daily Tribune. "Europe Buzzes With Mystery: 'Where's Hitler?'" April 25, 1945.

_____. "56th Birthday Finds Hitler is Still Mystery," April 21, 1945.

_____. "Goebbels Flees Panicky Berlin, Sweden Hears," April 23, 1945.

_____. "Goebbels Tells Germans: Scrap Warfare Rules," April 20, 1945.

_____. "Hitler Believed Running War at Berchtesgaden," April 22, 1945.

_____. "Hitler's Love Life is Told by His Valet," October 11, 1955.

_____. "1,000 German POWs Freed," October 10, 1955.

_____. "2d Army Frees 29,000 in Nazi Horror Camps," April 19, 1945.

_____. "Tribune Survey Bares Full Horror of German Atrocities," April 25, 1945.

Chicago Sunday Tribune. "Tells of Hitler's Suicide," October 9, 1955.

Chicago Times. "Hear Argentina Hides Hitler, Eva," July 16, 1945.

Chicago Tribune. "Autopsy on Hitler Released By Russ," August 2, 1968.

Chuikov, Vasily I. *The Fall of Berlin.* Trans. Ruth Kisch. New York: Ballantine, 1969.

Churchill, Winston S. *Memoirs of the Second World War.* Boston: Houghton Mifflin Co., 1959.

_____. *Triumph and Tragedy.* Boston: Houghton Mifflin, 1953.

Clay, Lucius D. *Decision in Germany.* Garden City: Doubleday, 1950.

Collier's Encyclopedia. Vol. XXIII. New York: Crowell-Collier and Macmillan, Inc., 1966.

Collin, R. "Hitlerism as a Sex Problem," *The Spectator* (January 19, 1934), 75–77.

Courier, Der (Toronto). "Adolf Hitler lebt in Suedamerika," December 20, 1956.

Craig, Gordon A. "What the Germans Are Reading About Hitler," *Reporter* (July 16, 1964), 36–38.

Daily Mail (London). "No, it's not Adolf, it's Albert," September 2, 1969.

————. "Secret Hitler Will Turns Up in Russia," May 7, 1963.

Daily Telegraph (London). "'Doctor Turned Hitler into Maniac' Claim," April 7, 1969.

————. "'Hitler Hoard' Dug Up," August 15, 1956.

————. "Is This Hitler?" December 9, 1944.

Daily Telegraph and Morning Post (London). "Hitler's Death Officially Announced," October 26, 1956.

Darmstaedter Echo. "Streit um die Stimme Hitlers," May 12, 1959.

David, Paul. *Am Koenigsplatz: Die letzten Tage der Schweizerischen Gesandschaft in Berlin.* Zuerich: Thomas Verlag, 1948.

Deane, John R. *The Strange Alliance: The Story of Our Efforts at Wartime Cooperation with Russia.* Bloomington, Ind.: Indiana University Press, 1973.

Delmenhorster Kreisblatt. "Keine Arbeitslosenunterstuetzung fuer Hitlers Kammerdiener," December 25, 1955.

Deutsche Allgemeine Zeitung (Berlin). September 20, 1944.

Deutscher, Isaac. *Stalin: A Political Biography.* 2nd ed. New York: Oxford University Press, 1967.

Dietrich, Otto. *The Hitler I Knew.* Trans. Richard and Clara Winston. London: Methuen and Co., 1957.

Doenitz, Admiral. *Memoirs: Ten Years and Twenty Days.* Trans. R. H. Stevens. London: Weidenfeld and Nicolson, 1958.

Ebermayer, Erich and Meissner, Hans-Otto. *Evil Genius: The Story of Joseph Goebbels.* Trans. Louis Hagen. London: Allan Wingate, 1953.

Edwards, Scott. "The Wonderful World of Garner Ted Armstrong," *The Humanist,* 38 (January/February 1978), 9–13.

Eisenhower, Dwight D. *Crusade in Europe.* Garden City: Doubleday & Co., 1948.

————. *Eisenhower's Own Story of the War.* New York: Arco Publishing Co., 1946.

Ergebnisse des Grossen Vaterlaendischen Krieges, Die. Vol. 5 of *Geschichte des Grossen Vaterlaendischen Krieges der Sowjetunion.* [East] Berlin: Deutscher Militaerverlag, 1968.

Evening Standard (London). "The body they cannot find," May 4, 1945.

————. "Himmler is still no. 1," May 2, 1945.

————. "Hitler lives," June 16, 1950.

————. "Hitler lives, say Nazis," May 12, 1950.

————. "Hitler mystery," May 4, 1945.

————. "Hitler not in Berlin," May 3, 1945.

————. "Hitler took poison and died in fire," June 6, 1945.

————. "Hitler was married, may be in hiding," June 9, 1945.

————. "Last throw to save the Hitler myth," May 2, 1945.

————. "Paris will believe it when they see body," May 2, 1945.

————. (Article title unavailable.) June 24, 1945.

Ewart, Andrew. *The World's Wickedest Men: Authentic Accounts of Lives Terrible in Their Power for Evil.* New York: Taplinger, 1963.

Fabricant, Noah D. *13 Famous Patients.* Philadelphia and New York: Chilton Co., 1960.

Farago, Ladislas. *Aftermath: Martin Bormann and the Fourth Reich.* New York: Simon and Schuster, 1974.

Fest, Joachim C. *Hitler.* Trans. Richard and Clara Winston. New York: Vintage Books, 1975.

Fortschritt, Der (Duesseldorf). May 5, 1955.

Frankfurter Allgemeine-Zeitung. April 12, 1973.

————. "Adolf Hitlers neue Revolution," April 13, 1957.

————. "Der bayerische Staat soll Hitlers Nachlass herausgeben," December 4, 1953.

————. "Entlassungen nach dem russischen Alphabet," October 10, 1955.

————. "Ermittlungsverfahren gegen Hitler," February 20, 1965.

————. "Das Herz in Deutschland," October 15, 1955.

————. "Ich habe Hitlers Leiche verbrannt," October 11, 1955.

————. "Nicht nur Kriegsgefangene," September 10, 1955.

————. "Pilger und Forschungsreisende," March 18, 1959.

————. "Seydlitz will sich politisch betaetigen," October 8, 1955.

————. "War Hitler gross?" April 11, 1969.

————. "Wieder ein grosser Heimkehrertransport in Sicht," October 15, 1955.

Frankfurter Rundschau. "In der 'Kareti der Boesewichte' stehen 52000 Namen," July 30, 1960.

————. "Millionen rollten fuer den Herrn vom anderen Stern," December 13/14, 1962.

Gallagher, Matthew P. *The Soviet History of World War II: Myths, Memories, and Realities.* New York: Praeger, 1963.

Gallup Poll: Public Opinion, 1935–1971, The. 3 vol. Vol. I, II. New York: Random House, 1972.

Gaxotte, Pierre. "Hitler-Boom," *Le Figaro,* November 3/4, 1973.

Genoud, Francois, ed. *The Testament of Adolf Hitler: The Hitler-Bormann Documents, February–April 1945.* Trans. R. H. Stevens. London: Cassell, 1961.

Gilbert, Felix, ed. *Hitler Directs His War: The Secret Records of His Daily Military Conferences.* New York: Oxford University Press, 1951.

Gimbel, John. *The American Occupation of Germany: Politics and the Military, 1945–1949.* Stanford: Stanford University Press, 1968.

Goerlitz, Walter and Quint, Herbert A. *Adolf Hitler: Eine Biographie.* Stuttgart: Steingruben-Verlag, 1952.

Goerlitz, Walter, ed. *The Memoirs of Field Marshal Keitel.* Trans. David Irving. New York: Stein and Day, 1966.

Goodman, Anne. Review of H. R. Trevor-Roper, *The Last Days of Hitler* (New York: Macmillan, 1947), in *New Republic,* CXVII (September 22, 1947), 29–30.

Gorbatov, A. V. *Years Off My Life: The Memoirs of General of the Soviet Army A. V. Gorbatov.* Trans. Gordon Clough and Anthony Cash. New York: Norton, 1965.

Great Britain. Ministry of Information. *News Digest,* Nos. 1744 54 (E.H. Series), April 26–May 8, 1945.

Greiner, Josef. *Das Ende des Hitler-Mythos.* Vienna: Almathea-Verlag, 1947.

Gronowicz, Antoni. *Hitler's Woman.* New York: Belmont Books, 1942.

Grothe, Peter. *To Win the Minds of Men: The Story of the Communist Propaganda War in East Germany.* Palo Alto, Calif.: Pacific Books, 1958.

Guderian, Heinz. *Panzer Leader.* Trans. Constantine Fitzgibbon. New York: E. P. Dutton, 1952.

Gun, Nerin E. *Eva Braun: Hitler's Mistress.* London: Leslie Frewin, 1969.

Hamburger Freie Presse. "War Hitler Jude?" August 27, 1949.

Hamburger Fremdenblatt. "Aus dem Fuehrerhauptquartier," July 31, 1944.

————. "Neujahrsglueckwuensche der Wehrmacht fuer den Fuehrer," January 5, 1945.

Harriman, W. Averell and Abel, Elie. *Special Envoy to Churchill and Stalin, 1941–1946.* New York: Random House, 1975.

Haupt, Werner. *Berlin 1945: Hitlers letzte Schlacht.* Rastatt: Erich Pobel, 1963.

Hegner, Hans, pseud. *Die Reichskanzlei, 1933–1945: Anfang und Ende des Dritten Reiches.* 3rd ed. Frankfurt/Main: Verlag Frankfurter Buecher, 1960.

Heiber, Helmut. *Goebbels.* Trans. John K. Dickinson. New York, 1972.

————, ed. *Hitlers Lagebesprechungen: Die Protokollfragmente seiner militaerischen Konferenzen, 1942–1945.* Stuttgart: Deutsche Verlags-Anstalt, 1962.

Heiden, Konrad. *Der Fuehrer: Hitler's Rise to Power.* Trans. Ralph Manheim. Boston: Houghton Mifflin, 1944.

Heim und Welt. "Hitler-Razzia auf Galapagos," 35 (August 31, 1952), 10.

————. "Ist Hitler wirklich tot?" 26–34 (June 29–August 24, 1952).

Howley, Frank. *Berlin Command.* New York: G. P. Putnam's Sons, 1950.

Hulme, George. *The Life and Death of Adolf Hitler.* Buckinghamshire, U.K.: Colin Smythe Ltd., 1975.

Imbert, G. *Les crimes d' Hitler: Le Procès d' Hitler et du nazisme.* Paris: Les Editions de Paris, 1945.

Infield, Glenn B. *Eva and Adolf.* New York: Grosset & Dunlap, 1974, and London: New English Library, 1975.

————. *Hitler's Secret Life: The Mysteries of the Eagle's Nest.* New York: Stein and Day, 1979.

International Military Tribunal. *Trial of the Major War Criminals.* Vols. XVII, XXXV. Nuremberg, 1947–49.

Irving, David. *Hitler's War.* New York: Viking Press, 1977.

Jacobsen, Hans-Adolf. "Historiker in Moskau," *Zeit,* May 7, 1965.

Jaenecke, Heinrich. "Wie tot ist Hitler?" *Stern,* No. 21 (May 15, 1975), 62–70.

Janssen, Karl-Heinz. "Das Phaenomen Adolf Hitler," *Zeit,* April 18, 1969.

————. "Wie starb Adolf Hitler?" *Zeit,* July 26, 1968.

Jerusalem Post. "'Acquittal' for Hitler," August 27, 1954.

————. "Dentist says he can solve Hitler death mystery," May 24, 1972.

————. "Hitler was shot after death by poison, Soviet probe finds," July 13, 1964.

————. "Hitler's Birthday Marked in Graz," April 21, 1953.

————. "Nazi Magazine is Sellout in Frankfurt," May 10, 1950.

————. "Nazis' New Empire?" June 16, 1950.

————. "New Doubts on Body of Hitler," November 26, 1971.

————. "Russians Examined Hitler's Skull," October 21, 1955.

————. "Shadow of Hitler in UN Debate," December 3, 1953.

————. "Soviets Admit Recovering Hitler's Body in Berlin," May 6, 1963.

Kaiser, David. "What Young Americans Know About Hitler," *Nation,* 225 (December 10, 1977), 613.

Kardel, *Adolf Hitler—Begruender Israels.* Geneva: Marva, 1974.

Kardorff, Ursula von. *Berliner Aufzeichnungen: Aus den Jahren 1942 bis 1945.* Frankfurt/Main: Buechergilde Gutenberg, 1962.

Kempka, Erich. *Ich habe Adolf Hitler verbrannt.* Munich: Kyrburg Verlag, 1950.

Kempner, Robert. *Das Dritte Reich im Kreuzverhoer: Aus den unveroeffentlichen Vernehmungsprotokollen des Anklagers.* Munich: Bechtle Verlag, 1969.

Kelley, Douglas M. *22 Cells in Nuremberg: A Psychiatrist Examines the Nazi Criminals.* New York: Greenberg, 1947.

Kelly, Elsworth K. "Adolf Hitler, His Dentist and His Dental Problems," *The Journal of the California Dental Association,* 41 (October 1965), 424–25.

Kesselring, Albert. *Kesselring: A Soldier's Record.* Westport, Conn.: Greenwood Press, 1970.

Khrushchev, Nikita. *Khrushchev Remembers.* Ed. and trans. Strobe Talbot. Boston: Little, Brown and Co., 1970.

Koelnische Rundschau. "Hitlers Inferno in der Rille," September 8, 1959.

————. "Hitler starb um 15.30 Uhr," October 26, 1956.

————. "Hunde-Freund und Henker," June 14, 1964.

———. "Kontroverse um Nazi-Platten," June 4, 1959.

———. "Die Meinung der anderen," April 22, 1959.

———. "Neue Sowjet-Version ueber Hitlers Ende," July 13, 1964.

———. "Wann starb Hitler?" March 29, 1964.

Koller, Karl. *Der letzte Monat.* Mannheim: Norbert Wohlgemuth Verlag, 1949.

Konev, I. *Year of Victory.* Trans. David Mishne. Moscow: Progress Publishers, 1969.

Krause, Karl Wilhelm. *Zehn Jahre Kammerdiener bei Hitler.* Hamburg: Hermann Laatzen Verlag, 1949.

Krosigk, Lutz Graf Schwerin von. *Es Geschah in Deutschland.* Tuebingen und Stuttgart: Wunderlich Verlag, 1951.

Kuby, Erich, ed. *Das Ende des Schreckens: Dokumente des Untergangs Januar bis Mai 1945.* Munich: Sueddeutsche Verlag, 1956.

———. *Die Russen in Berlin, 1945.* Munich: Scherz Verlag, 1965.

———. "Die Russen in Berlin," *Der Spiegel,* Nos. 19–24 (May 6–June 9, 1965).

Langer, Walter C. *The Mind of Adolf Hitler: The Secret Wartime Report.* New York: Basic Books, Inc. and New American Library, 1972.

Leahy, William D. *I Was There.* New York: McGraw-Hill, Whittlesey House, 1950.

Le Monde (Paris). "Adolf Hitler," May 3, 1945.

———. "Après la mort de Hitler," May 3, 1945.

———. "Découverte de documents dans l'abri souterrain de Hitler à Berlin," May 10, 1945.

———. "La dépouille de Hitler airait été retrouvée à Berlin," May 10, 1945.

———. "La dernière version de la mort de Hitler," May 25, 1945.

———. "La disparition de Hitler," May 3, 1945.

———. "La mort de Hitler," May 4, 1945.

———. "La saisie du livre 'Adolf Hitler, mon pere' sera-t-elle maintenue?" June 30, 1966.

———. "La tanière du Fuehrer," May 10, 1945.

———. "Le corps du Fuehrer reste introuvable," May 6-7, 1945.

———. "Le 'mystère Hitler,'" May 13-14, 1945.

———. "L'Enquete de 'Paris-Match' sur le néo-nazisme," July 2, 1966.

————. "Les derniers jours de Hitler," December 20, 1947.

————. "Les légendes ont la vie dure," December 10, 1947.

————. "Hitler ne serait pas mort . . . ," October 19, 1946.

————. "Hitler n'est pas en Espagne," June 12, 1945.

————. "'Hitler serait au pole sud' affirme un journal argentin," July 18, 1945.

————. "Petites depeches d l'etranger," September 26, 1945.

————. "Quatre cadavres pour un seul Hitler . . . ," May 12, 1945.

Lessner, Erwin. *Phantom Victory: The Fourth Reich, 1945-1960.* New York: Putnam's Sons, 1944.

Levin, Ira. *The Boys From Brazil.* New York: Random House, 1976.

Lewis, David. *The Secret Life of Adolf Hitler.* London: Heinrich Hanau, 1977.

L'Express. "Hitler: fin d'une longue enquête," (September 25–October 1, 1972), 35–38.

Life. "Amid Anguish, Homecomings: German PWs Return From Russia," XIL (October 24, 1955), 51.

————. "Did Adolf and Eva Die Here?" XIX (July 23, 1945), 26–27.

————. "Hitler's Last Stand Was in His Reichschancellery," XIX (July 23, 1945), 26–27.

————. "The Last Hours—and Some Last Words—of Hitler," XIL (October 24, 1945), 52.

————. "The Last Days in Berlin," XVIII (May 21, 1945), 41–44.

Life's Picture History of World War II. New York: Time Inc., 1950.

Linge, Heinz. "Valet's Own Story: 'The Hitler I Knew,'" *Chicago Daily News,* October 22–29, 1955.

Lochner, Louis P., ed. *The Goebbels Diaries.* Garden City: Doubleday & Co., 1945.

Loewenberg, Peter. "Psychohistorical Perspectives on Modern German History," *Journal of Modern History,* 47 (June 1975), 229–79.

Look. "The Insane World of Adolf Hitler," XXIII (January 6, 1959), 32–43.

Los Angeles Times. "Argentina Investigates Story of Hitler Haven," July 18, 1945.

————. "Arrests Linked to Nazi Underground," July 26, 1945.

————. "Astrologist Says Hitler Horoscope Denies Death Tale," May 3, 1945.

————. "Britons Read Hitler Death Report," May 2, 1945.

————. "Career of Hitler Founded on Hate," May 2, 1945.

————. "Coup of Ex-Nazi Officers Reported," April 18, 1945.

————. "Evidence of German Collapse," April 21, 1945.

————. "First Meeting of Allied Rulers Ends Abruptly," June 6, 1945.

————. "Four German U-Boats Still Unaccounted For," July 18, 1945.

————. "Fuehrer Death Report Brings Joy—and Doubt," May 2, 1945.

————. "General Eisenhower Finds Good Place to Hang Hitler," April 25, 1945.

————. "Germany is in the Bag," April 27, 1945.

————. "Goering Out; Rumors Rife About Hitler," April 27, 1945.

————. "Happy Grins Greet Hitler Death News," May 2, 1945.

————. "Himmler Escape Effort by Hitler Slaying Seen," April 29, 1945.

————. "Hitler Alone to Blame, Says Schuschnigg," June 9, 1945.

————. "Hitler Believed Hiding at Berchtesgaden," April 25, 1945.

————. "Hitler Body Found, Red Sources Claim," June 7, 1945.

————. "The Hitler Death Announcement," May 2, 1945.

————. "Hitler Escape by Sub? No, He was no Sailor," July 21, 1945.

————. "Hitler Refuge Denied by Japanese," April 27, 1945.

————. "Hitler, 'Wife' Reported Safe in Argentina," July 17, 1945.

————. "Japs Refuse Nazis Haven, Say Diplomats," April 27, 1945.

————. "Legionnaires Burn Swastika Raised by Soldiers as Joke," July 5, 1945.

————. "Leipzigers Say Hitler Married," April 21, 1945.

————. "Nazis Flying to Spanish Island, Moscow Reports," April 27, 1945.

————. "New Peace Move Hinted," April 30, 1945.

————. "Phantom Train May Have Whisked Nazis to Hideout," April 22, 1945.

————. "Reds Claim U.S. Coddling Nazi Chiefs," July 24, 1945.

————. "Report Hints Goering Flight," April 22, 1945.

————. "State Department Will Check Report," July 18, 1945.

————. "Struggle at Climax, Hitler Cries to Duce," April 24, 1945.

————. "Swiss Report Has Hitler Alive in Liechtenstein," July 16, 1945.

_____. "Truman to be Silent on Hitler Reports," May 2, 1945.

_____. "Yanks 'Duty' to Hitler Made Clear," April 20, 1945.

Luedde-Neurath, Walter. *Regierung Doenitz: Die letzten Tage des Dritten Reiches.* 3rd ed. Goettingen: Musterschmidt-Verlag, 1964.

Ludwigg, Henri. *L'assassinat de Hitler.* Trans. R. Jouvan. Paris: Editions France-Empire, 1963.

Mac, George. *La vie et la mort d'Hitler.* Paris: Editions Medicis, 1946.

Mad. "A Child's History in the Middle 1900s," 58 (October 1960), 21–23.

Manvell, Roger and Fraenkel, Heinrich. *Doctor Goebbels.* London: New English Library, 1960.

Maser, Werner. *Hitler.* Trans. Peter and Betty Ross. London: Allen Lane, 1973.

McGrath, George. "Hitler in Argentina," *Police Gazette* (December 1960), 6–7, 28.

McRandle, James H. *The Track of the Wolf: Essays on National Socialism and its Leader, Adolf Hitler.* Evanston, Ill.: Northwestern University Press, 1965.

Miami Herald. "Hitler's Last Word Stirs Nary Bidder," June 11, 1979.

Middleton, Drew. *The Defense of Western Europe.* New York: Appleton-Century-Crofts, 1952.

_____. *The Struggle for Germany.* Indianapolis, Ind.: Bobbs-Merrill, 1949.

Mason, Herbert Molloy, Jr. *To Kill the Devil: The Attempts on the Life of Adolf Hitler.* New York: Random, 1977.

Monde (Paris). "Il y a vingt ans, Hitler se suicidait," May 2/3, 1965.

_____. "Mort de Hitler: naissance d'un mythe," May 2, 1973.

_____. "Une procédure est ouverte contre Hitler," February 21, 1965.

Montgomery, Bernard Law. *The Memoirs of Field Marshal The Viscount Montgomery of Alamein, K.G.* Cleveland: World Publishing Co., 1958.

Moore, Herbert and Barrett, James W. *Who Killed Hitler? The Complete Story of How Death Came to Der Fuehrer and Eva Braun.* New York: Booktab Press, 1947.

Morgen, Der (Berlin). "Aufdeckung einer geheimen Nazi-Organisation," September 11, 1945.

_____. "Bormann angeblich verhaftet," January 3, 1946.

————. "Die Luege aus dem Grabe," January 4, 1946.

Morris, James. *The Preachers*. New York: St. Martin's Press, 1973.

Moscow News. "Battle of Berlin is One of War's Biggest," April 25, 1945.

————. "'Berlin' Is Stirring Documentary Film" July 4, 1945.

————. "Franco Spain—War Criminals' Hideout," June 2, 1945.

————. "General Dwight D. Eisenhower Holds Press Conference," August 15, 1945.

————. "German Capital in Soviet Hands," May 5, 1945.

————. "High Honors for Soviet Army Leaders," June 2, 1945.

————. "Pincers Dig Into Heart of Berlin," April 25, 1945.

————. "Reception in Kremlin in Honor of General Officers Commanding Red Army Troops," May 26, 1945.

————. "Red Army's Great Contribution to Victory," May 1, 1945.

Mosley, Leonard O. *Report From Germany*. London: Victor Gollancz Ltd., 1945.

Mueller-Gangloff, Erich. *Vorlaeufer des Antichrist*. Berlin: Wedding-Verlag, 1948.

Muellern-Schoenhausen, Johannes von. *Die Loesung des Raetsels Adolf Hitler: Der Versuch einer Deutung der geheimnisvollsten Erscheinung der Weltgeschichte*. Vienna: Verlag fuer Foerderung wissenschaftliche Forschung, 1959.

Muenchner-Merkur. "Hitler 'automatisch Kriegsverbrecher,'" July 19, 1952.

Murrow, Edward R., et al. *From D-Day Through Victory in Europe: The Eye-Witness Story as Told by War Correspondents on the Air*. New York: CBS, 1945.

Musmanno, Michael A. *Ten Days to Die*. 2nd ed. New York: Macfadden Books, 1962.

Nagle, John David. *The National Democratic Party: Right Radicalism in the Federal Republic of Germany*. Berkeley, Calif.: University of California Press, 1970.

Nation. "Nazi Post-War Strategy," 160 (February 10, 1945), 154–55.

National Police Gazette, The. "Hitler is Alive," CLXXXII (January 1977), 3–49.

Neue Zuercher Zeitung. "Eisenhower ueber die Zukunft Deutschlands," June 12, 1945.

————. "Hitler: Die letzten 10 Tage," October 6, 1973.

————. "Hitlers Wiederkehr," October 7, 1973.

————. "Die letzte Akt in der Hauptstadt des Dritten Reiches," June 15, 1945.

New Republic, The. "Is Hitler Dead?" CXI (November 20, 1944), 645–46.

News Chronicle (London). "The Last Days of Hitler," December 28–31, 1945.

————. "The Voice of Hitler is Back Again," April 24, 1959.

Newsweek. "He Saw Hitler Burned," LVI (October 17, 1955), 48-54.

————. "High Priced Hitleriana," XCIII (May 28, 1979), 23.

————. "Hitler's Last Gasp," XXVII (January 7, 1946), 35–36.

————. "Hitler: The Cremation," XXVI (July 2, 1945), 46.

————. "Missing: The Corpse," XXV (May 14, 1945), 35–36.

————. "Now You Find Him," XXV (June 18, 1945), 57–58.

————. "Obituary," LVI (September 26, 1955), 53–54.

————. "Springtimes for Hitler," LXXXI (April 30, 1973), 32–33.

————. "Uncle Adolf," XXVI (November 26, 1945), 48.

————. "What Long Teeth, Adolf," XXV (June 4, 1945), 56–61.

————. "The Wily Whatzit?" LV (February 22, 1960), 57.

New Yorker, The. "Letter From Berlin," XXI (November 24, 1945), 56–60.

New York Herald-Tribune. "Bavaria Letter-Writer Claims to Know Hitler's Whereabouts," January 22, 1953.

————. "Buchenwald's Hell Described By a Survivor," May 4, 1945.

————. "De-Nazification Trial of Hitler is Postponed," September 14, 1948.

————. "Final Ignominy Put on Hitler; His Will is Declared Invalid," December 2, 1947.

————. "Hitler Mystery Called a Matter of Deadly Seriousness to Allies," June 11, 1945.

————. "Hitler's First Plan Held to Flee Berlin by Car," October 21, 1955.

————. "Magazine Says Hitler Left Natural Son, Grandchildren," September 14, 1949.

————. "New Version of Hitler's Death: Himmler, Goering Killed Him," May 4, 1945.

————. "Sentiment in West Germany For 'New Hitler' at Low Point," August 31, 1962.

————. "Soviet Account Disputed," August 3–4, 1968.

New York Times, The. "Abetz Says He Believes Hitler Still Lives,"
October 29, 1945.

————. "Adolf and Marlene," March 18, 1977.

————. "Argentina Hunts Two More U-Boats," July 18, 1945.

————. "Army Curbs News in Reich as Result of Goering Report,"
May 27, 1945.

————. "A Rock Opera About Der Fuehrer," October 13, 1977.

————. "Asks Hitler Death Proof," May 26, 1948.

————. "'Benevolence' to Foe Decried by Moscow," April 13, 1945.

————. "Berliners Looting as Food Runs Low," April 28, 1945.

————. "Berliners Shoot German Soldiers," April 24, 1945.

————. "Berlin Falls to Russians; 70,000 Give Up," May 3, 1945.

————. "Bilbo Would Offer $1,000,000 for Hitler," August 14, 1945.

————. "The Bloody Dog is Dead," May 2, 1945.

————. "Camp Horror Films Are Exhibited Here," May 2, 1945.

————. "Churchill on Hitler," May 16, 1945.

————. "City Takes Report of Death in Stride," May 2, 1945.

————. "Clay Certain on Hitler," May 28, 1948.

————. "Congressmen Plan to See More Camps," April 27, 1945.

————. "Cremation Report Predicted," May 3, 1945.

————. "'Deep Satisfaction' is Felt by U.S. Troops at Death," May
2, 1945.

————. "DeValera Proffers Sympathy to Reich," May 3, 1945.

————. "Dittmar, Analyst for Nazis, Gives Up," April 28, 1945.

————. "Doctor Describes Hitler Injections," May 22, 1945.

————. "Eden Leaves Hitler's Fate to Troops Who Take Him,"
March 29, 1945.

————. "Eisenhower Didn't Say He Believes Hitler Alive," October
13, 1945.

————. "The End of Hitler," May 2, 1945.

————. "Enemy Says Hitler Took Own Life," May 16, 1945.

————. "Exhibit of Hitler Proposed," April 8, 1945.

————. "Film on Hitler to Open Fete," August 19, 1955.

————. "Foe Puts Russians Closer to Berlin," April 16, 1945.

————. "The Fuehrer's Double Gets a Careful Check," January 10,
1950.

————. "German Judge Confirms That Hitler Died as a Suicide in a Berlin Bunker in 1945," October 26, 1955.

————. "Germany Depicted as Land of Gloom," April 1, 1945.

————. "GI's Seize 285 Ribbentrop Aides Cowering in Refuge Near Weimar," April 11, 1945.

————. "Goebbels and Fuehrer Died By Own Hands, Aide Says," May 3, 1945.

————. "Goebbels' Escape Reported," April 6, 1945.

————. "Goebbels in Flight, Sweden Declares," April 23, 1945.

————. "Goebbels 'Virtually' Identified," May 16, 1945.

————. "Goering Suicide Rumored," April 28, 1945.

————. "Half-Brother of Hitler Seized," June 27, 1945.

————. "Hitler Alive in Records," January 8, 1954.

————. "Hitler Appeals to Army to Stay Loyal," July 23, 1944.

————. "Hitler Applauded for Last Act," May 4, 1945.

————. "Hitler Bars a Surrender, Warns Defeatists," January 1, 1945.

————. "Hitler Believed Alive, Eisenhower Tells Dutch," October 7, 1945.

————. "Hitler Bids Reich Die for Nazi Tenets," January 31, 1945.

————. "Hitler Birthday Ignored," April 21, 1950.

————. "Hitler Body Found, Russians Report," May 9, 1945.

————. "Hitler Body Proof Declared Fairly Certain by Russians," June 7, 1945.

————. "Hitler Cremated in Berlin, Aides Say," June 21, 1945.

————. "Hitler Dead in Chancellery, Nazis Say; Doenitz Successor, Orders War to Go On; Berlin Almost Won," May 2, 1945.

————. "Hitler Escapes Bomb, Purges Generals," July 21, 1944.

————. "Hitler Funds Reported," July 12, 1945.

————. "Hitler Imitation Reported Ready to Die in His Place," April 27, 1945.

————. "Hitler Kept Aide Ready to Kill Him," May 20, 1945.

————. "Hitler News Fails to Arouse Weimar," May 3, 1945.

————. "Hitler Not on Spanish Soil, Foreign Minister Says," June 11, 1945.

————. "Hitler Plan to Flee to Japan is Reported," October 16, 1945.

————. "Hitler Reported Alive," July 17, 1945.

———. "Hitler Reported Hid in Monastery," February 5, 1945.

———. "Hitler Rumors Circulated," September 11, 1945.

———. "Hitler Said to Be Dying," April 29, 1945.

———. "Hitler Shot Self, Berliners Believe," May 4, 1945.

———. "Hitler Sought in Boston," August 17, 1945.

———. "Hitler Took Cyanide, Soviet Inquiry Found," August 2, 1968.

———. "Hitler Valet Denies Account of Suicide," August 3, 1968.

———. "Hitler's Chauffeur Talks," June 21, 1945.

———. "Hitler's Gestures Believed Futile," April 29, 1945.

———. "Hitler's Pilot Says He Saw the Dictator Shoot Himself," October 9, 1955.

———. "Hitler's Private Will Found; Affirms His Suicidal Plans," December 30, 1945.

———. "Hitler's 70th Birthday Ignored," April 21, 1959.

———. "Hitler's Sister Fondly Recalls Adolf for British TV Audience," March 5, 1959.

———. "Hitler's Sister Seeks Proof of His Death to Get Funds," October 14, 1952.

———. "Hitler's Sister Under Arrest," May 28, 1945.

———. "How Will Hitler Meet End of Third Reich?" April 8, 1945.

———. "Is Hitler Dead or Alive?" September 16, 1945.

———. "Japanese Send Condolences," May 4, 1945.

———. "Jawbone Claimed to be Hitler's," July 31, 1945.

———. "Just a 'Fascist Trick,' Moscow Radio Asserts," May 2, 1945.

———. "Kesselring Praises Hitler," May 10, 1945.

———. "Killed for Gibe at Hitler," May 16, 1945.

———. "Leaders Reported in Berlin Exodus," February 3, 1945.

———. "Leaders Recently in Regensburg," April 28, 1945.

———. "Lest Hitler Reappear, Murder Case is Filed," February 20, 1965.

———. "Letter to Editor [from Hugh Trevor-Roper]," August 8, 1968.

———. "London Hears Hitler is Dying, Himmler Reported at Nazi Helm," April 12, 1945.

———. "Many Poison Phials Made by Germans for the Day," May 25, 1945.

————. "Moscow Urges Broader Hunt," May 14, 1945.

————. "The Nazi Legend," April 24, 1945.

————. "Nazi Resistance by Trickery Seen," May 3, 1945.

————. "Nazi Ruse is Seen in Hitler 'Death,'" May 2, 1945.

————. "Nazis' Conviction by Own Data Seen," September 9, 1945.

————. "Nazis Will Continue, Ley Tells Americans," May 18, 1945.

————. "New Berlin Search Fails to Find Hitler," May 8, 1945.

————. "No Hero's Death, Says Eisenhower," May 3, 1945.

————. "Paris Reports Assassination," May 3, 1945.

————. "Path to Berlin is Now Open, German Officer Tells Third," March 31, 1945.

————. "Pilot for Hitler Cites Rage at End," December 6, 1945.

————. "Pravda Says Spain Harbors 'Nazi Rats,'" May 7, 1945.

————. "Quick Trial for Goering Implied, As Allies Seize Henlein, Others," May 11, 1945.

————. "Re-Creating the Final Days of Adolf Hitler," April 8, 1956.

————. "Reich 'Through for Century' Say 12 Generals Here by Air," June 25, 1945.

————. "Reich Will Not Rise Again, Says Eisenhower in London," June 12, 1945.

————. "Reports on Hitler Vary," April 27, 1945.

————. "Russians Bore into Berlin, Swing North," April 24, 1945.

————. "Russians Encircle Berlin, Cross Elbe," April 26, 1945.

————. "Russians Find No Trace of Hitler in Berlin, Moscow Paper Reports," May 4, 1945.

————. "Russians Fly Victory Flag on Reichstag," May 1, 1945.

————. "Russians in Potsdam," April 28, 1945.

————. "Russians Probe Berlin Ruins," May 7, 1945.

————. "Russian Writes of Hitler's Death," February 22, 1964.

————. "Said to be the Last Picture of Adolf Hitler," May 17, 1950.

————. "Says Hitler Died in Mercy Killing," May 24, 1945.

————. "Shaef Aides Sure Hitler Died May 1," June 22, 1945.

————. "Shuster Doubts Theory Hitler was a Suicide," November 23, 1951.

————. "Soviet Report on Hitler Disputed by Historian," February 23, 1964.

————. "Soviet Sees Books on Hitler as Plot," January 28, 1974.

————. "Stimson Accepts Death Story," May 4, 1945.

————. "Stroke Is Doubted by Hitler's Doctor," May 7, 1945.

————. "Surrender Offers by Nazis Reported," April 28, 1945.

————. "Text of British Report Holding Hitler Ended His Life," November 2, 1945.

————. "Truman Believes Hitler Dead," May 3, 1945.

————. "Two Soviet Armies Join Inside Berlin," April 25, 1945.

————. "Underground Haven Found," May 9, 1945.

————. "U.S. and Red Armies Join, Split Germany," April 28, 1945.

————. "U.S. Deplores Lack of Agent in Berlin," June 3, 1945.

————. "Russians Tighten Ring on Berlin's Heart," April 30, 1945.

————. "Valet Says He Set Fire to Hitler's Body," October 10, 1955.

————. "World-Wide Search for Hitler Goes On," September 9, 1945.

————. "Writer on Hitler Fails to see Press," September 21, 1968.

————. "X-Ray of Hitler's Head Brings $375 at Auction," July 1, 1977.

————. "Zhukoff Says Hitler Wed Actress in Berlin, May Be Alive in Europe," June 10, 1945.

New York Times Magazine, The. "But the Hitler Legend *Isn't* Dead," January 20, 1946.

————. "Hitler Legends," May 1, 1949.

————. "Hitler's Hideaway," November 12, 1944.

————. "The Last Ten Days," March 25, 1956.

————. "The Nazis Dig in for World War III," August 6, 1944.

————. "Papa, who was Hitler?" October 28, 1973.

————. "Roosevelt Lives, Hitler is Dead," April 22, 1945.

————. "Schickelgruber: Alias—," October 8, 1944.

————. "Then and Now," August 21, 1955.

————. "When the Big One (Hitler) Got Away," May 24, 1964.

O'Donnell, James P. and Bahnsen, Uwe. *Die Katakombe: Das Ende in der Reichskanzlei.* Stuttgart: Deutsche Verlags-Anstalt, 1975.

Oven, Wilfred von. *Mit Goebbels bis zum Ende.* 2 vols. Buenos Aires: Duerer-Verlag, 1950.

Palestine Post, The (Jerusalem). "Hitler's Death Announced," May 2, 1945.

Parade. "Berlin Under the Russians," June 16, 1945.

————. "The Most Hated," April 10, 1977.

Payne, Robert. *The Life and Death of Adolf Hitler.* New York: Praeger, 1973.

Pelz, Werner and Lottie. *I am Adolf Hitler.* Richmond, Va.: John Knox Press, 1971.

Petitfrère, Ray. *Sous le signe du fusil.* Tamines: Duculot-Roulin, 1945.

Philadelphia Inquirer. March 22, 1945.

Picture Post. "The Last Two Photographs?" May 20, 1950.

Quick. "Der Mensch, der Adolf Hitler hiess," March 23, 1964.

Reader's Digest Illustrated Story of World War II. Pleasantville, N.Y.: The Reader's Digest Association, Inc., 1969.

Recktenwald, Johann. *Woran hat Adolf Hitler gelitten?* Munich/Basel: Ernst Reinhardt Verlag, 1963.

Reitsch, Hanna. *Hoehen und Tiefen, 1945-77.* Munich: DSZ-Verlag, 1978.

―――. "Mein Erleben im Hitler-Bunker," *National-Zeitung* (Munich), July 28, 1978.

Riess, Curt. *Berlin, 1945-1953.* Berlin-Gruenewald: Non Stop-Buecherei, n.d.

―――. *Joseph Goebbels.* London: Hollis and Carter, 1949.

―――. *The Nazis Go Underground.* New York and Garden City: Doubleday, Doran and Co., 1944.

Rjndt, Philippe van. *The Trial of Adolf Hitler.* New York: Summit Books, 1978.

Robinson, W. R., ed. *Man and the Movies.* Baton Rouge, La.: Louisiana State University Press, 1967.

Roehrs, Hans-Dietrich. *Hitlers Krankheit: Tatsachen und Legenden.* Neckargemuend: Kurt Vowinckel Verlag, 1966.

Rosanow, German L. *Hitlers letzte Tage.* [East] Berlin: Dietz Verlag, 1963.

Rosten, Leo. "Hitler's Jaw Was in Her Handbag," *Look* (April 4, 1967), 6.

Russia. Ministry of Foreign Affairs of the U.S.S.R. *Stalin's Correspondence with Churchill, Attlee, Roosevelt and Truman, 1941-45.* 2 vols. New York: E. P. Dutton, 1958.

Ryan, Cornelius. *The Last Battle.* New York: Simon and Schuster, 1966.

Ryder, A. J. *Twentieth Century Germany: From Bismarck to Brandt.* New York: Columbia University Press, 1973.

Rzhevskaya, Yelena. *Hitlers Ende ohne Mythos.* Trans. Werner Hanke. [East] Berlin: Deutscher Militaerverlag, 1967.

Saby, Edouard. *Le tyran nazi et les forces occultes.* Paris: Editions de l'Ecole Addeiste, 1945.

St. Louis Globe-Democrat. March 19, 1945.

San Francisco Chronicle. "Allies Set Up Four-Zone Occupation Rule in Reich," June 6, 1945.

_____. "All Out War Criminal Hunt Urged," April 25, 1945.

_____. "A Russian View on War Criminals," June 2, 1945.

_____. "Attempted Coup Reported as German Cities Revolt," April 29, 1945.

_____. "Berlin a Sea of Flame, Famine and Horror," May 5, 1945.

_____. "Can We Try Hitler?" May 30, 1945.

_____. "The Case Against Germany," May 6, 1945.

_____. "Colonial Discussion Blocked by British, Pravda Charges," June 9, 1945.

_____. "Dictators Fall," May 5, 1945.

_____. "Even Lesser Generals Win a Drink of Praise," May 26, 1945.

_____. "4,000,000 Crimes," May 8, 1945.

_____. "Hitler, Eva Suicides, Says Eyewitness," June 21, 1945.

_____. "Hitler Legend," June 12, 1945.

_____. "Hitler Pilot Says: 'I Know He Died,'" October 9, 1955.

_____. "How Hitler May Have Died," May 20, 1945.

_____. "Inferno and Fuehrer," April 24, 1945.

_____. "Izvestia Sees Nazi Scheme in Argentina," June 14, 1945.

_____. "Izvestia vs. Pro-Fascists in America," June 17, 1945.

_____. "Moscow Lists Big Three's Problems," May 18, 1945.

_____. "Moscow Radio Protests War Trial 'Hair Splitting,'" June 4, 1945.

_____. "Nazis are Reported Quarreling," April 21, 1945.

_____. "No Anti-U.S. Propaganda, Says Izvestia," June 8, 1945.

_____. "Out of Defeat—Nazis Winning Propaganda Battle," May 27, 1945.

_____. "People of Berlin Await Their Fate," April 22, 1945.

_____. "RAF Scores Bull's eye on Hitler's House," April 26, 1945.

————. "Recent Hitler Months were Rumor-Laden," May 2, 1945.

————. "Red Star: Hostile Press Seeks War," June 6, 1945.

————. "Russ Assail Allied Dealing With Doenitz," May 21, 1945.

————. "Russ Warn of the Poison in Nazi Lies," May 17, 1945.

————. "Soviets Renew Protest of Allied Abuses," June 7, 1945.

————. "Soviet Writer Stresses a 'Firm Peace,'" May 17, 1945.

————. "Today's Crop of Rumors," April 30, 1945.

————. "Truman Kills Peace Rumor," April 29, 1945.

————. "U.S. Delegation Stalled—Moscow's Replies Awaited," June 7, 1945.

————. "Views Clash Over Reports From Berlin," June 7, 1945.

————. "War Criminals," June 6, 1945.

————. "Who is the Fascist Enemy?" April 15, 1945.

————. "Whole World Sees Their Liberator in Us," May 17, 1945.

————. "'World' Supported Our Argentina Stand, Says Pravda," May 8, 1945.

————. "Yanks Discover Prisoners Burned Alive," April 19, 1945.

————. "Zhukov Calls Ike Among Greatest of All Time," May 10, 1945.

————. "Zhukov Sure Hitler Wed Eva and Fled," June 10, 1945.

Schaeffer, Heinz. *U-977—66 Tage unter Wasser.* Wiesbaden: Limesverlag, n.d.

Schellenberg, Walter. *The Schellenberg Memoirs.* Ed. and Trans. Louis Hagen. London: Andre Deutsch, 1956.

Schenck, Ernst Guenter. *Ich sah Berlin sterben: Als Arzt in der Reichskanzlei.* Herford: Nicolaische Verlagshandlung, 1970.

Schlesinger, Arthur, Jr. Review of H. R. Trevor-Roper, *The Last Days of Hitler* (New York: Macmillan, 1947), in *Nation,* 165 (September 20, 1947), 287.

Schmidt, Paul. *Statist auf diplomatischer Buehne, 1923–45: Erlebnisse des Chefdolmetschers im Auswaertigen Amt mit den Staatsmaennern Europas.* Bonn: Athenaeum-Verlag, 1950.

Schramm, Percy Ernst, et al. *Kriegstagebuch des Oberkommandos der Wehrmacht, 1940–1945.* Vol. IV. Frankfurt/Main: Bernard & Graefe Verlag fuer Wehrwesen, 1961.

Schultz, Joachim. *Die letzten 30 Tage: Aus dem Kriegstagebuch des OKW.* Ed. Juergen Thorwald. Stuttgart: Steingrueben-Verlag, 1951.

Schwarz, Hanns. *Brennpunkt F.H.Q.: Menschen und Massstaebe im Fuehrerhauptquartier.* Buenos Aires: Duerer-Verlag, 1950.

Semmler, Rudolf. *Goebbels—The Man Next to Hitler.* London: Westhouse, 1947.

Senior Scholastic. "Clear Up Hitler's Death," LXVII (October 20, 1955), 14–15.

Sharp, Tony. *The Wartime Alliance and the Zonal Division of Germany.* Oxford: Clarendon Press, 1975.

Sherwood, Robert E. *The White House Papers of Harry L. Hopkins.* Vol. II. London: Eyre and Spottiswoode, 1949.

Shirer, William L. *End of a Berlin Diary.* New York: Knopf, 1947.

———. *The Rise and Fall of the Third Reich.* New York: Fawcett Publications, 1965.

Sie und Er. "Aus dem Album der 'Braunen Eva,'" No. 47 (November 23, 1947), 6.

Smith, Jean Edward, ed. *The Papers of Lucius D. Clay: Germany 1945–1949.* Vol. I. Bloomington, Ind.: Indiana University Press, 1974.

Smoydzin, Werner. *Hitler Lebt! Vom internationalen Faschismus zur internationale Hakenkreuzes.* 2nd ed. Pfaffenhofen/Ilm: Ilmgau Verlag, 1967.

Sondern, Frederic, Jr. "Adolf Hitler's Last Days," *The Reader's Digest,* LVIII (June 1951), 113–18.

Sognnaes, Reidar F. and Stroem, Ferdinand. "The Odontological Identification of Adolf Hitler: Definitive Documentation by X-rays, Interrogations and Autopsy Findings," *Acta Odontologica Scandinavica,* XXXI (1973), 43–69.

Sognnaes, Reidar F. "Some Old and New Adventures in Dental Research," *Harvard Dental Alumni Bulletin,* 32, (1972), 56-59.

Sovetskaia istoricheskaia entsiklopediia. Vol. IV. Moscow: Gosudarstvennoe nauchnoe izdatel'stvo, 1961–63.

Soviet News (London). "Berlin Battle on the Screen," July 5, 1945.

———. "Marshal Zhukov's Press Conference in Berlin," June 11, 1945.

———. "Moscow Press Interviews Gen. Eisenhower," August 17, 1945.

———. "No Mercy!" August 31, 1945.

———. "Search for Hitler Goes on," June 16, 1945.

Soviet War News (London). "Above All—Allied Unity," June 8, 1945.

————. "Another Chance for German Imperialism?" July 12, 1945.

————. "At 3 P.M. on May 2 . . . ," May 4, 1945.

————. "Germany Must Pay in Labour, Too," May 16, 1945.

————. "Goering Should Be Swinging," May 14, 1945.

————. "How Weidling Capitulated," May 7, 1945.

————. "I Lunch in Hitler's Chancellery," May 14, 1945.

————. "No Mercy for War Criminals!" May 16, 1945.

————. "Report of Hitler's Death," May 3, 1945.

————. "Security in East and West," May 19, 1945.

————. "We Have Kept Our Oath," May 5, 1945.

Spandauer Volksblatt. "Um Hitlers juedischen Grossvater," May 6, 1956.

Speer, Albert. *Inside the Third Reich.* Trans. Richard and Clara Winston. New York: Macmillan, 1970.

Spiegel, Der. "Ad acta," No. 38 (September 13, 1961), 94–96.

————. "Adolf Hitler: Anatomie eines Diktators," No. 5 (January 29, 1964), 40–61.

————. "Adolf Hitler: Weder Held noch Schurke?" No. 48 (November 22, 1961), 45–46.

————. "Armer, armer Adolf," No. 16 (April 19, 1947), 5–6.

————. "Ein Stueck Stoff," No. 32 (August 5, 1968), 32–38.

————. "Es ist das deutsche Herz," No. 52 (December 22, 1954), 10–11.

————. "Der Fuehrer, wie ihn keiner kennt," No. 36 (August 30, 1961), 63.

————. "Heil Hygatt," No. 34 (August 14, 1967), 104–5.

————. "Hitlers Erben," No. 49 (December 3, 1952), 32–33.

————. "Ich reiche Nazis," No. 38 (September 15, 1949), 14–15.

————. "Die Kamera war dabei," No. 9 (February 24, 1954), 5.

————. "Kennwart Richthofen," No. 32 (August 3, 1960), 56–57.

————. "Mit Evas Monogram," No. 44 (November 1, 1947), 5.

————. "Die Spur Fuehrt zu Waldner 555," No. 2 (January 8, 1968), 22–24.

————. "Der Stenograf muss es wissen," No. 4 (January 24, 1951), 8–9.

————. "Story von Remarque," No. 7 (February 9, 1955), 34–35.

————. "Von Luther bis Hitler," No. 41 (October 4, 1961), 75–78.

————. ". . . worum dann ueberhaupt noch leben!" No. 3 (January 10, 1966), 30–47.

Springer, Hildegard, ed. *Es sprach Hans Fritsche: Nach Gespraechen, Briefen und Dokumenten.* Stuttgart: Thiele-Verlag KG, 1949.

Stalin, Joseph. *The Great Patriotic War of the Soviet Union.* New York: International Publishers, 1945.

Steel, Johannes. *Hitler as Frankenstein.* Adelphi, U.K.: Wishart and Co., 1933.

The Stars and Stripes (Paris). "Cremation of Hitler Believed Possible to Hide How He Died," May 4, 1945.

————. "Death of Hitler is Laid to a 'Mercy Injection,'" May 25, 1945.

————. "Goebbels Corpse Reported Found," May 8, 1945.

————. "Hitler, Goebbels Killed Selves, Russians Told," May 3, 1945.

————. "Hitler Papers Call Suicide 'Honorable,'" November 21, 1950.

————. "Russians Find Goebbels' Body," July 5, 1945.

————. "Says He Saw Fuehrer Burn," June 21, 1945.

————. "Uncertain Russians Ask Allies to Search All Areas for Hitler," June 22, 1945.

————. "Yank Who Saw Hitler Shelter in Berlin Doubts Fuehrer Died," June 12, 1945.

Steinert, Marlis G. *23 Days: The Final Collapse of Nazi Germany.* Trans. Richard Barry. New York: Walker, 1969.

Strasser, Otto. *Hitler and I.* Boston: Houghton Mifflin, 1940.

Studnitz, Hans-Georg von. *While Berlin Burns: The Diary of Hans-Georg von Studnitz, 1943–1945.* Englewood Cliffs, N.J.: Prentice-Hall, 1964.,

Sueddeutsche Zeitung (Munich). "Eines Tages verschwanden Sie im Nebel . . . ," December 30, 1953.

————. "Der Endsieg des Wahnsinns in der Reichskanzlei," January 25, 1961.

————. "Gefaelschte Briefmarken haben auch ihren Reiz," March 31, 1962.

————. "Hitler mit Backenbart," July 12, 1960.

————. "Nazi-Schallplatte jetzt in ganze Bundesgebiet," June 4, 1959.

Sunday Express (London). "Is 'Uschi' a Hitler?" November 18, 1945.

————. "My Last Words: by Adolf Hitler," April–May 1959.

Sunday Times, The (London). "'Deliberate Leak' that hastened Hitler's end," August 25, 1968.

Sunday Times Magazine, The (London). "The Home Life of Hitler," April 1, 1973.

Sydnor, Charles W., Jr. "The Selling of Adolf Hitler: David Irving's *Hitler's War*," *Central European History,* XII (June 1979), 169–99.

Szabo, Ladislas. *Je sais que Hitler est vivant.* Paris: Sfelt, 1947.

Tabori, Paul, ed. *The Private Life of Adolf Hitler: The Intimate Notes and Diary of Eva Braun.* London: Aldus Publications, 1949.

Tagesspiegel, Der (Berlin). "Akte II/52: Hitler endete durch Selbstmord," October 26, 1956.

————. "Frontstadt Berlin," April 23, 1946.

————. "Schrei aus der Hoelle," May 8, 1946.

————. "Spannungsreiche Tage in Nuernberg," March 9, 1946.

————. "Vor einem Jahr," May 1, 1946.

————. "Vor einem Jahr: Die letzten zehn Tage," May 3, 1946.

Telegraf (Berlin). "Auch Frauen kommen," October 11, 1955.

Telpukhovsky, B.S. *Velikaia otechestvennaia voina Sovetskogo Soviza, 1941–1945.* Moscow: Gosudarstvennoe izdatel'stvo politicheskoi literatury, 1959.

Thompson, Dorothy. "Was Hitler Really Crazy?" *Ladies Home Journal,* LXXII (October 1955), 11–23.

Thorwald, Juergen. *Das Ende an der Elbe.* Rev. ed. Munich/Zurich: Droemersche Verlagsanstalt, 1975.

Time. "Adolf Hitler's Last Hours," VL (May 21, 1945), 40f.

————. "Adolf, Where Are You?" VIL (December 25, 1944), 34.

————. "As Long as I Live. . . ," VL (May 28, 1945), 21.

————. "Historical Note: How Hitler Died," VIC (August 9, 1968), 29.

————. "The Hitler Revival: Myth v. Truth," CI (May 21, 1973), 81–82.

————. "Legends Never Die," XXII (November 12, 1945), 36.

————. "Nazi Revival?" IL (March 3, 1947), 30.

————. "Son of Hitler?" CX (November 14, 1977), 45.

————. Review of H. R. Trevor-Roper, *The Last Days of Hitler* (New York: Macmillan, 1947), L (August 18, 1947), 98–100.

————. "The Two Hitlers," C (October 2, 1972), 48–50.

————. "Where?" VIL (November 20, 1944), 35.

Times, The (London). "Adolf Hitler," May 2, 1945.

————. "A Hitler Rumour," July 18, 1945.

————. "Bavarian Emotional Excess," September 15, 1949.

————. "Bormann Inquiry to Be Reopened," June 2, 1960.

————. "Court Ruling Sought on Hitler's Death," October 15, 1954.

————. "Estates of Hitler and Eva Braun," November 27, 1947.

————. "German Youth Probe Hitler's Sway," March 19, 1964.

————. "Hitler and Mussolini in Stained Glass," September 18, 1953.

————. "Hitler at 80," April 18, 1968.

————. "Hitler Film Banned," November 21, 1953.

————. "Hitler's Bunker Blown Up," December 12, 1947.

————. "Hitler's Chauffeur at Nuremberg," July 4, 1946.

————. "Hitler's Confiscated Property," April 10, 1953.

————. "Hitler's Death," August 5, 1968.

————. "Hitler's Death Officially Established," October 26, 1968.

————. "Hitler's Fate," October 16, 1945.

————. "Hitler's Last Pilot," December 13, 1947.

————. "Hitler's Property to Be Confiscated," October 16, 1948.

————. "Hitler's Visit to Oder Front," March 10, 1945.

————. "Hitler's Voice," September 29, 1956.

————. "Hitler's Will," January 24, 1946.

————. "Hitler's Will Found," February 12, 1954.

————. "House of Commons," March 29, 1945.

————. "Jawbones Identified as Hitler's," July 9, 1945.

————. "Last Hours of Hitler," January 1, 1946.

————. "Mr. Khrushchev Adamant," August 14, 1957.

————. "News of Herr Linse," January 13, 1956.

————. "Riddle of Hitler's End," July 5, 1945.

————. "Russian Writer Throws New Light on Hitler's Death," August 2, 1968.

————. "Soviet Disclosures on the Death of Hitler," August 2, 1968.

————. "Teeth X-Ray Clue to Hitler's Body," November 27, 1964.

Timm, Albrecht. *Was weisst Du von Adolf Hitler?* Paderborn: Verlag Ferdinand Schoeningh, 1960 (?).

Toland, John. *Adolf Hitler.* Garden City: Doubleday & Co., 1976.
———. *The Last 100 Days.* New York: Random House, 1966.
Trevor-Roper, Hugh, ed. *The Bormann Letters: The Private Corre-spondence Between Martin Bormann and His Wife from January 1943 to April 1945.* London: Weidenfeld and Nicolson, 1954.
———. *Final Entries 1945: The Diaries of Joseph Goebbels.* Trans. Richard Barry. New York: G. P. Putnam's Sons, 1978.
———. "The Hole in Hitler's Head," *The Sunday Times* (London), September 29, 1968.
———. "Is Hitler Really Dead?" *Commentary,* XI (February 1951), 120–31.
———. *The Last Days of Hitler.* New York: Macmillan, 1947.
———. *The Last Days of Hitler.* 3rd ed. New York: Macmillan, 1965.
———. "The Last Days of Hitler," *Life,* XXII (March 17, 1947), 106–22.
———. "Last Days of Hitler," *New York Times Magazine,* April 24, 1955.
———. "The 'Mystery' of Hitler's Death," *Commentary,* XXII (July 1956), 1–12.
Truman, Harry S. *Year of Decisions.* Vol. 1 of *Memoirs by Harry S Truman.* Garden City: Doubleday, 1955.
United States. Department of State. *Foreign Relations of the United States.* Vols. II–III (1945). Washington, D.C.: U.S. Government Printing Office, 1960–68.
United States. Office of the Chief of Military History. *United States in World War II: The European Theater of Operations, the Last Offensive.* Washington, D.C.: Office of the Chief of Military History, United States Army, 1973.
United States. Office of War Information. Division of Press Intelligence. *International Affairs: Digests of Editorials and Columns from 75 Newspapers and of Opinion of About a Dozen Radio Commentators.* No. 420 (March 26, 1945).
U.S. News and World Report. "Goering's Unpublished Interview," XXXVI (May 14, 1954), 55–58.
———. "Satire, 'I Was Hitler's Toothbrush,' is German Magazine's Reply to Rash of Memoirs about the Fuehrer—But Trend Worries Allies," XXXI (November 18, 1947), 31.

Vernon, H. D. "Hitler, the Man—Notes for a Case History," *Journal of Abnormal Psychology,* XXXVII (1942) 295–308.

Vogel, Wolfgang. "Pandaimonium des Grauens," *Konkret: Unabhaengige Zeitschrift fuer Kultur und Politik,* IV (April 1964), 14–16.

Voelkischer Beobachter (Munich). March 1, March 10, 1945.

————. "Deutschland steht standhaft und treu zum Fuehrer," April 20, 1945.

————. "Berlin kampft entschlossen bis zum Einsatz," April 28, 1945.

————. "Der Fuehrer an die Ostfront," April 17, 1945.

————. "Der Fuehrer an Hanke und Koch," February 27, 1945.

————. "Der Fuehrer entflammt Berlin's Kampfgeist," April 25, 1945.

————. "Der Fuehrer in der Festung Berlin," April 26, 1945.

————. "Der Fuehrer Verteidiger Berlins," April 24, 1945.

————. "Glueckwunschaustausch mit dem Fuehrer," January 3, 1945.

————. "Neue Oberbefehlshaber der Luftwaffe," April 28, 1945.

————. "Rudel—der beste Flieger der Welt," January 4, 1945.

————. "Stunde der Bewaehrung fuer Berlin," April 23, 1945.

————. "Tapfere Jungen vor dem Fuehrer," March 21, 1945.

————. "Um Freiheit, Ehre, Zukunft!" February 1, 1945.

————. "Vidkun Quisling beim Fuehrer," January 30, 1945.

————. "Vom Fuehrer empfangen," February 27, 1945.

————. "Wir werden den Sieg erzwingen!" January 2, 1945.

Volkman, Ernie. "The Second Coming of Adolph Hitler," *Argosy* (December 1977), 36–41.

Wahl, Karl. '. . . es ist das deutsche Herz': Erlebnisse und Erkenntnisse eines ehemaliges Gauleiters. Augsburg: Self-Published, 1954.

Waite, Robert G. L. *The Psychopathic God Adolf Hitler.* New York: Basic Books, Inc., 1977.

Wallechinsky, David; Wallace, Irving; and Wallace, Amy. *The Book of Lists.* New York: Morrow, 1977.

Wallner, Albert. *Moench-Story: Hitlers Flucht aus Berlin am 30.4.1945.* Horn, Austria: Verlag Ferdinand Berger, 1968.

Warlimont, Walter. *Inside Hitler's Headquarters, 1939–45.* Trans. R. H. Barry. New York: Praeger, 1964.

Washington Times-Herald. March 25, 1945.

Weidling, Helmut. "Der Endkampf in Berlin (23.4–2.5 1945)," *Wehrwissenschaftliche Rundschau,* 12 (January–March 1962).

Weinberg, Gerhard, ed. *Hitlers zweites Buch.* Stuttgart: Deutsche Verlags-Anstalt, 1961.

Welt, Die (Hamburg). "Hitler auch amtlich tot," October 26, 1956.

Weltbuehne, Die. "Hitlers entraetselter Tod," No. 40 (October 1, 1968), 1253–56.

Westdeutsche Allgemeine (Essen). "Adolf Hitler schoss sich in die Schlaefe," October 26, 1956.

_____. "Wir sind zutiefst erschuettert," October 10, 1955.

Westdeutscher Rundschau (Cologne). "Bundesrichter hoerten Hitlers Stimme," May 14, 1960.

Wheeler-Bennett, John and Nicholls, Anthony. *The Semblance of Peace: The Political Settlement After the Second World War.* New York: Norton, 1974.

Weill, Gus. *The Fuehrer Seed.* New York: William Morrow, 1979.

Wiesenthal, Simon. "Doch die Moerder leben," *Der Spiegel,* No. 34 (August 14, 1967), 60–73.

_____. *The Murderers Among Us: The Simon Wiesenthal Memoirs.* Ed. Joseph Wechsberg. New York: McGraw-Hill, 1967.

Winkler, Hans-Joachim. *Legenden um Hitler.* Berlin: Colloquium Verlag, 1961.

Work, Robert E. "Last Days in Hitler's Air Raid Shelter," *The Public Opinion Quarterly,* X (Winter 1946–47), 565–581.

Yank: The Army Weekly. "Berlin Today," August 10, 1945.

_____. "Eisenhower Discusses the War," July 20, 1945.

_____. "The Fall of Germany," June 1, 1945.

Zeit. "In Flensburg diskutieren Schueler den 20. Juli," March 15, 1956.

_____. "Die letzten Soldaten des Grossen Krieges," October 13, 1955.

_____. "Mangels berechtigten Interesses. . . ," August 16, 1968.

_____. "So starb Adolf Hitler," August 6, 1968.

Zhukov, G. K. *The Memoirs of Marshal Zhukov.* Trans. Novosti. New York: Delacorte Press, 1971.

Ziemke, Earl F. *Battle for Berlin: End of the Third Reich.* New York: Ballantine Books, 1968.

Zoller, Albert. *Hitler privat: Erlebnisbericht seiner Geheimsekretaerin.* Duesseldorf: Droste Verlag, 1949.

Index

263